THE LIVING CHRIST

And I say to thee,
Thou art Peter,
And upon this rock
I will build my Church.
Matthew 16:18

✝ ✝ ✝ ✝ ✝

THE LIVING CHRIST

JOHN L. MURPHY

THE BRUCE PUBLISHING COMPANY
MILWAUKEE

NIHIL OBSTAT:

JOHN A. SCHULIEN, S.T.D.
Censor librorum

IMPRIMATUR:

✠ ALBERTUS G. MEYER
Archiepiscopus Milwauchiensis

Die 13ª Martii, 1956

Acknowledgment is gratefully made to the publishers for permission to cite certain passages from:

The Mystical Body of Christ, by E. Myers (New York: Macmillan Company, 1931)

The Spirit of Mediaeval Philosophy, by Etienne Gilson (New York: Charles Scribner's Sons, 1940)

Growth or Decline? by Emmanuel Cardinal Suhard (Chicago: Fides Publishers, 1948)

The Mystical Body of Christ, by John C. Gruden (St. Louis: Herder, 1938)

Is There Salvation Outside the Church? by J. V. Bainvel (St. Louis: Herder, 1923)

Catholicism, Henri de Lubac, S.J. (London: Burns, Oates & Washbourne, 1950)

Key to the Doctrine of the Eucharist, by Dom Anscar Vonier (Westminster, Md.: The Newman Press, 1946)

The New Testament, translation by the Confraternity of Christian Doctrine (Paterson, N. J.: St. Anthony Guild Press, 1941)

The New Testament, translation by Ronald Knox (New York: Sheed and Ward, 1946)

Catholic University of America Dewey Classification: 260

© 1956 BY THE BRUCE PUBLISHING COMPANY
MADE IN THE UNITED STATES OF AMERICA

(Second Printing — 1956)

To Mother and Dad

THE LIVING CHRIST

THERE is a special reason for designating this work as THE LIVING CHRIST. There have been many books about Christ, but what follows has been written not only that the reader might understand the God-Man better, but also that he might understand himself somewhat better. The reader himself is also the subject matter of this book, for it is a work about Christ: the Mystical Christ, as He lives on in the members of His Mystical Body. Because of a very special and intimate union with Christ the God-Man, we can say of these men and women and children that they represent Christ in the world today.

The *Church,* in Bossuet's beautiful definition, is *"Jesus Christ prolonged in space and time, and communicated to men."*[1] Poetic as it may appear, it is not sheer poetry. It is a reality, no less real than that car passing by your house, or that dog barking down the street, or those people with whom you work day by day. And it is of that reality that I intend to speak.

Christ appears in space and time in the personages of many people: of bishops, above all the Pope in Rome; of priests, Sisters, doctors, lawyers, and bank clerks; of factory workers and teachers, typists and bus drivers, scrub women and short-order cooks. All of these bear the person of Christ according to their role in life, and all are important, for, as the body is one and has many members, and all the members form but one body, so also is it with the Church of Christ.

It is not to the learned that I would speak in THE LIVING CHRIST. There are scholarly books for them. It is to the ordinary reader that this work is directed — to all those members of Christ who are striving to live according to His command, and who, by their lives, show that they wish to gain a deeper, more profound understanding of their Catholic faith. I am writing especially for those men and women belonging to the laity, who are anxious to understand the Church better, and who are willing to spend a certain amount of time and energy in studying this doctrine of the Mystical Body.

It has been difficult at times to put things down simply. Human language, when dealing with a mystery of revealed religion, is bound to stagger beneath its load in attempting an explanation. Yet I hope that, for the most part, what follows will be of help to the serious reader in his pursuit of the doctrine of the Mystical Body of Christ.

This attempt to explain so profound a doctrine in simple terminology will account for the style and form of the writing. If to some it may appear that I have adhered to a rather legal, point-by-point manner of presentation, I can only reply that it is my firm belief that a solid understanding of the doctrine demands such an approach. This explains also the extended background material in Chapters V and VI. It might be presumed by many readers, but since it is so essential to an adequate grasp of the Church's role in the whole work of salvation, it seemed best not to take it for granted for the ordinary reader. Possibly some matters treated here might have been left out of a book like this, but they have been added for the sake of completeness. If they should prove too frightening, I hope those who find them so will pass over them, and hasten on to what might prove helpful to them.

Since this is not a theological treatise, all footnotes have been omitted, except for direct quotations. Most of the references are to the encyclical of Pope Pius XII, *On the Mystical Body of Christ,*[2] or to Sacred Scripture. The work has been based almost entirely upon the outline for the first part of the encyclical; I have not treated the other two sections expressly. The scriptural quotations have been included in hopes that the reader may learn to know and love the pages of the Bible, particularly the New Testament.

We hear much of the Mystical Body today, all of us do. We are often told that we should build up our religious life upon that doctrine, but the only solid basis for any devotional life is a good understanding of the doctrine beneath it. We can imagine the confusion of a man who, when asked to take a train trip, not only has no idea what a train schedule is, but even has vague notions as to what a train is. Yet the situation in the spiritual life is not dissimilar. A person asked to model his life according to the doctrine of the Mystical Body must have a clear idea first of all as to what the Mystical Body is. Thus the purpose for writing this particular work has been to *teach* doctrine, reserving for a later book the beautiful and soul-stirring applications of this teaching to everyday life and the liturgy.

Much of the criticism leveled against Liturgical and Catholic Action groups has really been aimed at those in the groups who attempt to apply the doctrine of the Mystical Body before they are quite sure what this doctrine is. Little wonder, then, that there is confusion, even dangerous confusion, at times. There is no real need for vagueness in the teaching of the Mystical Body, at least not after the recent encyclical of Pope Pius XII. Fully understood, it is profound and it does involve many mysteries of faith, but yet we can see it all clearly enough to be able to say with certainty *what* the mystery is. A proper understanding of the doctrine will not result from mere study, however, but rather from thought and prayer devoted by each individual to the subject. Study is the beginning but not the end, for while a man may know the basic points of any doctrine, they will sink in and become vital and real and meaningful only through a life of prayer aided by the grace of God.

The aim of the following chapters will be achieved if, at the close, the reader will possess a clear and correct answer to that often-asked question: "Just what *is* the Mystical Body of Christ?" He will not understand it perfectly; no man ever will. But he can know enough about it to go out and pattern his life upon this truth which so moved the mind and heart of St. Paul.

* * *

I wish to take this opportunity to express my gratitude to the many individuals who have assisted in any way in the publication of this book, above all to my former professors at the Salesianum.

First of all, to the Most Rev. Albert G. Meyer, S.T.D., S.S.L., whose course in Fundamental Theology first awakened my interest in this subject and served as a continued source of inspiration; to the Most Rev. John B. Grellinger, S.T.D., Ph.Mag.Agg., whose graphic examples in teaching philosophy set an example I have tried to follow; to the Rev. John A. Schulien, M.A., S.T.D., who was of assistance both in class and in his painstaking reading of the manuscript. All of these, I am sure, will discover echoes of their own statements on these pages. Acknowledgment is due also to the following for their friendly encouragement and their assistance in many ways: the Rt. Rev. Msgr. Frank M. Schneider, M.A., S.T.D.; the Rt. Rev. Msgr. Peter Leo Johnson, S.T.D.; the Rt. Rev. Msgr. John J. Barry, Ph.D.; the Rev. Robert J. Mullins, M.A.; as well as my colleague, the Rev. John T. Donovan, J.C.D., for his help in the task of correcting the proofs.

I also wish to thank the Dominican Sisters of Racine for my early training, and particularly, in this instance, Sister Mary Celeste, O.P., head of the Department of English of Dominican College, for reading the entire manuscript.

NOTE TO SECOND EDITION

IN THIS second edition, I have made a number of changes. For the most part, they are small ones, with but three exceptions. Chapter IV and Chapter V in the first edition have been revised, and combined into one chapter; the book now has sixteen chapters instead of the seventeen in the first edition. Two other chapters have been considerably revised also: Chapter IX, "The Church and Salvation," and Chapter XIII, "The Infallible Church." These were formerly Chapter X and Chapter XIV respectively. In this regard, I would like to thank the Right Rev. Msgr. Joseph C. Fenton, S.T.D., whose review of the present Chapter IX was of great help in clarifying the issues; and also the Rev. John J. Galvin, S.T.D., whose comments aided greatly in reworking the present Chapters III and XIII. In general the very favorable reception of the book has been most encouraging, and it is my hope that the revisions included here will add to its usefulness.

J. L. M.

CONTENTS

THE LIVING CHRIST

ENCYCLICAL LETTER

on the Mystical Body of Jesus Christ
and on our union with Christ in it . . .

(N.C.W.C. edition)

COMMENT

THE Holy Father has divided his subject matter into three sections. The first is more closely akin to the usual treatise *On the Church* (*De Ecclesia*), but viewed in the light of St. Paul's metaphor. It is this section that we discuss in the pages which follow. It is the section which tells us *what* the Mystical Body is, *how* it is organized, and *who* are its members. It tells us something of the special prerogatives enjoyed by this Church, and it stresses above all the inner nature of this Church. This is the longest and, by far, the most basic section of the encyclical.

We have not gone into a further discussion of Parts Two and Three for two reasons: first, the book is already long enough; but, second, and more fundamental, it seemed better to separate a discussion of the more inner, theological bonds which unite the members of the Church from the more outward, legal requirements for membership. It appears to be the best way of avoiding confusion in a book of this nature.

We do not say much, as a result, about the inner life of faith, hope, and charity in the Church, nor of the effect of these virtues in making the Church a community of love, such as it is. We have not devoted any special section to a discussion of the Eucharist and the Mass, although, as Pius XII points out, it is in the Holy Eucharist that "this union during this mortal life reaches, as it were, a culmination" (paragh. 81). This also belongs to the inner bonds of union; even more, the Mass and the Eucharist are so important and yet so complex in regard to the union of all the faithful, that it seems they could be treated far better at another time in a separate work.

We would not like to leave the impression, however, that these more or less external bonds of union which we discuss here are intended to go no further. What we are trying to portray for the reader is a solid grasp of what the Church is. THE LIVING CHRIST is, in a way, the equivalent of the seminary tract on the Church. But the life of the Catholic is destined to touch other depths. This union of all in Christ is supposed to bear fruit in the world of grace, and to flower forth in a lively faith, a confident hope, and an all-consuming love. It is to take root especially in the liturgical life of the Church, the official public and social worship of the Mystical Body.

When we describe what things are required to *be* a member of the Body of Christ, we do not want to imply that they exhaust the meaning of membership. The life of the Catholic, and his union with Christ and in Christ, implies far more. Our purpose is to discuss the juridic bonds by which the visible body of the Church is constituted. "These juridical bonds in themselves far surpass those of any other human society, however exalted," as Pius XII remarks; "and yet another principle of union must be added to them in those three virtues, Christian faith, hope and charity, which link us so closely to each other and to God" (paragh. 70). A *full* Christian life demands the flowering of these virtues; the life of the Mystical Body cannot be all that it should be without them. To these elements then, God willing, we may be able to return at another time.

CHAPTER I

IT'S THE CHURCH WE'RE
TALKING ABOUT

ABOUT the most frequently asked question in regard to the doctrine of the Mystical Body is: "What is it?" It is a good question, and things would be much clearer for a good many people if they had stopped at the very beginning to ask that same question. His Holiness Pope Pius XII has stated the answer very clearly in his encyclical letter, *The Mystical Body of Christ,* issued on June 29, 1943: "If we would define and describe this true Church of Jesus Christ — which is the One, Holy, Catholic, Apostolic Roman Church — we shall find nothing more noble, more sublime, or more divine than the expression 'the Mystical Body of Jesus Christ.' "[1]

If we turn the above definition around we have our own definition: *The Mystical Body of Christ is the One, Holy, Catholic, Apostolic, Roman Church.* If the reader leaves this book with no other thought than that, the writing of it will not be in vain. As we shall see later on, there has been a great deal of confusion on this one point, and a very understandable reason for this confusion at that. Since the publication of the epic-making encyclical of Pius XII on the Mystical Body, however, there is no doubt as to just what the Mystical Body is, and we can follow this definition without fear and without more confusion than we might find in any other study of the Church, limiting ourselves, as does the encyclical, to a consideration of the Church Militant.

THE CHURCH

It is best to emphasize at the outset that we are speaking about the Church in this book. But we are *not* speaking about a building, although that is perhaps the image that comes most commonly to mind today at the word "church." We at once think of good old St. Thomas' Church where we were baptized as infants; where we made our First Holy Communion; and where, one slumbering August morning, we joined hands with the man or the woman who was to be our spouse for life. The color of those not too artistic but beloved stained-glass windows seems once more to capture our eye; the fragrance of the Benediction incense floats upon the air while the organ gently sings. That is the church to which we once "belonged." Whatever may be the church that comes to mind — a small country chapel, a big city church a block long, the cathedral church itself — we only too easily come to think of it as something *outside* ourselves. We "belong" to that church because our name appears on the register, and we receive each year a set of envelopes to facilitate making our contributions for the support of "the church."

There is also the tendency on the part of the laity to think of the Church as something *outside* themselves by identifying the entire Church with that part of it which is formed by the Holy Father, the bishops, and their priests. It is this attitude which might be reflected in such statements as "Why does the Church do this or that?" or, perhaps, "Why doesn't the Church change her view on this matter?" Actually, the clergy did not make up the beliefs of the Church any more than did the laity; the hierarchy are simply the custodians of those truths which God Himself has revealed.

One who really wishes to understand the Church must go far beyond these notions, for they but touch the surface. Assuredly, there is a place for organization and for officials and for buildings in our view of the Church; the Church is a visible body. But we must not stop there, for it is far more than that.

THE CHURCH IS PEOPLE

This idea is profound. The Church is a group of human beings, some of whom are to govern and others who are to be governed, but *altogether* they form the Church. This Church is not some tyrannical force outside the people, as many who misunderstand her would have it. The Church is not a body of priests and bishops who dominate the lives of the less forceful any more than it consists solely of the laity without these rulers. There *is* a power outside all of them, but that power is God, and it is not a tyrant's power but the power of Love. If some among the members have more power and authority than others, it is by no means to their own credit. They all make up the Church, and the authority which certain ones may possess is not their own, but rather the power of God, and it is for that reason that these men are respected and obeyed. Yet they, no less than the governed, are but members of the Mystical Body; and all the members are important. Authority in the Church simply indicates that the Church is a social body, a group of people; and in all such groups of human beings on this earth there must be those who lead and direct. The Church is no exception. The fact, however, that one is not a bishop or priest does not mean that that individual is not an integral part of the Church, any more than a child ceases to be a member of a family because his mother and father have authority over him, or than a woman ceases to be a member of the Altar Society when she is not elected president.

This organic notion of the Church is important to keep in mind because it is so easy to talk about "the Church" and forget that one is talking *about oneself.* It is a common failing to speak thoughtlessly in what philosophers call "abstract terms." We can all speak of "whiteness," and we know what we mean. But did anyone ever see "whiteness" apart from an object? Surely, we have seen white snow and white dresses and white frosting on cakes, but no one has ever seen just plain "whiteness." It is always some white *thing* which we see, yet we still speak of "whiteness." It is an abstract term, something that exists as such only in our minds — abstracted from real things. Or again, we may order an ice-cream soda. When we say "ice-cream soda," we all know what is meant without saying just what kind of soda it is. Actually we have always had chocolate sodas or vanilla or raspberry or pineapple sodas; we have never had just an "ice-cream soda." But we are able to abstract from the kind of soda it is and talk about sodas in general; we can talk in abstract terms.

Now, it is possible for us to speak about the Church in this way too. We can talk so much about the Church in vague terms that we gradually get the idea that the Church is not real. We miss the reality itself. We do that especially when we begin to think and speak of the "Church" as something vague and mysterious; something outside ourselves, something that we can stand aside and talk about, but on which we cannot quite put our finger — very much like "whiteness."

We would find, perhaps, that only too many people fall into one of two errors: either they mistake one small part of the Church, which they can see, for the whole Church; or they decide that the whole Church is something that they cannot see. The one who thinks that the Church is nothing more than priests and bishops or buildings, doesn't go *far enough,* while the other person, who seems to think the Church is only something to talk about, but not to see, *misses things* right in front of his eyes. Both are wrong, for they are talking about parts of the Church rather than the whole reality.

In the Church of Christ we find two distinct elements, yet so closely are they interwoven that they merit comparison between the human and divine nature in Christ. Cardinal Suhard has described this very beautifully in his pastoral letter, *Growth or Decline?:* "In Christ two natures were united: He was man and God. In the same way two worlds are closely united in the Church: the invisible reality and the visible Society, the community of the faithful. If we forget one of these two aspects we suppress the Church. Without a visible organization, without institutions, a hierarchy, the sacraments, etc., Christ is no longer incarnate on earth, the Church is no longer a body. But, on the other hand, to stop at the juridical organization and go no further than external appearances is to replace the Body of Christ by a corpse of the Church."[2]

THE VISIBLE SOCIETY

The visible side of the Church will take on slightly different forms from century to century, but it always has one thing that is unchanging and unchangeable: it is made up of people. They are the Church.

At times they will be highly organized, as in many countries today, divided into archdioceses and dioceses and individual parishes. They will have beautiful buildings called churches, but so called only because the Church (this is, the people who make up the Church) worships there, priests and laity together. They will have ecclesiastical offices with elaborate systems of filing the hundreds of papers concerning marriages, baptisms, and the like. They will publish newspapers and magazines; they will broadcast over the radio and television. There will be much system. But we must not confuse the system within the Church with the Church herself.

Buildings called churches are most useful for worship, but if these do not exist, the *Church* — the people and their priests — will continue to worship anywhere: on boxes of ammunition piled on bloody battlefields, in empty store buildings, in the basements of factories, in the sand pits of Rome. The Church lives on as long as the people hold fast to the word of God. In the persecuted countries of Europe and Asia today, with the church buildings taken away or destroyed, with the system of organization disrupted, with even the leaders — the bishops and priests — driven from the land, the Church lives on. There are members of the Church today in Russia who hold fast to their Catholic faith, and though the governing body of their group has been taken away, they still await with great hope the return of their pastors so that the Church might worship again in her official act of sacrifice, the Mass. But we may be sure that the Church in Russia is not dead; it lives on, without buildings, even without priests, and it prays for the day when it may again come, not to life, but simply out of hiding.

It was this notion of the Church that Pope Pius XII had in mind in speaking to the newly-created Cardinals in 1946: "The faithful, and more precisely the laity, are in the front line of the Church's life. . . . Accordingly they — especially they — must have an ever clearer sense not only of *belonging to* the Church, but of *being* the Church, the community of the faithful on earth under the guidance of the common head, the Pope, and of the bishops in communion with him."[3]

The Church of the year 35 was certainly no less the Church of Christ and His Mystical Body than the Church of 1900. There were no churches then such as we know today, but the Church met and prayed: first in an upper room borrowed for the occasion; and in the homes of the faithful, over the tombs of the deceased; and even in the cells of the imprisoned. Neither was there the complex organization of today, but there were then — as there will be always — bishops, priests, and laity, united under the headship of Christ and his vicar on earth, the Pope. And that is the Church.

The complex organization and growth and development of the Church is something added, something accidental. It is adapted according to the needs and demands of the day, and thus it will at times vary. The external, passing things will change from century to century, but the Church will remain the same, like the motionless depths of the sea beneath the constantly changing waves above. St. Paul never filled out a marriage questionnaire such as the Church demands today before allowing the ceremony to take place, yet he was no less a priest, and the marriage was no less a sacrament, nor the Church any different from what it is today. It is simply that the circumstances of our times and a modern world require these added precautions. Thus has it always been. The Holy Sacrifice of the Mass is the same always and everywhere, yet the external rites have varied, and though it is usually said in Latin today, there are still places where it is offered in Greek and other Oriental languages; and it is not impossible that some day it may even be offered in such modern tongues as English, French, or German. As Cardinal Suhard wrote: "The Church takes men as they are with their heredities, their languages and customs. She has become incarnate in time as well as in space. She has traversed, and adapted herself to all the successive civilizations of History. She has accommodated herself to the age as well as to the place. Each age has lent her its stature and its countenance."[4]

When we speak of the "Body" of Christ, then, it is of this that we speak: the visible, Roman, Catholic Church, living throughout the ages. We are speaking of people, priests, and laity, under the headship of Christ and His vicar on earth, the Pope; we are speaking of Jesus Christ prolonged in space and time through those who make up His Body, and of Christ communicated to men in this Body.

THE INVISIBLE REALITY

To explain how this is all possible, how this group of people, despite the changing faces from century to century, can still remain the same Body of Christ; to understand how this unbroken unity has continued for nearly 2000 years; to grasp what is the bond of union between all these people through all these years we must look beyond the outward appearances. We must look further than the people who make up the Church, because the question will always remain. Why is it only *this* group of men can attain to such unity despite time and place? *How* can this be accomplished? Why can they alone, amid the ever changing things of life, somehow stay the same from century to century?

The only answer is that there exists a Power which is outside each of these men, and outside of them all taken together: the Power of God. That alone can explain the continued life of the Church, despite the changing rounds of people who make up her membership. It is that Power which makes all the difference in the world, for without it the Church is no different from any other group of men — more organized than a mob, perhaps, but beyond that, the same. To say that it is the Body "of Christ" would then sound pretty, but it would mean nothing, because any group of men might call themselves the same thing. Actually *to be* the Body of Christ, a group must have more than the desire, or the boast, that it is so.

It is the divinity of Christ which makes all the difference in the Church of Christ. This all-important invisible element comes to the Church from its divine Head, for Christ is God. There is, therefore, a divine element within this Church itself which is the Body of Christ.

It is this element in particular that we are to study in learning about the Mystical Body of Christ. When we speak about the Mystical Body we are speaking about this and nothing more: the Roman Catholic Church. But we are speaking about a side of the Catholic Church which many perhaps have failed to notice at all, or to which they have given but slight attention — this inward, supernatural life. The doctrine teaches nothing really new, for the Church has always been the Body of Christ. What is important, however, is that through it we catch a glimpse of the Church in her full glory, in the fullness of her life.

THE CONSTANCY OF THE CHURCH

The *fact* of the Roman Catholic Church is indisputable; its history of almost 2000 years is recorded for all to read, and a magnificent thing it is. Believers and nonbelievers alike must stop to marvel at what they see. They are all accustomed to the changing things of life. They have seen organizations rise in their own lifetime and disband within that same period. They have seen countries surge to power, only to fall into insignificance. They can read the pages of history and ask themselves what became of the great Persian Empire, and the Greek and the Roman. They can study the teachings of influential religious leaders who said that "Faith without good works is sufficient," and they can see their followers today teaching the exact opposite: "Good works without faith" — at times not even faith in Christ. Human nature and human organizations are very changeable things.

When mankind meets up, then, with a very unique group of men that has remained intact for twenty centuries, *despite* the difficulties at times within the group, and *despite* the avowed intention of persecutors from without, to blot the very memory of that body from the face of the earth — when mankind comes upon such a group, it cannot help but stand aside and marvel at it. And this is the question they put to themselves: "Why is this one group so permanent, so enduring?" The greatest political and military powers in history have expended their tremendous force to destroy this organization. Why, then, does it *still* continue; how can it be? What is the secret behind the Roman Catholic Church?

TWO ANSWERS

There are two answers and those two answers represent two completely different fields of human thought. *First,* there are those who accept the possibility and who believe firmly in the actuality of a divinely sustained Church. They are the ones who see beyond the outer shell of the Church and grasp the invisible reality; that Power outside of these men which keeps this Body alive; that Power which makes the Roman Catholic Church the Body "of Christ." For these the words of the Vatican Council have real meaning: "The Church *herself* is a tremendous and perpetual motive of credibility and an undeniable proof of her divine mission, [because in the life of the Church we see such marvels] as her remarkable propagation [throughout the world], as her extraordinary sanctity and inexhaustible fruitfulness in all good things, as her unity throughout time and space and her unconquered stability."[5] The fact that the Church has remained throughout all these years is a miracle in itself, and a proof to these people, as it was to the Fathers at the Vatican Council, of the divine power that sustains her.

Second, there are those others, who for one reason or another, either false philosophies or misunderstandings or bigotry, reject even the possibility of such an explanation. For them, there just can be no question of a divinely sustained body. And yet the fact of the Catholic Church's continued existence faces them and demands an explanation. For these the answer lies in the "political power and organization" of the Papacy.

There is much talk today about such supposed political power. This is really quite understandable, for the Church today cannot be ignored. Yet if the first explanation be rejected, what other one is possible? Everyone must take his choice of one or the other; it is either the Power of God or the power of politics that accounts for the stability of the Roman Catholic Church. To debate point by point the different activities of the Church with people who hold this second view will be useless. It is in the basic viewpoints that the differences lie. Until such persons will consider at least the *possibility* of a divinely sustained Church, there can be no hope of agreement. These two opposite viewpoints will result in two different interpretations of everything the Church does. If the Church is presented as a powerful opponent of Communism, the first group will see in that a reflection of the power of God behind the Church, while for the second, it will be only an added indication of ecclesiastical politics.

When men speak about the tyranny of the "Church"; of its "Fascist" ways; or when they call it an "exalted form of totalitarianism," they give evidence of this second way of thinking. It is the deeper, more basic viewpoint which colors all of their thinking, according to which they firmly believe that the Roman Church is sustained by no divine power, but rather by the most efficient and ingenious bit of politics ever known to mankind: sly, scheming, shrewd, but always successful. Macaulay's statement well expresses their view: "It is impossible to deny that the polity of the Church of Rome is the very masterpiece of human wisdom. In truth, nothing but such a polity could, against such assaults, have borne up such doctrines. The experience of twelve hundred eventful years, the ingenuity and patient care of forty generations of statesmen have improved that polity to such perfection that among the contrivances which have been devised for controlling mankind, it occupies the highest place."[6]

It is a rather left-handed compliment, forcing the Machiavellis and the Hitlers of all ages to take a poor second place. In a world which sets such high values upon political power, it might not be a poor compliment, and one might imagine that, with the added experience since the time of Macaulay, the polity of the Church of Rome would be the last word in perfection. It is not acceptable, however, because it is given only as a second choice. Macaulay and others like him find it better to admit political supremacy than to speak of the Church as a divinely sustained institution. The choice is made reluctantly for the sly, shrewd, scheming, but always successful power; for to admit the possibility of a divinely sustained religion would lead to the humbling admission that *Something* besides such a polity could, against such assaults, have borne up such doctrines for 2000 years, and with that admission would come the loss of their creed of unbelief.

When Christ declared His power to teach, to rule, and to sanctify men, there were those, who, seeing only His humanity, and failing to pierce through to His divinity, called out that He blasphemed. And so today, when Christ continues to teach, to rule, and to sanctify through His Church, the men who see only the feeble humanity of those who make up that Body, and who fail to pierce through to the divine power which sustains it, cry out against what appears to them as arrogance. They call them tyrants, perverters of the truth, obstacles to the free approach to God — all because they do not look deep enough to see Christ in His Church.

The Creed of the Catholic Church contains, in addition to a belief in the Trinity and a belief in Christ, a rather unusual phrase: "I believe in the one, holy, catholic, and apostolic Church." If we can see behind the Church the power of God, we can understand this. Faith is the acceptance of a truth on the word of God. When I believe that Christ is God, I accept His word for that, and it is easy because He performed miracles to prove the truth of His statement. His argument was this: "If I can work these wonders that you see, or read about, then My words can also be accepted without fear. These miracles prove that I am what I say, that I am God; and thus what I teach is of God also."

So it is with the Church. We cannot see the divine element in the Church directly; we see only men. Yet, with the eyes of faith, we can look beyond them. We have the word of Christ that He will be with us all days, and that the gates of hell shall not prevail against His Church because the divine power will sustain it. And it is easy to believe that, because the Church itself *does* live on, and the gates of power or politics or military might or hell itself cannot prevail against it. It is in that divine power of the Church that a Catholic believes, that power which Christ has promised: the divine element in the Catholic Church which makes it the Body of Christ. It is this that makes all the difference in the world between this group of men known as Catholics and any other organization of men throughout the world. It is this that forms our explanation for the stability of the Church of Christ.

CHAPTER II

WHAT'S THIS "MYSTICAL" ABOUT?

For most people the most confusing term in studying the doctrine of the Mystical Body of Christ is the word *mystical*. From what was said in the preceding chapter, it would seem that we are talking about something very definite — the Roman Catholic Church. Yet today the word *mystical* carries with it the notion of something "vague" or "ghostly" or "unreal"; something we cannot see; something on which we cannot quite put our finger.

The Mystical Body is none of these things. It is something real, as real as yourself, as real as your parish church. If you want to *see* the "Mystical" Body for yourself, you need only walk into your parish church and see the people kneeling there as the priest and they offer the Sacrifice of the Mass. That is the Mystical Body of Christ at prayer.

USE OF THE WORD "MYSTICAL"

Perhaps it would help matters to state at once that the word *mystical* has nothing to do with this doctrine as such; in fact, St. Paul, who wrote constantly about this teaching, got along very nicely without ever using the word, and so did some twelve centuries of Catholics who followed him. It was only later, probably about the thirteenth century, that the word *mystical* was added to the Pauline phrase "Body of Christ" in reference to the Church; but that was before the word "mystical" carried with it the notion of something "vague," which it has acquired in our time. Previously the writers had spoken of the Church as a "spiritual" body or as a "spiritual" temple, expressing the same idea intended by the use of the word *mystical* today. They had referred to the "mystery" of the Church, and had gone so far as to speak of the "mystical church," as did St. Augustine, and of the "mystical union" with Christ in that Church, as did St. Cyril of Alexandria. These terms expressed the same general notion, but it was not until much later that the term *"mystical body"* was first used in reference to the Church. There had been a gradual development in the use of this term, also, for at an earlier date the phrase "Mystical Body" had been applied to the Eucharist, to distinguish It from the physical body of Christ in heaven. Gradually a transition was made to the Church, and since that time the term *mystical body* has been the usual manner of referring to the Pauline concept of the Church as the body of Christ. Perhaps we today would not have chosen the word at all; but it's there, and it is a good word, a time-honored word; it is only necessary that we learn to understand it properly.

UNITY, ONENESS, IS THE MAIN POINT

As we shall see in greater detail as we go along, the use of the term *Body of Christ* in reference to the Church is actually somewhat poetic. Not that it is sheer poetry; by no means. It describes a reality. What it intends to stress really exists. Yet the term itself is a figure of speech, and as with all figures of speech, we must make the proper adjustments to avoid confusion.

The *reality* that St. Paul saw, and which he wanted to bring into clearer light, was the "intimate *union* between Christ and the members of His Church." *Union, oneness;* these are the words to remember. St. Paul lived by this truth — a truth which God presented to his mind so vividly the first time that he couldn't have forgotten it if he had tried.

THE ROAD TO DAMASCUS

St. Paul, as we know, was not always a Catholic. Until he was about thirty years old, he was a Jew, and a very fervent one at that. His zeal for the Temple went so far that he actively engaged in the persecution of a new group called "Christians" (after their founder, Christ) who were breaking away from the teachings and practices of the ancient Hebrew religion. Saul (as he was known in those days) had set out for Damascus from Jerusalem in order to capture more of these Christians, and to bring them in bonds to Jerusalem. "Still breathing threats of slaughter," Saul drew near to Damascus, when suddenly a light from heaven shone around him; and falling to the ground, he was struck blind. Then he heard a voice saying to him, "Saul, Saul, why dost thou persecute me?" And Saul asked, "Who art thou, Lord?" And he who was speaking to Saul answered, "I am Jesus, whom thou art persecuting."[1]

Paul was stunned. That was the beginning of an entirely new life for him. He was baptized, and became a great apostle for Christ, the Apostle of the Gentiles. The memory of the incident on the road to Damascus, however, never left him. He pondered it over and over, analyzing each word. He had actually seen Christ, and he saw and heard Him ask, "Why are you persecuting *me?*" Yet Paul had not even touched Christ; before this incident, he had not even seen Christ. But he had persecuted the followers of Christ. Why, then, had not Christ asked, "Why are you persecuting my followers?" But He had said: "I am Jesus, *whom thou art persecuting.*"

THE MEANING OF WHAT HAPPENED

Gradually Paul saw the meaning behind it. He realized that Christ was God as well as Man, and that through some divine power He had established some sort of special relationship between Himself and those who became members of the Church He established. There was a bond of "union," of "oneness," between them and Christ, unlike that found anywhere else in the world. This formed the basis of all of Paul's teaching. His epistles are filled with this truth, above all those which he wrote in his later years, while he was in prison in Rome, the Letter to the Ephesians and the Letter to the Colossians.

No doubt, as Paul talked with the Christians, asking about Christ, some one of the disciples (maybe Peter) told him of what our Lord had said one day after they had left the temple. They had asked Him about the end of the world, and, among other things, He told about the last judgment, mentioning how some people would be brought to Him, and He would praise them, because when He was hungry, they had given Him food, and when He was thirsty and homeless, they had given Him to drink and had taken Him into their homes and given Him clothing to wear. And these people, who would be seeing Christ for the first time, would be puzzled, and ask: "Lord, when did we see thee hungry, and feed thee, or thirsty, and give thee drink?" adding perhaps, "We have never seen thee before." And answering, the King will say to them: "Amen, I say to you, as long as you did it for one of these, the least of my brethren, you did it for me."[2] That is the same union between Christ and His followers that Paul had learned of on the road to Damascus. To take pity on one of those members of Christ's Church is the same as taking pity on Christ Himself — just as persecuting those same members means persecuting Christ.

"What does it all mean?" thought Paul. "Why is there such a difference between being a follower of Christ and a follower of some other man?" The followers of the Greek philosophers — Socrates, Plato, Aristotle — none of these claimed such intimate union with their leader; none of these philosophers ever claim it for their followers. Certainly, if I kill a king's messenger, I do a dishonor to the king, but I do not really harm the king himself. Of course, following a manner of speaking, the king might *consider* it as done to himself, and might say, "You have harmed the king in slaying his messenger"; but here in this case Paul clearly sensed that Christ had in mind something more than a way of speaking. He later found out more surely that this was true. When the messenger of the king is slain the king himself does not suffer death. There is nothing in the messenger that unites him to his master so closely that they might actually *be* one; it lies entirely in the mind of the king, who decides to consider it as done to himself. In regard to Christ and the members of His Church, on the other hand, there is something more. Here something happens to the individual; he is changed *in himself*. He becomes something different; there is a real and an intrinsic change in the man himself, and because of that, he is actually one with Christ. It is not all in the mind of Christ, but it is in the soul of the individual as well. Christ favors that soul with special gifts and unites it, in a very real way, to Himself.

Baptism makes one a member of the Church of Christ, but it also changes the individual himself. The followers of Christ, then, really put on Christ, as St. Paul expressed it: "For all you who have been baptized into Christ, have *put on Christ*."[3] Stamped with the seal of Christ, they have put Him on, not merely in some outward fashion, but in the very depths of their being. Paul strains language to the breaking point in his efforts to bring home to his Christians the greatness and completeness of this change. Later centuries found a new word to express this idea. They used the verb *to christen*, that is, to make one "Christ-ed." Today we might hear such words as *configured* to Christ, or *incorporated* into Christ, expressing the same notion of actual oneness, even of identity, with the God-Man.

PAUL'S TEACHING

In his attempts to get this idea over to his people, Paul looked about for the best means to be used. The idea of "union" and "oneness" with Christ filled his mind. He could have spoken about it in just those words, but they seemed not graphic enough. When a man has something to say that he wants to impress deeply on the minds of his hearers, he will turn to graphic, vivid speech. The human mind is greatly attracted by such an approach, and in that lies the teaching value of stories. That is the reason why our Lord spoke so often in parables. Christ might have spoken to the multitudes simply about how the heavenly Father will forgive us our sins if we are sorry. To make His point strong, however, He told the story of the prodigal son; in it we see all with the eyes of our mind. We see "sin" — a floundering, foolish, and inexperienced youth chasing after the glittering things of earth until they have changed into mud and swine. We see "sorrow" trudging down the road, head bent, tears streaming from his eyes, crying out, "Father, I am no longer worthy to be called thy son!" And we see "forgiveness" running down the road to "sorrow," and catching him up into his arms, kissing him as he calls out to one and all "to make merry, because this my son was dead and has come to life again."[4]

It is in this way that those notions become alive for us. And that is what Paul wanted to do with his message. He already had at hand the examples Christ had used, above all His beautiful comparison between the vine and branches:

> Abide in me and I in you.
> As the branch cannot bear fruit of itself
> unless it remain on the vine,
> so neither can you
> unless you abide in me.
> I am the vine,
> you are the branches.
> He who abides in me, and I in him,
> he bears much fruit;
> for without me you can do nothing.[5]

Our union with the God-Man is as close as that. Paul grasped the import of that metaphor, and even made use of a similar idea in his Epistle to the Romans, when he wrote, thinking of an olive branch: "And if the root is holy, so also are the branches."[6]

Christ also had compared His mission to a wedding feast, implying that the union between Himself and His followers was similar to the union between man and wife. Some disciples of John the Baptist had come and asked of our Lord: "Why do we and the Pharisees often fast, whereas thy disciples do not fast?" And Jesus answered them: "Can the wedding guests mourn as long as the bridegroom is with them? But the days will come when the bridegroom shall be taken away from them, and then they will fast."[7] In other words, Christ had come down from heaven to unite Himself to mankind most intimately. His brief sojourn upon earth was likened to the wedding feast, when all celebrated the union; it was a time of joy. When after His death, the Bridegroom would leave the world, then would come the time for penance.

Paul made use of this same comparison in his Letter to the Ephesians, a text which is used by the Church in her marriage ceremony:

> Be subject to one another in the fear of Christ.
> Let wives be subject to their husbands
> as to the Lord;

because a husband is head of the wife,
     just as Christ is head of the Church,
          being himself savior of the body.
But just as [we are] subject to Christ,
     so also let wives be to their husbands in all things.
Husbands, love your wives,
     just as Christ also loved [us],
     and delivered himself up for [us]
Even thus ought husbands also to love their wives
     as their own bodies.[8]

We can see, in passing, what a lofty concept of marriage was to be found in the mind of Christ and St. Paul in making these comparisons.

At other times, Paul tried to express this idea of union between Christ and the members of His Church by comparing it to the unity found in a building, stone united to stone to make the grand structure, and "Christ Jesus himself as the chief corner stone"[9] upon which all depends. The "spiritual temple," or the "spiritual house," comparison is used by St. Peter to express the same thing: "Be you yourselves as living stones, built thereon into a spiritual house, a holy priesthood, to offer spiritual sacrifices acceptable to God through Jesus Christ."[10] This was the notion St. Paul had in mind when he also asked of the Corinthians: "Do you not know that you are the temple of God and that the Spirit of God dwells in you?"[11]

St. Paul also compared the union between Christ and the Church to the oneness and identity of the Eucharistic Bread, of which all partake: "Because the bread is one, we though many, are one body, all of us who partake of the one bread."[12] The same Christ is present in all the tabernacles throughout the world; and as He is one in Himself, so are we all one in Him.

FAVORITE COMPARISON: BODY

Above and beyond all of these comparisons, however, one became the favorite of St. Paul; one which he repeated over and over again, which through the centuries has become the favorite of the Church as well. It is the comparison of the union between Christ and His Church to the union between the head and the body of a human being.

Paul had learned from Christ Himself the truth of this very special and unique union, this "oneness" between Catholics and Christ. One of his particular works in the Providence of God was to lay special emphasis on this inner life of the Church, this special union which makes this particular group of men unique and different from any other group of men on the earth. And it was this image of the "Body of Christ" that was to be his most favored tool in performing that work: Christ the Head, and the Roman Catholic Church the body. This comparison, perhaps better than any other, brings to light the *reality* of that inner union in Christ.

As Paul looked about for a means whereby he might best express this idea of oneness, his keen eye was quickly attracted by the unity of the human person. Men had always marveled at it, and all men knew about it. What simpler then, than to lead their minds gradually from an understanding of that union to an understanding of their union with Christ in His Church. All good teachers try to proceed from the known to the unknown in their instructions, and Paul was a good teacher.

Here we have the human body, the physical body of any man. It is something real, tangible — something you can see, and not just an idea. It has many different parts, some of them bigger and others smaller, but all of them necessary in order to have a *perfect* human body. And most remarkable of all, no doubt, is the fact that these many different parts make up a perfectly grouped and organized whole. Every part has its role to play, and altogether they make the body what it is.

This *unity* of the different parts of the body is a very noticeable truth in something as simple, for example, as a sudden flush of anger or fear in a person. The emotion will arise from an external cause which seems to threaten the individual in some way, but it will give way almost at once to certain physiological changes in the entire body. The fear arises in the mind, but the body shares in it. The heart beats faster, the blood pressure rises, blood is shifted from reservoirs in the vegetative area to the muscles, the sugar level of the blood increases, digestion ceases, the individual becomes alert and irritable. These changes all have a clear-cut biologic process: to prepare the individual for action or fighting or other suitable behavior. It all tends toward securing the survival of the whole body, so that the different parts are forgetful, as it were, of their own individual processes for a moment.

Paul saw all of this, then, and transferred the idea to the notion of the Church. The Church of Christ is *like* a human body. It is not the same by any means; it is a group of people, not a composite of physical organs; but we can see the similarity. Just as when we say of someone that he is a "bear for work," we do not mean he is an animal, but that his tenacity and endurance for work suggests the power and endurance of a bear.

As we shall see later, Paul worked out this comparison in considerable detail, and it does bring home in an admirable fashion the idea of the union between Christ and the men who are His Church.

VALUE OF THE TERM

Confusion is always a dangerous thing in theology as well as anywhere else. That became clearer in this matter as men began to confuse the different uses of the term *body of Christ*. We have first the physical body of Christ, derived from the body of the Blessed Mother; that body in which Christ appeared among men some 2000 years ago. It was a perfect human body, yet no different in its physical aspects from the body of any other man. Today, after the Ascension, that body is in heaven where Christ sits at the right hand of the Father. That physical body is present in heaven; but also, in the Blessed Sacrament, that same identical body is present upon thousands of altars throughout the world, wherever the Sacrifice of the Mass is offered.

On the other hand, we have the term *body of Christ* as referring to the Church. To help avoid confusion between the two, we now have the word *mystical* added to the phrase *body of Christ,* and we know at once that we are speaking about the Church. For that reason the word *mystical* is a good word, one that helps us to keep our thinking straight. As soon as we hear someone mention the "Mystical Body of Christ," the idea of this unique organization of men comes to mind rather than the physical or Eucharistic body of Christ.

ANOTHER DISTINCTION

Pope Pius XII mentions another value in the use of the term *mystical* which he tells us is more important than the one above in view of certain modern errors. It is that it helps us to keep the Church separate in our minds from any other physical or moral body in the world. *Physical* bodies would be, for example, stones, buildings, the human body; a *moral* body would be an association of men in some group, such as the American Legion or the Sodality or governments of nations. There are important differences between the Mystical Body and either of these two types of bodies, physical and moral. And it is these differences which make the Church such an unusual organization, unique among all the groups on earth.

PHYSICAL BODY

As was mentioned before, the phrase *Mystical Body* intends to say only that the Church is like a human body; it is not a human body actually. Thus we must note certain things in which it is *unlike* a physical body also, points on which the comparison would not apply.

First of all, in a physical body the different parts live *only* for the good of the whole body. The tail of a dog is nothing if considered apart from the dog; it is just the tail of the dog, and has no personality and no existence of any sort of its own. In the Church, however, we have a union of different members, but each member is a person in his own right, and is not so immersed in the whole body that he loses his individuality. Every member, while he is linked intimately to other members, still remains something very important in himself. He keeps his own individual personality. Some people failed to keep that in mind, and as a result, the Pope had to condemn those who, when speaking of the Mystical Body, failed to make the correct distinctions — those who tried to "make the Divine Redeemer and the members of the Church coalesce in one *physical* person."[13]

So also, in a physical body, the various parts act for the good of the whole body alone. The eyes, the ears, the hands of a man have no special interest of their own apart from the body itself. The members of the Catholic Church do, however, have their own interests. The ultimate purpose of the Mystical Body includes the spiritual advancement of all in general and of each single member in particular; and no member can ever become so engrossed in the welfare of other souls as to completely forget his own interests — an error into which some have at times fallen.

MORAL BODY

There is a far greater tendency today, however, to confuse the Mystical Body with other groups that we call "moral bodies." The word *moral* indicates here a group which is joined together through an agreement of their minds and wills. The word *moral* in this case has nothing to do with "goodness" or "morals." Here it merely refers to the fact that the existence of the group depends upon the *will* or agreement of its members. A society to promote artificial birth control could be called a "moral" group in this sense, although, in an ethical sense, it is organized for highly immoral purposes.

We also refer to governments as "moral" organizations — that is, that they are groups of people which exist only because the will of the people decrees it. We even call these groups "bodies"; the legislative body in Washington, for example. The dictionary explains this use of the word *moral* as referring to "a unit formed of a number of persons; a collective whole; so called because of the moral unity of their wills."

It is perhaps easy to confuse the Church with such moral bodies, because the two things are very close: the Mystical Body actually is a moral body, but a moral body *plus* something else — and it is that "plus" that makes all the difference in the world. The Church of Christ is a moral body since it is a group of men, united for a common goal or purpose. But that is not enough. In a *mere* moral body (one that is such and nothing more), the principle of union, the thing that binds the members together is found *only* in the common purpose and the common co-operation of all under authority to reach the goal set by that body. In the Church, we have this, but we have something more, namely, a distinct, *internal* principle — an inner life — that exists in the Church taken all together, and also in each one of the members. It is something unique, something that is possessed by no other moral body in the world. It is something distinct from the members; it is something supernatural, and, as we shall see more fully later, it is essentially something infinite and uncreated: the Holy Spirit Himself.

It is this inner spark of life, over and above the common interests and goals and labors of the members, which makes the Body of Christ different from any group of men in the world. It is this which makes it different from all non-Catholic religions as well. Separated from this inner principle, these other groups remain merely moral bodies. These men are joined together by a community of mind and will, but they lack this further, inner principle of life which is the true source of changelessness and stability in the Church of Christ. "What makes Christ's Mystical Body so very different from any mere moral body of men," writes Archbishop Myers, "is the character of the union existing between Christ and the members. It is not a mere external union, it is not a mere moral union; it is a union which, as realized in Christ's Church, is at once external and moral, but also, and that primarily, internal and supernatural."[14]

To remind us of this, then, and to help us distinguish the true Church from all other moral organizations, we now have the word *mystical,* and, we repeat, it is a good word. The Church is a visible body, but we cannot understand it perfectly if that is all we see. We cannot explain the Church in the natural order alone, because part of it — and the most important part of it — lies in the supernatural order. When we hear the phrase the "Mystical Body of Christ," then, we think not simply of the organization, but more especially of the inner life of this Church which makes her so different from all other groups of men. The union of men in the Mystical Body is far superior to the union and oneness found in any other human organization, hence "this word [mystical] in its correct signification gives us to understand," as Pius XII writes, "that the Church, a perfect society of its kind, is not made up of merely moral and juridical elements and principles. It is far superior to all other human societies; it surpasses them as grace surpasses nature, as things immortal are above those that perish."[15] Thus once again we see the value of the phrase "Mystical Body of Christ" in its proper designation. It does not indicate something vague or unreal, but it does serve to distinguish this body properly.

If once we begin to grasp the deeper shades of meaning hidden in this doctrine, it will gradually capture our entire spirit. Little by little we will see, with the help of God, the full force of the words of His Holiness who tells us that "nothing more glorious, nothing nobler, nothing surely more honorable can be imagined than to belong to the Holy, Catholic, Apostolic and Roman Church, in which we become members of one Body as venerable as it is unique; are guided by one supreme Head; are filled with one divine Spirit; are nourished during our earthly exile by one doctrine and one heavenly Bread, until at last we enter into the one, unending blessedness of heaven."[16]

CHAPTER III

I NEVER HEARD OF IT

THERE are a good many Catholics who had never heard of the Mystical Body of Christ until recent years, and it is somewhat of a problem for them to explain why they had not heard of it. When, after an explanation, they discover that it is just another name for the Roman Catholic Church, their most common reaction is, "Why didn't you say so the first time?"

The reason for using this other name for the Church today, however, is not merely a sudden enthusiasm for the phrase. It has its basis both in history and in the peculiar circumstances of our own time. It has been suggested that the doctrine of the Mystical Body is receiving so much attention today for much the same reason that Communism is attractive to men of our century. It fills a need of the times. Our world today has inherited the highest aspirations of the spirit of the nineteenth century — a spirit of collectivism; and this approach to the Church emphasizes her social nature. The aim is not, of course, to present to the world a new Church; it seeks merely to point out one particular aspect of that Church — an aspect which has been somewhat neglected during the past few centuries. The inner life of which it speaks is nothing new. It was present there always, as it always will be, even though men might not speak too frequently of it.

EARLY USE OF TERMS

In the early days of the Church reference to the Church as the Body of Christ was very frequent, especially so in the writings of

St. Paul and in the works of such of his great disciples as St. Augustine and St. John Chrysostom. St. Thomas Aquinas and others in the middle ages used the terminology also. With the coming of the Protestant Reformation in the sixteenth century, however, a new problem arose. This was the first large-scale falling away from the Catholic Church which had ever been experienced in the West. The sixteenth century was a time of general unrest and revolt against tradition and authority; and Luther, Calvin, and others capitalized upon this circumstance. As a matter of fact, the interests of the Revolt were largely secular rather than spiritual, and today Protestant as well as Catholic historians admit that the religious elements of the movement have been greatly overestimated. The fact is frankly acknowledged by this statement of the *Encyclopaedia Britannica:* "Had the German princes not found it to their interests to enforce his principles, Luther might never have been more than the leader of an obscure mystic sect."[1]

In its religious teachings Protestantism spoke out against authority — the Pope, bishops, priests. It preached the doctrine of private interpretation of the Scriptures and of salvation by faith alone without good works. And as for an organization, its main teaching was that a *visible* church was not the thing that mattered. Christ, they contended, did not found any visible church to assist mankind in working out its salvation; He supposedly instituted only an invisible church, a church of faith, and it was that alone that mattered.

Such an invisible body has no need of priest, bishop, or Pope; any lay person can exercise the priestly function. Ceremonies and exterior worship are neither essential nor useful; religion is entirely a thing of the heart, a private affair between God and the individual, and the individual is free to interpret revelation as best suits him.

THE POSITION OF THE CHURCH IN THE SIXTEENTH CENTURY

We can easily see, then, the position of the Catholic Church in such an historical setup. Thousands of her subjects were giving up the truth of Christ and turning to these false beliefs, newly formed in the sixteenth century. Others in her membership were in danger of being at least partially influenced by them so as to water-down their Catholic belief. The Church had a problem on her hands; the truths which Christ had revealed to man were being attacked, and as His representative upon earth, she had a battle to fight. And that is exactly what she set about doing. Since the big attack was upon authority and a visible Church, it was precisely those points upon which she laid special emphasis. The whole Catholic apologetic (that defense of one's beliefs in speech and writing) was geared to defend the visible side of the Church, and it still is generally.

As for the inner life of the Church, while it was never in any way denied by Catholics, it was just not spoken of too often. It is only natural to lay particular stress upon one side of an argument when one is trying to make a point, so much so that any truth on the other side seems to be entirely excluded. The so-called Reformers repeatedly denied the need of a visible church in every book they wrote, in every word they spoke. To disprove their statements the defenders of the Catholic doctrine often spoke only of the exact opposite: the *need* of the *visible* elements in the Church.

The basic teachings of Protestantism lead unremittingly to the admittance of an invisible church. They began by denying the need of a visible hierarchy; there was to be no Pope, no bishops, no ordained priests. The liturgical ceremonies of the Church were gradually abandoned. While Catholics had always thought of these rites as an outward expression of their faith, it was taught that particular ceremonies of one type or another were not necessary, and it was left to the individual groups to use such rites as they desired. All of the visible elements of an authoritative Church were abandoned. The Catholic Church requires for membership what is known as the Triple Bond: baptism, adherence to the true faith, and submission to the rule of the Pope. As we shall see, these are all visible elements. The Augsburg Confession, however, written in 1531 to express the doctrinal views of the Lutheran church, described the church of Christ as "the assembly of all the faithful."[2] In this way, it made "faith" the one sole requirement for membership in the church: faith understood, however, as a trust in the saving power of Christ rather than an expression of belief.

In the doctrine on the church, however, the Protestant distinction between the invisible and visible church was first clearly formulated in the Westminster Confession of 1647. This expresses views which were largely Calvinistic. "The Catholic or Universal Church," it says, "which is *invisible,* consists of the whole number of the elect that have been, are, or shall be gathered into one, under Christ, the head thereof; and is the spouse, the body, the fullness of him who filleth all in all."[3]

It can be seen, then, why the doctrine of the Mystical Body might be neglected in such historical circumstances. The teaching of St. Paul on the Church calls our attention especially to that side of the Church which Protestants were exaggerating completely, that is, the invisible element, so that to speak of the Church in that way might open the path for further confusion. These disputes naturally had a reaction in the field of Catholic thought. "The negation of the visible character of the Church of Christ, and of its hierarchical constitution," writes Archbishop Myers, "has led to such stress being laid upon the visible, tangible aspects of the Church that those who are not Catholics have come to think of it in terms of its external organization and of its recent dogmatic definitions." Even more, as he goes on to say, "Not a few Catholics, concentrating their attention upon the argumentative, apologetical, and controversial side of the doctrine concerning the Church, have been in danger of overlooking theoretically — though practically it is impossible for them to do so — the supernatural, the mysterious, the vital, the overwhelmingly important character of the Church as the divinely established and only means of grace in the world, as the Mystical Body of Christ."[4]

THE SITUATION TODAY

This reaction has continued to our own times, so that people today are still accustomed to think of the Church first of all in its visible aspect. If you ask the average Catholic what the Church is, almost naturally the first thing that comes to his mind is the picture of the visible, human organization. It is the idea with which he is best acquainted. The average catechism will answer the question something like this: "The Church is the congregation of all those who profess the faith of Christ, partake of the same Sacraments, and are governed by their lawful pastors under one visible head." A good answer, as far as it goes, for it clearly separates the Church of Christ from all other religious bodies. Yet it does not go far enough; it separates in our mind the Roman Catholic Church from other churches, but it fails to tell us very much about the inner life of the Catholic Church herself. It is a definition geared to offset the claims of the Protestant Reformation. Much of our writing even today gives evidence of that tradition; it is aimed at proving that someone else is wrong, rather than at exposing the Catholic faith as a massive spiritual and also humane force.

When asked what the Church is, a man could also answer, however, that the Church of Christ here on earth is the Mystical Body of Christ: a body, since it is the visible organism instituted by Christ and directed by Him in a visible manner through His vicar, the Pope; but called the "mystical" body of Christ, since that organization in itself, in its varied organs, in its members, is unified and vivified by an invisible principle of life. That would call attention to both sides of the Church, the visible and the invisible elements. The catechism definition in the paragraph above is speaking about the same *reality,* but it simply takes for granted this inner life, without mentioning it expressly. It describes the externals: a congregation of people, profession of faith, reception of Sacraments, rule by lawful pastors under one visible head — all of which are manifestations of this inner life. To define the Church in terms of the Body of Christ is to speak of the same reality, but to lay special emphasis upon that inner life which is all-important. When one does grasp the true meaning of the phrase "Mystical Body of Christ," he will not find a new Church, but will come only to realize more vividly what he should have understood all the while by the phrase "Roman Catholic Church." It will bring to light an aspect of the Church which perhaps he has been neglecting. And that is the need of the times.

INDIFFERENTISM TODAY

Protestantism has to a great extent run its course as an enemy of the visibility of the Church. The attack will never entirely cease, of course, but it is not so strong as it was. Indifferentism is the great error of the present century: "one religion is as good as another." When you live by that philosophy, you have no fight left in you; you just don't care. It is like playing golf. If your next-door neighbor wants to play, well let him play; if he doesn't want to, so what? The same is true with religion in this view. It is purely a matter of private choice. What disputes do arise are based not on doctrinal difficulties so much as on biased fears of so-called "ecclesiastical politics" and "totalitarian churchmen." There are at times bitter denials of the Catholic way of life, but very little positive development of doctrines which, while remaining Christian, would replace those views.

Actually this spirit is a direct outgrowth of the earlier attacks on the visibility of the Church, except that now it is accompanied by an "I don't care" attitude. It is taken for granted by many now that there must be some kind of visible organization, but it is not important whether that group be Catholic or Lutheran or Anglican or Seventh-Day Adventist, provided no one group obtains too much power. There are a multitude of visible churches now, some claiming to be Christian and others not. In many points of doctrine they agree while in others they are in complete disagreement, yet that is all a matter of preference, and certainly not anything to fight about. The High Episcopalian Church even now publishes books that read almost exactly like Catholic books; their churches and ceremonies are often almost the same as the Catholic ones. What, then, is the difference?

Such is the typically modern attitude. It explains the first reason for the great growth in interest concerning the doctrine of the Mystical Body. It is an answer to that question; it tells what the difference actually is. It is an answer to the desire in many for something deeper, something more meaningful in religion; for something beyond surface differences. The most important difference between the Catholic Church and other religious groups is something *internal,* her inner life. That is the point on which we cannot be indifferent. There is no danger in speaking about this today in an age of religious indifference and superficiality. On the contrary, there is a great need for bringing out the teaching to make men conscious of what the true Church really is in her entirety; it is something, further, which appeals to the Catholic and the non-Catholic alike, since it plunges beyond the surface and shows the real meaning of the religion which Christ gave to mankind. And men do want to discover that today.

SOCIAL-MINDEDNESS

The second reason for the current interest in the doctrine of the Mystical Body is also a child of our age; this is the social-mindedness of men on all sides. It is evident everywhere, in business, labor, politics. In it lies the strong appeal Communism has on the minds of many today. It parades under a "pseudo ideal of justice, of equality, and fraternity," as Pope Pius XI has stated in his encyclical on Atheistic Communism.[5] Communism seeks to give a false brotherhood to men, and many are accepting it, while the Church, "with her doctrine of peace and Christian brotherhood," is being ignored. To be truthful, there is no unity possible among men that can compare with the union with Christ and with one another "in Christ" in the Mystical Body. It is not something merely external; it is not simply a banding together in a moral body for some common purpose. Rather it goes to the very roots of the soul, and catches it up on a bond of union far surpassing any of which a human being could ever of himself conceive. While others may dream visions of One World, the Catholic Church already knows it as a reality, as an actual, palpitating union of men which *does* exist and is existing now throughout the world. It is a union, not of politicians nor of capitalists nor of laborers nor of world conquerers. It is a union of ALL "in Christ." It leaps beyond the boundaries of individuals and nations; beyond the boundaries of politics and of self-aggrandizement. It dissolves the bonds of hate in order to draw all men together in the heart of Christ. Indeed, if there is any spirit of unity among men which can meet the surging wave of the sickle and hammer, it is the Spirit of Christ, it is the reality of the Mystical Body, which is the Roman Catholic Church.

GROWTH OF INTEREST

The pages of Catholic literature produced fifty years ago did not contain very much about the Mystical Body. The turn of the century saw the first beginnings of a great and impressive movement, marked by a reawakened interest in this total view of the Church. The late Archbishop Goodier recalls how "to be enthusiastic about the doctrine of the Mystical Body of Christ" at that time "was to be thought in dangerous proximity to the heresy of Modernism."[6] Unused to hearing this terminology, it struck harshly on the ear of many a Catholic in the nineteenth and early twentieth centuries. They were afraid of it.

Within the past three decades, however, it has taken on a new life. Articles, studies, books of all kinds are appearing throughout the world in greater and greater numbers, explaining the teaching and applying it to various phases of Catholic life. Men like Abbé Anger, Emile Mersch, Ernst Mura, and Ferdinand Prat led the way in France; Sebastian Tromp of the Gregorian University in Rome; Cuthbert Lattey and Hugh Pope in England; Karl Adam in Germany; Hermann Dieckmann in Switzerland; Franc Grivec in Yugoslavia; Joseph Bluett, Joseph C. Fenton, Fulton J. Sheen, and John C. Gruden in America — to mention just a few of the many — have done much in recent years to add to a proper understanding of the doctrine. The climax of all of this was reached in the encyclical letter of His Holiness, Pope Pius XII himself, in 1943, hailed by theologians as one of the greatest which has come from the Holy See.

During these same decades there were others who admittedly feared the doctrine. They felt that it was something vague and uncertain, and therefore dangerous. Still others looked upon the entire question rather humorously. They could scarcely restrain a smile when they heard the phrase "Mystical Body," thinking how foolish it was to be enthusiastic about such an indefinite belief. Today, however, no man need fear this teaching, or consider it humorously. Provided he follows the direction of the Pope in understanding it properly, there is no reason for any vagueness or confusion.

We might ask why there ought to have been any confusion at all. The answer lies in the nature of both the Church and Revelation. Some men think of Revelation as something that was given to mankind by God, once and for all, in its final form. For them, the role of the church would consist merely in passing on that rather dead and lifeless message from century to century. They can envision no growth or development whatsoever.

On the other hand, the Modernist heresy of the early part of the twentieth century went to the opposite extreme. They could see *nothing but* change. For them there was no stable, unchanging truth given to men by God; quite the contrary, religious truth was to change from century to century. The Church was simply the means of proposing this changing truth; it was to adapt itself to the changing beliefs of men.

DEVELOPMENT OF DOGMA

It is in between these two extremes that we find the true answer to our problem. There is such a thing as the legitimate *development of dogma*. The pages of Scripture do not give a full and complete account of what we are to believe. Revelation was entrusted to two sources: to the *Bible* and to *Tradition*. But Tradition is nothing other than the "teaching of the living Church." In that teaching, the Church does not act simply as a lifeless mouthpiece, repeating what has been revealed. It also has a vital role to play in unfolding the full content of revealed truth. It is an ever present duty of the Church, a task that extends throughout all the centuries of her existence.

Revelation itself ended with the death of the last Apostle, St. John. Since that time, there has been nothing added to the essential content of revealed truth. When Revelation came to a close, all supernatural truth we were to know was contained either in Scripture or in Tradition — the Church. But since that time, the Church has plumbed the greater depths of those truths. What was contained in germ, as it were, at that early date, has later flowered forth. Even Scripture depends upon the Church. It is the Church's book. Under God she wrote it, and she alone has the right to explain it in the name of Christ; she must do this, in fact, because many of the things that were written down demand some authoritative explanation. This is the work of Christ's Mystical Body and its teaching authority. Tradition thus came before Scripture since the Church existed before the New Testament was even written. It is also something more complete than Scripture, since not everything that Christ taught was written down.

There is, then, life and vitality in the doctrinal role of the Church. We need not say, as some would, that the Apostles had explicit knowledge of all the dogmas of our faith, but that they handed down to their successors only certain principles. As Father Galvin remarks, "This theory appears unlikely and offers no real solution to the problem of the development of doctrine."[7] It is simply too easy an answer to say that the Apostles just neglected to pass on the full understanding of the truths that they taught. We must look further.

We find, then, that there has been a gradual clarification of revealed truth. Just as there has been a legitimate development of doctrine in the teachings concerning Christ or the Blessed Mother or our understanding of the Eucharist and the Mass, so also, through the centuries, has there been progress and development in regard to the Mystical Body, the Church. As Carl Feckes notes: "The tiny understanding of man can always comprehend only one or another side of a mystery of faith, or at least it can only devote itself fully and completely to one or another side. Hence there is the possibility that one generation turns to this side, and a later generation, neglecting those things customary up until that time, will turn to another side, as their talents and the current of the times determine. So it happens that there is a relative change in the course of Christian history, but it is a changing that is guided by the Holy Ghost and that must serve the full development of divine revelation."[8]

GROWTH OF KNOWLEDGE

In a way, this growth is a parallel in the supernatural order of the ordinary human growth of knowledge. It does not mean that the men of earlier centuries were wanting either in learning or mental acuteness. There are simply certain things which take a longer time and much discussion to clear up in order to set forth in an orderly fashion the contents of Revelation. The ordinary scientist today may know more about atoms than the ancient Greeks, but that does not make him more intelligent than they were. Today's scientist has everything they ever discovered and a lot more besides to work with before he even begins his own labors. The same is true in under-understanding the truths revealed by God to man. Many of the greatest minds of the Church belong to the first four centuries, yet almost anyone today can easily understand things which were great problems for them, because today we have the results of their labors. They had to do the spadework.

Thus it is with the doctrine of the Mystical Body. As Feckes notes: "The later generations ever face the increasingly difficult task of setting in harmony with their own new insights all of those sides worked out by earlier generations; for it is obvious that only a combined view of the manifold findings of each of many generations and ages can approach the exalted reality of the mystery."[9] The encyclical of Pius XII presents just such a synthesis. With it as our guide, we need have no fear. Even more, every Catholic today *should* become acquainted with this sublime teaching. As the Holy Father tells us, "Mysteries revealed by God cannot be harmful to men; nor should they remain as treasures hidden in a field, useless."[10] This is especially true in this case. The doctrine of the Mystical Body has come into its own again in our times.

CHAPTER IV

HOW CONFUSED SHOULD WE BE?

If we would trace out this growth of the doctrine of the Mystical Body, we will note that it grew and developed according to the special view of the Church current in each century. At some times the metaphor of the Body was used frequently because it served well the needs of the time. It was an effective tool in answering the objections of certain heretics, or for emphasizing a special truth for the good of the faithful in that century. At other times, the comparison of the Church to a body was passed over almost entirely because of special concerns with another element of the doctrine of the Church. This is what happened during the 400 years following the Protestant Reformation. In stressing the visibility of the Church, the metaphor of the Mystical Body — which stresses its *inner* life — would not have come to mind so easily. It was this fact that made the doctrine appear "new" to some people today. In the heat of battle, it had receded into the background somewhat.

All of these various disputes and discussions, however, were preparing the way for a more complete understanding of the Church as the Mystical Body. The encyclical of Pius XII gives a composite picture of all these views of the Church, and phrases it in the metaphor of St. Paul. It does condemn some errors which had crept into certain explanations of the doctrine, but that is a minor purpose of the letter. Its chief aim is to set forth a *positive* presentation of what the Church is as the Mystical Body of Christ.

THE LESSON OF TRADITION

In order to make such a synthesis, we must, of course, look to the Tradition of the past. Tradition is not concerned with the teaching of the Church at only one age of her history. It is not something limited to the first few centuries of the Christian era; it is something that exists today and always. Since the Church's teaching is always faithful to itself, however, and does not change essentially, we naturally look first to the past in order to solve the problems of the present.

Most important are the official statements of the teaching authority of the Church throughout the centuries. These are the direct exercise of the teaching authority of the Church under the guidance of the Holy Spirit. Where they exist, they naturally give us our best directions. But we also give special importance to the writings of the early writers and scholars of the Church, men whom we call the "Fathers of the Church." These were men like St. John Chrysostom, St. Athanasius, St. Cyril of Alexandria, St. Gregory of Nazianzus, and the great St. Augustine, most of whom lived in the first five hundred years of the Christian era. We look to their writings especially to see what the living Church taught in those early centuries close to the time of Christ, when many of the most basic truths of the Church were being keenly debated. Their writings, as well as the prayers or ceremonies used in church, or the inscriptions we find, mirror that teaching for us.

The doctrine of the Mystical Body has been current in the Church throughout the centuries.[1] There were times when the metaphor was used to express slightly different notions, however. This came about in those eras before men fashioned those exact concepts in which we now phrase the tract on the Church. A man would take one particular element in the life of a Christian, for example, and speak of it in terms of the Mystical Body. In the light of further developments of the doctrine on the Church, we had to narrow down certain concepts; we had to be very precise, for example, in stating our requirements for membership in the Church. This was not so necessary before the time of the Protestant Reformation, and especially in the very early centuries of Christianity. At those times there was but one

Church claiming to be Christian. Anything else a man might say about life in that Church quite naturally would apply to those who belonged to that visible body.

PRIMARY AND APPLIED CONCEPTS

As a result, we can distinguish between the *primary* concept of the Mystical Body, and the extended or *applied* concepts. The primary concept is that one which we find in Scripture first of all, and which has been gradually clarified even more through the ages; it is the one outlined by Pius XII which states that the Mystical Body and the Catholic Church are identical.

The applied concepts speak of some notion of union with Christ that is proper to the Christian, but which might admit of a broader meaning. The type of union spoken of might include others who are not actual members of the visible Church. This became clearer as we emphasized the visible elements in the Church after the time of the Reformation. These applied concepts, of course, are perfectly legitimate, but we must not confuse them with the more precise notion outlined in the encyclical. In point of fact, it was a confusion between some of these broader notions and the more exact one which brought about the uncertainty evident before the encyclical of Pius XII.

WHAT IS A METAPHOR?

To understand this better, we must remember that St. Paul was using a *metaphor* when he spoke about the Mystical Body. A metaphor is a figure of speech that expresses a comparison between two things. Instead of coming right out and saying it, however, the metaphor prefers to leave us guessing a bit. We say it is an *implied* comparison, because it takes the comparison for granted without expressing it. If we read somewhere that "the ship plows the water," we all know what is meant. The word "plow" refers to a machine cutting up earth, but the furrows made by a sailing ship suggest the same things to us. We could say that "the furrows made in the water by a ship are like the furrows made in the earth by a plow," but that wouldn't sound as nice, nor would it bring out the ideas as well; we would become too involved with words. That is the very advantage of a metaphor: it brings out its point more graphically, with more emphasis, than would a direct comparison.

There are always three things required in such a figure of speech: the object you are talking about, the thing you are comparing it to, and some *basis* for the comparison. Take something in everyday language. We say to someone, "You're a dirty rat." This is an implied comparison; we don't use any "likes" or "similars." We do not mean that the person *is* a four legged rodent, however. We have three things in mind: the person, a rat, and something in the man that is similar to something which we dislike in the rat. It is this "something" which we dislike in both of them which gives us the basis for the comparison.

THE IDEA OF UNION

Turning then to the Mystical Body, it is clear by now that we are comparing the *Catholic Church* to a human body. Those are the two things we have in mind. The basis of the comparison, however, which is the most important item, is the *union* found in both. We say that the union between Christ and His Church is like the union between the head and the body. Because we are using a metaphor, however, we leave out the "like" and say simply that the Church is a body. We do not mean that it is actually a physical body, with hands and feet, with head and ears and eyes. We mean simply that it is similar to a human body in one way or another.

It is at this point that difficulties began. There are different ways of looking at that term *union* between Christ and men. As soon as you change the basis for the comparison, you change the comparison itself; thus such different notions could arise. Some of the Fathers spoke of the union between Christ and men that comes from "faith" or "grace" rather than actual membership in the Church. These gave rise to what we now call the applied concepts. We find the same thing when people speak of the *Church* "in the wide sense," or "in an extended sense." Strictly, the Church is only the Roman Catholic Church. In an extended sense, someone might say that all those who have faith in Christ are members of His Church, even those in the Old Testament. There is nothing wrong in this, provided that we always keep in mind that we are using an extended sense. The confusion arises when the primary concept and the extended senses are all mixed up: when different people understand different things by the phrase "Mystical Body." Their discussions cannot help but be a bit confusing.

ANALOGIES

The doctrine we know as the primary concept is the *Primary Analogy;* the applied concepts we call the *Secondary Analogies* or, more properly, *Analogates.* We use the word "horse" somewhat like that. Besides the animal itself, we also use the word to designate the "horse" or frame used to support planks for a painter or a table at the church bazaar; here the basis for the comparison would seem to be the four legs. So also the "horse" used in the gymansiums for vaulting exercises and the like. On the other hand, basing a comparison on the idea of power and strength, we often say that a man is a veritable "work horse." Students at times go out in search of a "horse," meaning the translations sometimes used as an aid to translate their homework; it helps them as the animal helps the farmer. Or those who play chess may refer to the knight pawn as a "horse" because of the figure of a horse head on it.

In all of these examples, the word "horse" means something different, yet all have some element in common with the animal. The same thing is true of this much more important matter of the concepts of the Mystical Body. While using the same words, the different authors had different things in mind. It is important to note that they all considered some *union* with Christ, however, as the starting point, the basis of their comparison. But in each case it was a different kind of union they were thinking of.

The most important value of the encyclical of Pius XII was that, as Father Bluett states, "It cuts through the confusion and uncertainty which were associated, in the minds of many, with this sublime doctrine. The very richness and splendor of the doctrine of the Mystical Body produced, in the course of the centuries, a variety of interpretations and analogous, extended uses of the term 'Mystical Body of Christ.' Most of them were theologically sound, and many of them surpassingly beautiful, but their abundance did introduce an element of confusion into much of what was written about the Mystical Body. The new encyclical re-enthrones, in its unique majesty, the original meaning with which the doctrine of the Mystical Body of Christ came from the lips of our Saviour and His inspired Apostle, Saint Paul."[2]

In order to understand the entire matter better, then, it would be good to take a closer look at some of these various applied concepts of the Mystical Body. In a brief form, we might summarize the more important ones as follows, basing it upon the important work of Father Sebastian Tromp.[3]

THE UNION OF CHRIST WITH MEN IN THE MYSTICAL BODY

We may look at each of these separately to understand them better.

*   *   *

A. Union in the Mystical Body Because of Creation

In this applied concept of the Body of Christ, we think mostly of Christ as the Second Person of the Trinity. In some mysterious fashion, the Second Person of the Trinity, born of the Father from all eternity, represents in Himself all of creation, and contains in Himself the pattern, as it were, of all those things to be created in time. He is the Wisdom of the Father, the living Image of His infinite perfection.

When an artist goes about painting his masterpiece, he keeps before him at all times a master idea that will guide his every action. No less is this true in the great work of creation. The world is but a reflection of the glory of God. His perfections are seen throughout the world, one in this creature, one in another, but all telling us of God in whom we find every perfection in its highest — its infinite — degree. It is in Christ, the eternal God, equal to the Father and the Holy Spirit in all things, that we find in a certain way the full expression of this divine beauty which is reflected in nature. He is the living Idea; or the expression of that Idea, the Word: "and the Word was made flesh."[4]

Being thus "the image of God,"[5] "the brightness of his glory and the image of his substance,"[6] we can truly say that "in him [Christ] were created all things in the heavens and on the earth, things visible and things invisible. . . . All things have been created through and unto him."[7] There is nothing existing which is not related to Christ in this way as the Second Person of the Trinity. "All things," as St. John tells us, "were made through Him."[8] Even the darkest pagan, the most violent atheist, and inanimate creation itself bear a relationship to Christ the Son of God.

Some began, then, to speak of this relationship with Christ by using St. Paul's terms concerning the Mystical Body. Since the basis for this union with Him was so general, they were able to speak of everyone as a member of Christ, even, in a way, of inanimate creation. But that is not exactly what St. Paul had in mind when speaking precisely of the Mystical Body of Christ, for he was considering only members of the Catholic Church. Thus, it is an applied concept. It was used to meet the arguments of certain heretics, and it is a good and useful argument, provided one keeps in mind, of course, that it is not the primary concept itself. We can see how easily confusion might arise about the doctrine when one would speak of the members of Christ in His Mystical Body meaning only Roman Catholics, while others would speak of the entire human race, or even of the entire created universe, as a member of Christ. Each one has a different concept in mind.

B. *Union in the Mystical Body Because of the* Incarnation of Christ *and* His Death *on the Cross*

In this concept of the Mystical Body we have a different basis for the union with the God-Man, but the membership is just as extensive: the entire human race.

Christ became man in order to save all men without exception. From the very first moment of His Incarnation, all men were included in that divine intention. "Therefore in coming into the world, He says: 'Sacrifice and oblation thou wouldst not, but a body thou hast fitted to me,'" in order that we might all be "sanctified through the offering of the body of Jesus Christ once for all."[9] Thus it was that on Calvary we were all most closely united to Christ; it was the climax of His Incarnation. Apart from Christ there is no salvation, "for there is no other name under heaven given to men by which we must be saved."[10] The all-important truth of Christianity is that "there is one God, and one Mediator between God and men, himself man, Christ Jesus, who gave himself a ransom for all."[11]

This, then, is a bond of union between us and Christ, and if we choose, we might speak of all of us — the entire human race — as being members of Christ because He, as our Head, died for His "mystical body." We can see again that the term "body" in this case does not mean the Roman Catholic Church, for it includes in its number many who never were and never will be members of that Church. It is then an applied concept, and hence the danger if it be confused with the more strict, revealed notion.

CHRIST, THE MORAL HEAD OF MANKIND

This manner of speaking is based on a distinction which theologians refer to today in speaking about the "Headship" of Christ. When they speak of Christ as being the Head of *all* mankind (because He became man for them and died upon the cross for all), they refer to Him as the "Moral Head." When they speak of Him as the Head of the Mystical Body of Christ in the *strict* sense, that is, the Roman Catholic Church, they call Him the "Mystic Head."

In all of these applied concepts it is really only as the Moral Head that Christ represents all men. It means that He took all of us to Himself in some way, so that He could act in our name. It was as Moral (or Juridic) Head of mankind that Christ redeemed us. As a result, every single human being who ever lived or will live is *able* to be saved. Some will actually accept that supernatural life of grace; others will refuse it. Yet all are redeemed in the sense that they can enter the gates of heaven if they will. As Moral Head of mankind, Christ embraces all of mankind entirely; as Moral Head of mankind, He paid the price for all, He redeemed everyone. As Moral Head, Christ is united to all men, although in a more or less intimate degree, depending upon the acceptance or refusal of grace on the part of each individual.

CHRIST, THE MYSTIC HEAD

To have Christ as our *Mystic Head* (in the strict sense) something very special is required. It is a unique relationship, one that endures even should the person lose the state of grace through sin. It means becoming a member of His Mystical Body, the Roman Catholic Church. It is a mark of special love and favor on the part of God, and it demands special love and gratitude in return. It is a relationship with Christ which is established by a Triple Bond: baptism, adherence to the true faith, and acceptance of the rule of the Vicar of Christ. Those who live in a relationship of this sort to Christ are privileged to "bear the person of Christ" in a special manner on this earth, in a way not given to others outside the Church. They are Christ prolonged in space and time and communicated to men. Though others may bear the grace of Christ within their souls, no others will bear so intimately the very *person* of Christ on this earth as those whose glory it is to be called members of the Mystical Body of Christ which is the Church, and who can, therefore, look to Christ as their Mystic Head. It is an honor to be appreciated, and one that carries with it special duties for all and a heavy responsibility.

In applying the fruits of redemption to the souls of individual men, God could have imparted these graces to mankind directly. Actually, as Pope Pius XII tells us, "He willed to do so only through a visible Church made up of men, so that through her all might co-operate with Him in dispensing the graces of Redemption."[12] Why God chose to do this only through a visible Church, no one knows, for "who has known the mind of the Lord or who has been his counsellor."[13] But we do know that He did so ordain. Ideally, every man in the world today should know Christ not only as Moral Head but as Mystic Head as well; every man should be a member of the Mystical Body, which is the visible Church. To join all men freely and willingly to the Mystic Christ is the very purpose for all the apostolic and missionary work of the Church. One cannot help being a member of Christ the Moral Head; as long as one is a member of the human race, Christ became man and died for him. For an adult to enter into union with Christ as Mystical Head, something more is required: the free will of man. He must will to be baptized, to believe, and to accept the rule of the Roman Pontiff.

Even in reading the Letters of St. Paul, we must remember that his thought also developed gradually with the passing of years, and became more exact. So also do we note that he spoke of Christ both as the Moral Head of mankind and as the Mystical Head of His Church. Often he failed to give the reader a clear indication that he was changing from one to the other, but he did refer to both. This is another of the things which add to the difficulty of ferreting out the primary concept of the Mystical Body. St. Paul never wrote an orderly treatise on the subject, but spoke of it in passing, we might say, while treating of the questions proper to whatever particular church he was writing. Thus we can see again the importance of keeping our notions clear and avoiding any confusion between the applied concepts and the primary one.

C. Union in the Mystical Body Because of Faith in the Redeemer

Faith is defined as an act of the intellect, moved by the will (under the inspiration of grace), to assent to a truth because it has been revealed by God. It is more than trust; it is a firm adhesion to a truth. Because a person recognizes the authority of God behind that truth, he can accept it completely and without fear. It is something supernatural; without the grace of God such firm acceptance of a truth which is not perfectly clear to natural reason is impossible.

Faith is the beginning, the foundation, and the root of justification, requiring, of course, the practice of other virtues to complete it. Because it is of prime importance, however, it was only natural that some writers should desire to lay special emphasis upon it, and this they did by speaking again in terms of the Mystical Body of Christ. The bond of union in this instance was *faith* in Christ; and those who believed in Him were then said to be members of His body. It is another applied concept, since more is required to be a member of the Catholic Church than faith alone.

Some of these writers included those in the Old Testament who had faith in the *coming* of Christ, the Messias; it was through this faith that they were to be saved, just as those in the New Testament were to be saved through faith in Christ the Son of God who *had come*. In this way we hear certain of the Fathers speaking about "the church from the time of Abel." Abel, the good son of Adam and Eve, killed by his brother Cain, is taken as the first of a long line of just people who believed in Christ. Together they form the "Universal Church," the same in both the Old and the New Testaments.

This notion had a danger if it were confused with the more strict notion spoken of in the Letters of St. Paul, for this union of those who believe is first of all something *invisible* and extends far beyond the limits of a visible Church. It includes those men who accept Christ as the Redeemer, but who, perhaps through no fault of their own, fail to grasp the fullness of Christian revelation. Thus if one were to speak of the Church simply as a mystical person of some sort, identical in both the Old and New Testaments, we would conclude almost at once that the visible organization of the Mystical Body of Christ is something secondary in importance — something "tacked on," as it were, to this invisible union.

Other writers limited this union of faith to those who came after the time of Christ, but the danger of confusion still remained. If it were understood as more important than the primary concept of St.

Paul, it would give first place to an invisible union with Christ and make the visible organization here on this earth seem comparatively unimportant.

D. Union in the Mystical Body Because of Sharing in the Grace of Christ

This is the most common of the applied concepts found in the literature of our own century. For practical purposes, in fact, until the encyclical of Pius XII on the Mystical Body, the field had been narrowed down to two schools of thought about the teaching of this doctrine, one group basing it upon this application, and the other limiting it to the visible Church.

The difficulty arose mostly out of the fact that St. Thomas Aquinas wrote about *grace* in terms of the *body of Christ,* so that whoever possessed grace was thereby a member of the Mystical Body. Although he lived in the thirteenth century, no single man has had a greater influence on modern-day Catholic thought. He did not write expressly on the Church as such; he lived before the Protestant Revolt when the special need arose for a clearer explanation of what the Church is. Thus, what he wrote about the Mystical Body was really an applied concept. Even St. Thomas — beautifully as he has written about the Mystical Body — would have written quite differently if he had the encyclical of Pius XII to guide him, for it is here that we find clearly stated just what is the primary concept.

The problem up to this time has been to ferret out the basic concept from the many notions about the Mystical Body. It was not an easy task. There were great minds on both sides; one group convinced that the meaning of St. Paul was to limit the Mystical Body to the visible Church, and the other holding that he intended to include others in that Body besides Catholics — that he included anyone who shared in the grace of Christ. Father Tromp, Father Dieckmann, Father Gruden, and Father Grivec were some of the men who held that St. Paul intended to equate the Mystical Body and the Church. Yet, on the other hand, the brilliant French theologian, Father Mersch, among others, disagreed with them, and believed that they "force the meaning of the Pauline text, 'The Church which is

His body,' and of certain other texts similar to it."[14] Father Mersch wrote, of course, before the encyclical on the Mystical Body. It is apparent that since 1943, however, no one should speak of the Mystical Body in any other way than to limit it to the Catholic Church. Once singled out as the primary concept, this view must be accepted by all, and the teaching of St. Thomas and those who followed him must be considered as an applied concept.

It is important, then, to keep all of this in mind when reading books printed before the year 1943, for many of them speak of the Mystical Body in terms of grace, and consider this the primary notion, rather than that which identifies the Mystical Body and the visible Church. It is for that reason that we at times read such statements as this: "The body of Christ extends beyond the boundaries of the visible Church, which is universal and includes an incalculable multitude from all nations and ages and religions, 'baptized and unbaptized, circumcised and uncircumcised, all those whose intentions are good and who maintain an inner communion with God and Christ.' They are, in their entirety, the real members of the one mystical body, of the new race in Christ."[15] This can be true only of an applied concept; taken in opposition to the primary truth, as presented by Pius XII, it is completely erroneous.

Similar statements may be found in other works, many of them not as direct as this, but all giving the notion that more people belong to the Mystical Body than to the Catholic Church. At times such writers may make a distinction between the Church and the Body of Christ, similar to that made formerly by Father Mersch: "In the ordinary language of the Church, the term 'mystical body' signifies the ensemble of those who live of the life of Christ, a life, of course, which admits of degrees; on the other hand, the word 'church' represents the society of the baptized faithful under their legitimate rulers."[16]

Because he had in mind a union established by faith and grace alone, the author could make, with perfect accuracy, this distinction between the Mystical Body and the Church. Pope Pius XII, on the other hand, does not speak of the union in the Mystical Body as being established by grace alone, that is, "the life of Christ." Rather, he tells us that membership in this Body demands that same Triple Bond which makes one a Roman Catholic. He equates the Roman Catholic Church and the Mystical Body as spoken of by St. Paul; these other notions, based on the teaching of St. Thomas Aquinas especially, must be then applied concepts. There is nothing incorrect about them, provided these teachings are understood as applied concepts. But we must not try to apply all the words of St. Paul to such secondary notions, and thus seem to make this union in faith or grace alone appear more important than the visible Church. St. Paul was speaking about just that: a visible Church, and as Father Tromp says, "the Pauline metaphor of the body is fully verified solely in the Catholic Church."[17] It is only when speaking about that group that we can really understand and appreciate the words of St. Paul. None of these applied concepts will match the picture on all points.

The result of this encyclical on the Mystical Body has been to remove the confusion prevalent before. We now know just what is the primary concept. Because it was not always clear before, there were two schools of thought about it. Today there is agreement. The encyclical has been a valuable aid to those writing on the Mystical Body of Christ. Today readers can be reasonably sure that by the term Mystical Body, the author means the Roman Catholic Church, and that in the phrase "members of Christ," he has in mind all and *only* Roman Catholics.

E. The Church

It might be well to add a few words concerning the word *Church*. In its proper and strict sense it means the organization established by Christ and existing here on earth. It is this organization of which the Pope speaks in his encyclical, in which he examines and explains "above all what concerns the Church Militant."[18] It is called "militant" because it is still fighting a battle for eternal salvation here in the world.

At times we hear the terms *Church Suffering* and *Church Triumphant*. The first refers to the souls in purgatory and the second to those in heaven. Neither of these are visible bodies, although the Church Triumphant will become visible after the final resurrection at the end of the world. These are extended uses of the word *church* also.

It is only the *Church* in the strict sense which coincides with the Mystical Body, and it is only of this that we shall speak in the following chapters. The Church Militant and the Church Triumphant are not one and the same "organization." The organization is the Church on earth. Perhaps we could speak of the visible group in heaven at the end of the world as "an organization," but it will be essentially different in form from the organization of the Church as we now know it. The words of St. Paul concern the Body of Christ on earth; the Glorified Body of Christ on the Last Day will be far different.

THE COMMUNION OF SAINTS

The term *Communion of Saints* refers to an invisible union with Christ through grace and to our union with others through Christ. It coincides with one of the applied concepts of the Mystical Body which speaks in terms of grace, but it is not the same as the Mystical Body in the sense described in the encyclical of Pius XII. The Communion of Saints is not visible; it is not an organization that we can see. Baptism of water is not necessarily a requisite for entrance into the Communion of Saints, which includes many who, though through no fault of their own, do not hold to the Catholic faith or accept the Catholic rule. In the Communion of Saints we may include the saints in heaven, the souls in purgatory, as well as those who possess sanctifying grace (or at least faith, the root of that grace) here on this earth. The bond of union here is something invisible, that is, grace.

The Communion of Saints differs from the Church in this, that while the Church is intended as the medium of salvation — *the way* to attain grace and heaven — the Communion of Saints *presupposes* that one has grace (or at least holds to the true faith), and thus its purpose is to enable the members to share in the spiritual treasures held in common, to pray for one another, to assist one another. Thus those on earth may pray for others on earth as well as for those in purgatory; and they may pray to the saints in heaven and be helped by them; and even the souls in purgatory, we are told, can assist those of the Church Militant by their prayers. This participation in the spiritual treasury of Christ and His saints implies the distribution, the interchange and application of all of the spiritual gifts, graces, and fruits of meritorious works to all the members who might be in need of them. One is *not* saved, however, *through* the Communion of Saints; on the contrary, one is a member of the Communion of Saints *because* he is saved (in heaven or purgatory) or is on the way toward being saved (through living a life of faith and grace on this earth). The Communion of Saints is not "another" Church. There is only one Church, and it alone is to be the means, the way, of reaching heaven, and it includes, strictly speaking, only those on this earth who are associated with that visible body.

* * *

This will suffice for our study of the different notions of the Mystical Body; it should help us to understand how confusion might have arisen in the past, and why even now we may find statements which describe the Mystical Body in vague terms. If we keep in mind simply the fact that the Mystical Body here on this earth is the Roman Catholic Church, we will not be confused, and we will at the same time come to appreciate what the Church is, and learn to know and understand with all our heart what great favors God has given us in making us members of His Body. We will see in full force the meaning of Pius XII in saying: "Surely nothing more glorious, nothing nobler, nothing surely more honorable can be imagined than to belong to the Holy Catholic, Apostolic and Roman Church."[19]

AND ADAM ATE OF THE FRUIT

A JEWEL, although beautiful in itself, is never at its best outside of its setting. The same is true with the Church. In order really to appreciate her role in the plan of salvation we should stop for a moment to get a bird's-eye view of the entire picture. That plan itself is something wonderful, so that a study of it will be well worth the time.

There is, first of all, a common misconception to clear up. God did not have, as some may think, two different plans for mankind — the first one being his original plan, and the second being some sort of a patched-up affair, made necessary when Adam and Eve interfered with the first one by sinning in the garden of paradise. Such a concept fails to see God as He is entirely. It is impossible for Him to change His mind; it is equally impossible for any creature to interfere in any way with His plans so as to cause Him to change them.

The truth is that God had but one single plan from all eternity, and that plan included the garden of paradise as well as the sin of Adam, and the payment on the part of Christ for that sin. It is more than just a cold idea that we are concerned with here. God is love, and, because of that, this whole story is a story of love. Let us trace it down from the very beginning.

THE ETERNAL GOD

From all eternity, endlessly, ages upon ages before creation, there was God. Before the first ray of light, before the first song of a bird, the first faint flicker of a star, God the Almighty dwelt in the realm of love, Father, Son, and Holy Ghost. He had no beginning, as He also shall have no ending. He came from no one, depended upon no one; He is sufficient to Himself, for He is God.

But then God decided to create in order to manifest His perfection in the goods given to creatures. He had nothing to gain from creation; it could offer Him nothing which He did not already have. Love, however, like good, tends to diffuse itself, and so God decreed that He would share His life and love with others. The whole of creation was to be an image of God, a true expression outside Himself of His own infinite perfections. No single creature, of course, could mirror the limitless perfection of God, for every creature by its very nature has to be limited. And so God *divided* this created image of His Goodness among many creatures and among many levels of creatures: the earth and the waters and the minerals were to show forth the very existence of God by existing themselves; the trees and the flowers and the plants were to tell of the vitality of that life by growing and increasing and developing in themselves; and the animals and the birds and the fishes were to show the power of that life by hearing and seeing and moving from place to place. When all of these were made, however, God wished to place yet another creature upon this earth which would include in itself all of the things possessed by these others on a lower level, but which would express besides the greatest perfection of the life of God: it was to possess something spiritual as well as material, it was to have a body and an *immortal soul,* endowed with an intellect and a free will. And this creature was man.

MAN — THE IMAGE OF GOD

Man has been created more truly than any other being on this earth after the image and likeness of God, because he contains in himself the very thing that makes God so marvelous. Man is, in part, a spirit; he can think, and he can will to do or not to do things. No other creature on earth has been given that perfection. The trees, the plants, the animals, like the very stars themselves, can serve God only by doing what they *have to do.* By a certain necessity, coming from the fact that they simply exist and do as God decrees, they worship Him. Apart from this blind necessity, however, they are speechless before their Maker.

But it is different with man. He, of course, also worships God by this necessity. By the very fact that he exists, he, as a creature, gives honor to the Creator, an honor that man can never take from God, not even the man in hell. Over and above this, however, God made it possible for man to give a higher and more noble kind of worship: a free worship. Man alone, of all the creatures on the earth, can speak up before God and give himself to God, not simply because he must, but because he wants to. He *wants to* adore, to honor God. And to be able to make this choice, he must be free, and that means, also, that he must be able to refuse such honor. To endow man with a free will is the only way that God might receive this high and more noble form of worship, even though it involves, in this life, the possibility of sin. God did not give man a free will so that he might be able to sin. God gave him a free will primarily to enable man to give free worship; to be able to sin is only the other side of being able to love freely.

Man has become the king of the universe for that reason. He was given charge over all the earth; all things were his to use: "Let us make man to our image and likeness; and let him have dominion over the fishes of the sea, and the fowls of the air, and the beasts, and the whole earth, and every creeping creature that moveth upon the earth. And God created man to his own image."[1] When man willingly uses these things for the honor of God, he becomes the spokesman of all creation, rendering free worship to God. Man was granted an intellect that he might know God; a will, that he might serve Him. It was for this that he was created, and he is most a man when he uses his mind and will as God intends. If he does give himself freely to God, he most completely fulfills that purpose for which he was made, the very purpose for which he was given a free will. If, on the other hand, he refuses such service, and he turns against God, he also turns against himself and his nature, against the very purpose of humanity; and no matter how long he may continue in that direction, if he but gives Truth a chance, he will sooner or later begin to feel that dissatisfaction, that feeling of misdirection which overwhelmed St. Augustine, crying: "Our hearts were made for Thee, O God, and they shall not rest until they rest in Thee!"[2]

THE LIFE OF GRACE

God was not content, however, even with this greatness given to man. He wished to give him more. He wished to make man not only mirror the perfection of God, but rather actually *share* in the divine life itself: to make us "partakers of the divine nature."[3] For that reason, when God created man, He also raised him to the level of supernatural life; He created man endowed with the gift of sanctifying grace.

Mankind has always been in some way or another completely wrapped up in the supernatural. There never has existed a purely "natural" man; that is, a man who possesses only what comes with a body and a human soul, and nothing more — a man who is destined for the natural goal of that body and soul, and nothing more. Mankind has always had but one single goal, and that is completely supernatural: union with God in the beatific vision. To understand better just what we mean by the "supernatural" gifts, we at times talk about nature as though it existed apart from supernature. When we do so, we are only pretending that this is the case. Mankind in its present historic state does not have any merely natural goal in life. We either reach heaven through grace or enter hell for want of it. Even in discussing the fate of unbaptized infants, theologians resort to a distinction made necessary by the unicity of our supernatural goal. The child cannot achieve his supernatural goal without grace, and in the present state of man, we cannot miss our supernatural destiny without at the same time missing any natural one that might have been. Yet "between these two extremes (damnation in the strict sense and natural beatitude)," writes Pohle-Preuss, "there is conceivable a third state, *viz.:* a condition of relative beatitude *materially* though not *formally* identical with natural beatitude so called."[4] Since there is, formally, no purely natural goal in our present state, the author goes on to explain what he means. "As there is no *state of pure nature,* so there can be for the unbaptized infant no *beatitude of pure nature.* But materially he may enjoy all those prerogatives which in some other economy would have constituted man's natural end and happiness."[5] Original sin touches upon only our supernatural gifts, so the unbaptized infant might still have such happiness. Nevertheless, the very use of this distinction underlines the sad fact that the child *has* missed that one goal in life, common to all men in our present state; even though he knows no sadness for it, he *has* missed a far greater happiness that might have been his.

*Super*natural, of course, means something *above* or *beyond* nature. In the idea of nature we include everything that God owed it to Himself to give man, once He had decreed that He would create him: a human body, a human soul that is spiritual and endowed with an intellect and a free will. Once it was determined that mankind was to exist as it is, God, in a certain sense, had to give every man these things. Strictly speaking, God could no doubt have left it at that, and given mankind a purely natural goal in life. If a man used that intellect and will properly, God could have rewarded him in a way that was proportionate to that nature: the knowledge and love of God coming from the use of these natural powers alone.

Actually God did not do that. He gave mankind a more lofty goal: to know and love Him in a higher and more intimate manner. To do this, man needed a new and higher power; and this power of the soul is grace — a power to know God and love Him as He is *in Himself,* and not simply as we might know Him through created things. It is a new life entirely, supernaturalizing our nature and giving it a power to perform actions which would take effect in heaven — supernatural actions. It is a life that leads us to this more intimate and noble knowledge and love of God for all eternity.

SUPERNATURAL GOAL

We might bring this distinction out a bit more clearly by asking ourselves four questions.

1. *What* do we ultimately aim for in life? — If we were living on a merely natural level, it would be to know God by the use of our human mind alone. On a supernatural level, however, it is to know God as He is in Himself, and to be happy with God forever in

heaven. This is brought about through faith in this life or the Beatific Vision in heaven.

2. *Who* directs us and enables us to attain this goal? — Again as regards a natural goal, it would be God as the author of natural life, who created us and keeps us in existence; and also we ourselves, using as well as we could, our human mind and will, but nothing more. So that we might attain our supernatural goal, it is God, acting also as the author of supernatural life, who directs us: He who endowed our soul with this new life of grace; and also we ourselves, living this new life, and making use of its new powers over and above those of our human mind and will.

3. *How* do we get to know about this goal? — We would come to a knowledge of a natural goal through *created things*. For example, through the stars, the plants, animals, and our own existence, we would come to the conclusion that God exists and that we should love Him. In coming to the knowledge of our supernatural goal, however, we must use more than our natural mind. We must turn to the truths which God has *revealed* about Himself and this higher goal, and accept them and live by them. These are truths which we cannot know by our human minds alone; God must tell us of them.

4. *What laws* do we have to guide us so as to reach this goal? — If we were concerned with a purely natural goal, the law of nature would suffice — that law which God put in all men in creating them. It is in the power of reason to make proper judgments about moral problems. As regards our supernatural goal, on the other hand, we have, in addition to a more perfect understanding of the law of nature, the further special commandments and precepts which God has given us for living a supernatural life.

This general outline must not be understood, of course, as though there really are two separate goals in life. The natural and the supernatural *orders* are completely distinct, but for mankind today there is only *one goal:* a supernatural one. From the first moment of human creation, God gave man this higher goal in life. The supernatural revelation of Himself and His laws to mankind began at once, and increased progressively in depth and content until it reached its high point in Christ: "God, who at sundry times and in divers manners spoke in times past to the fathers by the prophets, last of all in these days has spoken to us by his Son. . . ."[6] Although men learned to know more about God in Himself, and the laws which He wished mankind to follow, there was always, even from the beginning, some knowledge of a supernatural religion in the world. It was all a part of that one grand, unified plan of God.

In living this supernatural life, however, man does not undertake a new life, completely distinct from the natural. Rather, through grace, these natural powers are *supernaturalized;* it is the natural powers themselves which are changed. The supernatural is built upon the natural, and it is through these natural powers of man that he lives his new life of grace. Even more, with sanctifying grace, these various activities of man can also become meritorious. Outwardly, his life might not seem any different from that of a man who is not in the state of sanctifying grace. Actually, so far as eternal merit is concerned, it is as though one were vitally alive and the other completely dead. Both may use their minds, their wills, and their bodies, but the actions will be meritorious only for one. Both may labor side by side in a factory, doing the same work, hour by hour. For the one, that labor can be a labor of supernatural love, and have great meaning before God in heaven. For the man who does not love God, however, that same labor is nonexistent in the order of strict merit.

The world, then, has been re-created by Christ, and it is through that supernaturalized world, of which we are a part, that we must attain salvation. Everything in the world that God created, shares in this. Thus the proper attitude toward food and drink, and sex, and work, and recreation is not that it is so terribly human that a man must be ashamed of it and pretend it does not exist. Far from it, a man must accustom himself to dealing with all of these elements of real life in a supernaturalized fashion. Work and play, and even sex in its proper place, can be a supernatural act, pleasing to God. The supernatural life is not limited to saying prayers and going to church. Headaches and toothaches, though they seem dreadfully human, can have a place in the life of grace and share in the supernatural value of suffering.

It is for this reason, too, that a man of faith judges the success or failure of other men on the basis of what they really *are* in the only order that really matters, rather than what they might appear to be. A scrubwoman living the life of grace may be far more important supernaturally than the president of the company whose floors she scrubs, and vice versa. Worldly honor or lack of it is of small account to the man of faith who "seeks the things that are above."[7]

ORIGINAL JUSTICE

Adam and Eve, then, were the first two human beings on this earth; they were also the first two bearers of these supernatural gifts to help them reach their supernatural goal. We say that they were created in the state of *Original Justice;* they were given all the helps they needed to attain their goal. The most important of these helps, of course, was sanctifying grace. It was this which made their supernatural life possible. In connection with this gift, Adam and Eve also received other gifts which we call "Preternatural Gifts." Just as sanctifying grace made the soul subject to God, so these gifts made the lower nature of man subject to the sanctified soul. We call them *preternatural* because they simply perfect the natural failings of human nature; they fill in the loopholes, as it were, of our nature. They are not so far beyond us as to be called supernatural; they still remain within the limits of our nature.

Man is composed of a body and soul; of matter and spirit. The normal and natural result of this situation is a constant warfare between the two. The flesh has its own appetites, and it strives to satisfy them. It is the animal part of our nature, and in that regard we are like animals: our body of itself knows no law, our body itself does not think. It is in the soul that we find thought and judgment; it is there that a man decides what is good for him to do and what is bad. The only difficulty is that the body and soul do not always agree on the matter. The body will crave one thing while the mind will say it is bad; the body will rebel at another thing which the mind sees as good. A little child, for example, follows only the dictates of his appetites. When he sees a piece of candy, he reaches out at once to catch hold of it. That same child, when he reaches the age of reason and his mind begins to work, may still want to reach out for a piece of candy, but his mind will dictate a strong "no," since it might bring on a punishment. The child has given the matter some thought.

Again, there is, in a way, the same conflict between the immortal soul and the material body in this, that the material body will of necessity know the weakness of matter, and will naturally fall victim to sickness and suffering. This will eventually end in the final collapse of the material body in death, and the separation of the deathless soul from that body. It is found, too, in the process of learning, for while the mind is a spiritual power of the soul, it can come to learn only through the physical body, so that the process of learning, from childhood on, is a long and often tiresome thing, constantly hindered by the weakness of the body.

GIFT OF INTEGRITY

All of this is true in the hundreds of other big and little difficulties in life. Man may always crave something which his mind forbids. A man adrift on the ocean may crave the salt water; a man may desire another man's wife; but the mind says "no." It is the old battle of which St. Paul spoke when he wrote: "For I do not do the good that I wish, but the evil that I do not wish, that I perform."[8] It is a warfare known to every person in the world, just as we are all acquainted with sickness and death and the difficulty of learning. We know these things today since, because of original sin, the weakness of nature is allowed to harass mankind. Adam and Eve possessed, as all men do, a human nature with a body and a spiritual soul, so that they also would have been subject to these difficulties, but in their case, an exception was made. We say that they were created in the state of *Original Justice,* and, because of that, they not only possessed sanctifying grace, but this natural conflict was stilled by virtue of special gifts known as the preternatural gifts. Adam and Eve were given four "preternatural gifts" which supplied for the defects of human nature in itself. This included four things: (1) freedom from concupiscence, (2) the gift of wisdom, (3) freedom from suffering, and (4) freedom from the necessity of dying. The first part of this gift gave man control over his lower nature and its desires, so that it always coincided with the dictates of reason. The second part gave our first parents infused knowledge; they did not have to learn some things as we do, but this information was infused into their minds. God simply put knowledge into their intellects, thus supplying for the natural defect of human nature in that it knows nothing at birth, and must learn slowly by this long process of reasoning. The third part, freedom from suffering, supplied for the weakness of human nature in wearing out and becoming sick; it helped man to continue in health, and both to avoid mistakes which bring on suffering from within and to overcome obstacles which cause suffering from without. By virtue of this gift, Adam and Eve were going to be able to avoid just such sufferings, and the result of this was to be the fourth gift. It ordained that instead of allowing nature to run its course, and the body to wear out completely and end in death, Adam and Eve would know no death; their bodies would continue to function properly always, and when their period of trial was over they would simply be transported to their heavenly reward without having first to die.

SPECIAL CONDITION

Sanctifying grace and all of these preternatural gifts were totally free gifts from God; He is not obliged to supply for the failings in the nature which He created, for human nature is good in itself. When He did choose to give these gifts, and to go further, and raise man to the supernatural level, it was for the same reason that He deigned to create: it was because of His great love.

God gave these gifts of Original Justice (sanctifying grace and the preternatural gifts) at the same time, and He made a special condition for both. They were totally free gifts, and God wished to give them in a special way, and under special conditions — and who can deny the giver of a gift the right to do that? It was not a question of justice; men had no right to demand these things from God just because they were to possess a human nature. They were gifts, and so mankind had to accept the terms of the Gift Giver.

The *condition* given to Adam was this: if Adam were to remain faithful to one special command given to him by God, he would keep these gifts, and all of those born after him would also be born with these same gifts, the gift of wisdom excepted. Sanctifying grace and the other three preternatural gifts, therefore, were not simply private gifts to Adam and Eve; they were *social* gifts intended for all of mankind. Thus, had Adam not sinned, every man would have possessed grace in his soul at birth, and would have been free from concupiscence, from suffering and death. Others would still have had to learn things for themselves as human beings, since the gift of wisdom was not for all. It would have been far easier, however, for a man to learn, and his knowledge would have been more complete, for the other gifts would have aided him. There would have been a period of trial for every individual before entering heaven, however, even if Adam had not sinned, and, as a result, there would have been the possibility of failure for each.

But had Adam fulfilled his condition, others would be born with grace; and the trial would not have been beset by all the weakness within and the difficulties without that man knows today.

THE SIN OF ADAM

Actually Adam failed and ate of the forbidden fruit. All of mankind thus lost these gifts of God, above all that one which we need so dearly to reach our heavenly goal in life: sanctifying grace. Our unfortunate state was something like the situation of a farmer's children in such a case as this. We can imagine some great benefactor saying to a farmer that, provided he send him a bushel of wheat each year for ten years, the farm would be his. And then after a few years the farmer failed to send the wheat, and he lost the farm, as did those who would have inherited it from him. It is not the fault of the great benefactor that the children lose out, but rather of the farmer who failed to keep the one simple condition established. That is what happened in the case of Adam. God gave mankind a free gift through Adam, and in so doing He chose His own conditions; the guilt lies on the shoulders of Adam.

The one important difference, however, between these two cases is that the farmer's children did not have to be farmers, and could get along somehow by doing work other than farming. But mankind *must* get to heaven and just cannot get there without sanctifying grace. Every human being has a goal assigned to him in life, a super-natural goal which he absolutely must reach; and to reach that goal, it is not merely "nice" to have grace, it is also absolutely necessary. It is something, further, that we are *supposed* to have; something everyone *should* possess. And because we do not have it when we are born, we are in the state of original sin. Adam committed the *act* of original sin; the result of that (the guilty lack of sanctifying grace that we *should* have) is what all possess: the *state* of original sin, or as we usually refer to it, simply "original sin."

Through original sin, mankind lost not only sanctifying grace, but also the preternatural gifts, so that "original sin" means that also. God took away, in other words, those extra helps which Adam and Eve had at first, and He allowed nature to take its own course. The defects in human nature, which had been supplied for by these four extra gifts in the Garden of Paradise, came into prominence. Since this happened because of the sinful act of Adam, it is also a punishment for that sin. Whether original sin had an extrinsic influence on man's mind and will by making it more difficult to know and do good is a disputed question, but we do know that the grace of Christ more than supplies for all the effects of the sin of Adam.

It is true that God did not give back the preternatural gifts at once when He restored the life of grace. Original sin has left its mark upon us, and we must all know suffering and death, even though we live the life of grace. Yet these things are left to us as a reminder of our sin, and since they are left "for the battle," as the Council of Trent tells us,[9] they can harm only those who give in to them and who fail to put up a fight against them with the help of the all-powerful grace of Christ.

The fact that such a thing as original sin is possible for us proves that God never for a moment took mankind out of the supernatural order. If man had simply a natural goal in life, there could be no such thing as original sin; man would always be able to reach that goal. As it is, mankind ended up in a very difficult situation: it seemed as though man was expected to do something he just was not able to do. Man had to be on the supernatural level and Adam lost the grace which put him there; he had to attain a supernatural goal, and he had lost the only means with which to attain it. It is like a man who is expected to ride the elevated train when he can't find any stairways or elevators leading up to it, and it is too far to jump; he doesn't know what to do. And so also was it with mankind, for grace is the one and only way to heaven.

THE INCARNATION

The solution to this seemingly insoluble problem lies in the Love of God. God never intended to place men in an impossible situation, and no sooner had the sin been committed than God promised to send a Saviour who would restore grace to men, and enable them once again to reach the goal of heaven. For centuries the world lay in great expectation for the coming of the Saviour, but when Christ actually came, He did far more than simply restore mankind to grace. Christ was God, and in coming into the world, He made it possible for men to be united even *more intimately* to God than was possible before. Our condition after the coming of Christ meant more intimate union with the Divinity than we would have otherwise known.

It is only in the light of the Incarnation that the fact of original sin is understandable. On the occasion of so great an evil as the sin of Adam, God wrought the greatest good of the coming of Christ: the assuming of the human nature by God Himself, the intimate union between God and the members of that race. It is for this reason that the Church calls the sin of Adam a "happy fault" in her Holy Saturday liturgy: "O happy fault which merited such and so great a Redeemer!"[10] We know from Scripture and the teaching of the Church that God actually did not allow original sin to fall upon us without, at the same time, preparing the grace of salvation. He did not permit Adam and Eve to bring sin into the world with all its far-reaching consequences, without considering the greater good that was to result, without promising the greater return of grace. Thus St. Paul shows the closeness of these two events in the classical text on original sin in the Epistle to the Romans:

Therefore as through one man sin entered into the world
　　and through sin death,
　　and thus death has passed into all men
　　　　because all have sinned. . . .
But not like the offense is the gift.
For if by the offense of the one the many died,
　　much more has the grace of God,
　　　　and the gift in the grace of the one man Jesus Christ,
　　abounded unto the many. . . .
Therefore as from the offense of the one man [Adam]
　　the result was unto condemnation to all men,
so from the justice of the one [Christ]
　　the result is unto justification of life to all men. . . .
But where the offense has abounded,
　　grace has abounded yet more;
so that as sin has reigned unto death,
　　so also grace may reign by justice unto life everlasting
　　　　through Jesus Christ our Lord.[11]

Such would have been the state of man had God not intervened.
Had Christ not come, there would have been no hope for mankind,
for in Christ alone is there salvation. "For we know," as St. Paul
tells us, "that all creation groans and travails in pain until now";[12]
and it is Christ alone who will turn that pain into tears of joy.

CHAPTER VI

SALVATION THIS WAY

"REMEMBER that Jesus Christ rose from the dead and was descended from David; this is my gospel."[1] With these words, St. Paul sums up the two chief points in the coming of Christ and the salvation of mankind: Jesus Christ was both God and Man.

The whole stage was set for the coming of Christ. Adam had failed, and mankind lay helpless, so it seemed, before the throne of God, unable to reach the goal set before it. Absolutely speaking, God could have done other things to restore man to grace. He might simply have forgiven the offense when man was sorry. Or He might have demanded some particular satisfaction from each individual; or He might have chosen but one of them, or perhaps sent an angel, to represent the others and thus make up for the sin of Adam.

THE PERFECT SOLUTION

We know, however, that in the plan of God something far more wonderful than all of these was to occur: God Himself, the Second Person of the Holy Trinity, was to become Man and die for our sins. It was God who was offended, and, yet, through the divine mercy, it was God who was to atone for that offense; however, it was man who had sinned, but it was also a man who was doing the atoning. It was the perfect solution for balancing the scales of divine justice. We measure the offense by the dignity of the one offended, and so it was only God who could make up completely for the offense to

70

the dignity of God Himself; all others are as nothing before the face of God. And still, if it is to be a real "satisfaction," a real making up for the offense, it must come from the part of those who committed the offense; otherwise it is simply a "forgiving," a "pardoning" on the side of God alone. Christ was able to join those two together. As the Son of God, He was equal to the Father, but, as the Son of Mary, He was a true member of the human race. He became the linking bond, the bridge between God and man. "For there is one God, and one Mediator between God and men, himself man, Christ Jesus, who gave himself a ransom for all. . . ."[2]

The coming of Christ has quite naturally come to be considered as the central point in all history; it is from that day that we now number our years, and rightly so. If original sin and its consequences upon our supernatural goal in life is a fact of history, then the birth of Christ is an even more important fact, for it put us back on the way to heaven. Before His birth all eyes were turned toward His coming; since that time, all eyes look back upon His days on earth.

THE OLD TESTAMENT

Scarcely had the sin of Adam been committed when God promised to send a Saviour, when He said to Satan: "I will put enmities between thee and the woman, and thy seed and her seed: He shall crush thy head, and thou shalt lie in wait for His heel."[3] And through the centuries which followed, God continued to tell the Jewish people more and more about this Saviour, until at last, when, somewhat after the manner of a great mosaic, all of the particular pieces of information were put together, the people had a fairly accurate picture of the Messias or Saviour. We speak of these bits of information as the "Messianic Prophecies." They told us, for example, thousands of years before Christ was born, that the Messias would be a descendant of Noe, Abraham, Isaac, but even more closely, that He would be a descendant of King David. It was revealed that He would be born of the tribe of Juda, of a virgin mother, in the little village of Bethlehem. Long before the unhappy events ever occurred, the Scriptures told us that the Saviour would be handed over to His enemies for thirty pieces of silver, that they would pierce His hands and feet and cast lots over His garments; but also that He would rise again from the dead and bring about the conversion of Jew and Gentile alike.

The entire history of the Jewish race in the Old Testament is bound up with these two themes: (1) they were to keep alive on this earth the belief in the one true God, and (2) they were to keep alive the hope for the coming Redeemer.

To help them fulfill that first purpose, God worked many marvels among them. The Jewish people were a small group, surrounded by large groups of unbelievers — pagans, who bowed down to many false gods. Only too great was the danger that close contact with these people would bring for the Hebrews — the danger of forgetting the one true God and of worshipping graven images. God therefore protected them, leading them through deserts, and giving them power to conquer far superior forces in battle. He sent great leaders and great prophets to guide them, to keep strong their belief in the one true God. Thus we have the historical books of the Old Testament, recounting the progress and the military advances of the people under the Providence of God.

Much of their life, though, was to be lived in hope, the hope of things to come with the birth of the Messias. To keep alive that hope, God spoke to them often through His prophets, telling the people more and more about this Saviour. He did so especially when their spirits were low and their hope was languishing. By the time Christ came, people should have been able to recognize Him; it was for that reason that God had spoken. Christ Himself repeatedly called the attention of the people to these prophets. The first time He spoke in the synagogue at Nazareth, He made use of one of the prophecies to tell His friends and neighbors of His mission. The practice was followed in the Jewish services of having someone read a text from the Scriptures, and then comment upon it. Christ was asked to read a section from the prophet Isaias. He read a section concerning the Messias, in which it says: "The Spirit of the Lord is upon me; because he has anointed me; to bring good news to the poor he has sent me, to proclaim to the captives release, and sight to the blind; to set at liberty the oppressed, to proclaim the acceptable year of the Lord, and the day of recompense."[4] The people had always understood this as referring to the Messias, and they marveled at what followed the reading. St. Luke relates it for us: "And closing the volume, he [Christ] gave it back to the attendant and sat down [that is, to begin commenting upon the text]. And the eyes of all in the synagogue were gazing on him. But he began to say to them, *Today this Scripture has been fulfilled in your hearing.* And all bore him witness, and marvelled at the words of grace that came from his mouth."[5] Christ told those of His native village that He was the Messias in the plainest terms possible, but they rejected Him, and He passed on to preach to others. The woman at the well said to Jesus: "I know that the Messias is coming (who is called Christ), and when he comes he will tell us all things"; she had read the prophets. But Jesus answered her: "I who speak with thee am he."[6] He could not have spoken more plainly. But many did not listen, as many since then have not listened. It is a pity, for the Jews knew the Scriptures well. Even the worldly King Herod knew something about the prophecies, for when the Magi came, asking where they might find the "king of the Jews," Herod called in the chief priests and scribes to learn what the Scriptures told about the birthplace of the Messias; and they told him: "In Bethlehem of Judea; for thus it is written through the prophet."[7]

One of the most interesting references which Christ made to the prophets was in foretelling His own Passion and death. He was speaking to the twelve Apostles, and said to them: "Behold, we are going up to Jerusalem, and all things that have been written through the prophets concerning the Son of Man will be accomplished." He then went on to describe what would take place, enumerating some of the things which these prophets had actually foretold: "For he will be delivered to the Gentiles, and will be mocked and scourged and spit upon; and after they have scourged him, they will put him to death; and on the third day he will rise again."[8] Yet even at that time, as St. Luke relates, the Apostles "understood none of these things." But the day did come when they could not help but see that all these prophetic texts referred to Christ.

THE MYSTERY OF CHRIST'S COMING

While God could have simply forgiven the offense of mankind, and restored man to grace, He did not choose to do so. God wanted to join Himself intimately to our human nature by becoming one of us, "one tried as we are in all things except sin."[9] He assumed our flesh and blood, and at once that same identical human nature possessed by every man born into this world was beatified, honored in a way even above that of the angelic nature, for God deigned to become a man, not an angel. In assuming a perfect human nature, Christ took on all that went with it: a body, a soul, mind, will, and emotions. He was a true member of the human race. We may sometimes fail to appreciate this, and think of Him as some unique, unreal individual. Actually He was just like us; he felt fatigue and hunger and pain; he shivered in the cold; he had emotions of love and fear —emotions always controlled, but the same as we have nevertheless. His human will felt repugnance, as the night before He died. Were we to meet Him today as He appeared when He traveled along the dusty roads of Palestine, we would see Him as no different from any other man we might meet—a very attractive personality, no doubt, and an air about Him which would speak of something wonderful, but apparently the same as all others. We could go up to Him, and greet Him and shake hands, and spend the night in conversation with Him as Nicodemus did one night long ago. And if we were not very careful, we too might miss the very divinity hidden beneath that humanity; we too might cry out in surprise at His first claims, as did His neighbors in Nazareth: "Where did he get this wisdom and these miracles? Is not this the carpenter's son?"[10] He was so human that those who did not look deep enough saw only that humanity and nothing more.

THE HYPOSTATIC UNION

Christ became Man, but He was also God; for He always was and always will be. Only 1900 years ago did the Second Person of the Trinity assume to Himself a human nature. It is the great mystery of the Incarnation, and at the very heart of that mystery we have what theologians refer to as the "hypostatic union." We will never be able to understand it perfectly, but we should know what it is.

Hypostatic union refers to a joining together of two completely separate things in their very being, in the depths of what they are. The term "hypostatic" comes from the Greek word *hypostasis,* which gradually came to mean the same thing as "person." Thus, the phrase "hypostatic union" refers to the union, in the one divine *person* (hypostasis), of two separate natures in Christ, the divine and the human. We find in the God-Man a perfect *human* nature, and yet without confusion, that nature is joined to the *divine* nature of Christ. The result of this is not simply that this humanity of Christ acts with God, or is penetrated by God, or simply joined to God, but rather that this Man Christ *is* God, in the very depths of His being. As St. Paul expresses it: "Have this mind in you which was also in Christ Jesus, who though he was by nature God, did not consider being equal to God a thing to be clung to, but emptied himself, taking the nature of a slave and being made like unto men."[11]

Perhaps a few words of explanation will help. A "nature" is that which makes a thing what it is: the nature of a cat is different from the nature of a man; the nature of man is different from the nature of God. It is because we have a human nature that we can think, while cats cannot. It is because we have a human nature that we can freely choose to do what we will, while animals cannot. God also has His nature: a perfect, all-powerful nature; God can do anything. That is the divine nature. And between God and man we know also that there exists the angelic nature.

A "person" means a complete individual being, intellectual in nature and master of its actions. A person is termed, technically, "a suppositum which can think." Everything that exists as something complete in itself may be called a *suppositum:* an animal, for example, or even a stone. In the depths of their being they *are* something, independently of everything and everyone else. A *suppositum* is the subject to which all activities are referred, since the thing is complete in itself; it is whole and entire, and is not a part of anything else by its nature, nor does it belong to anything else. It acts for itself. A cow may be a member of a large herd, but, in itself, that cow is independent; it possesses completely the animal nature of a cow, and is distinct from all the others; it is, therefore, a suppositum. If a suppositum possesses an intellect, we might call it a "thinking suppositum." Actually we have another word for it in that case: we call it a *person,* or an *hypostasis.* Every man, since he has an intellectual soul, is called a person or an hypostasis, since he is a "thinking suppositum."

The idea might be expressed in this way also. If we see a figure far off in the distance we might ask at once, *"What* is it?" We are asking then, "What *nature* does it possess?" As the figure comes a bit closer, we can see the general outlines, and we answer that it is a man — something possessing the nature of a man. We then proceed further and ask, *"Who* is it?" We are wondering which particular one it is, out of all those who possess human nature; we are asking then about the *person.* When we actually are speaking to the individual, we known that what we saw off in the distance is a man (nature), and more, an individual man named James Taylor (person).

THE EXCEPTION

Every individual human nature has one human person to go along with it; we have no other experience with human nature except in human persons. But there was one exception. In the case of Christ, it was *not* true that, because He had a perfect human nature, He was also a human *person,* independent from all other things and persons; it was not true that there was attached to, or involved in, that particular human nature a human person, that is, some thinking suppositum (an hypostasis) which was the subject to which all his activities were referred. This was not true because the *human nature of Christ* was not complete, whole, nor separate or independent in itself. Christ had a human nature actually and truly, identical with the nature possessed by every other man, up until the very last point: the giving of the title of "person" to that nature. At that very point, it was the *divine Person* which took over. Because of the close union between the human nature and the divine nature in Christ, He had no *human* "person," but rather the place of a human person was taken by the eternal, divine "Person" of the Son — the Second Person of the Trinity.

Thus, if asked what Christ is, we would say from appearances that He is a man, and that is absolutely true; through faith we would later learn that He is also God. When asked "who" Christ is, however, it would be absolutely incorrect to say that He is a human "person"; as we learn again through faith, the only correct answer to that question is, "He is the Second Person of the Trinity." This is what is meant by the term "Hypostatic Union": that marvelous and intimate union of two complete, yet separate natures, in the one single Person (hypostasis) of the eternal Son of God.

This is the only instance which we have of such a union. There are other types of unions in things with which we come in contact. There is, first, what we call an "accidental" union, a passing, superficial type of union. Such, for example, would be the union between a pile of stones or the parts of a watch or the man and the automobile he drives. The man gets up, leaves the car, and there is no more union.

A substantial union is something more profound. In this case, the union of two distinct elements (substances), in their very being, produces something lasting, some new thing. All things, scholastic philosophy tells us, are composed of two elements: matter and form. The union of these two will result in a new *thing,* such as a flower, a dog, a stone. And since this thing which possesses the nature of a flower or dog or stone is also independent and self-possessed, it is also a "suppositum."

When we talk about man, we also have a union of two distinct elements, resulting in an individual human nature. Here the "matter" is the *human body;* but the "form" is not something material (as in the case of the flower or the dog or stone), but something immaterial, something "spiritual." This "form" is the *human soul,* endowed with an intellect and a free will. And since this rational human nature is also independent and complete in itself and for itself, the result is also an "hypostasis" or "person" — a "thinking suppositum."

The hypostatic union, however, is something far different from any of these. "Matter" and "form" are what we call *incomplete* substances. To have a perfect human nature, we must have both the body and the soul; they complete one another. Since Christ possesses a human body and soul, He has a true human nature resulting from a substantial union of the two. In the case of Christ, however, we have something more. There we find two absolutely distinct natures each complete in themselves, yet united in the Second Person of the Trinity. Not only does Christ possess this human nature, but He has the divine nature as well. These two do not complete one another; they remain absolutely distinct, but yet they are united. The divine Person takes over this human nature, the human nature of Christ, so that it has no "personality" of its own: it is not whole and entire in itself, and therefore it is not a "thinking suppositum" or "person." When the human nature of Christ thinks, it is not a human *person* which thinks; it is *God,* thinking in *His* human nature.

Unlike the soul and body, these two natures in Christ do not *have to* be united; it is solely because God deigned to assume this human nature. But from then on, when this human nature "thinks" or "wills" or does anything else, it is God who does it. The *body* and *soul* are ordinarily joined together so as to form a new *person.* In the Incarnation of Christ no new person was formed. There was a permanent, substantial, intimate union of body and soul as well as a union of two complete natures, but always a union in a *pre-existing person,* the person of the Son of God. The sole example we have of an hypostatic union is in Christ, and we can learn of it only through Revelation.

RESULTS OF HYPOSTATIC UNION

There are far-reaching results of this hypostatic union. A man is responsible for his acts, because he is a person. If one were to thrust his fist suddenly through his neighbor's window, and then disclaim any blame for it by responding that, "I didn't do it; it was my fist that did it," he would be laughed to scorn. He is the complete, incommunicable, self-possessed individual, the *person,* and not his fist; and it is he who receives the credit or blame for what his fist might do.

The basic notion of a person as a separate, independent being carries with it the idea of responsibility for one's actions. It implies that one can receive blame or credit for what he does. This juridic notion of a person is really contained *in* the other, more basic notion, known as the ontological person. It is rooted in his very being. Every human being, by virtue of his human nature, is endowed with natural rights, and correspondingly, also, with certain duties. These rights are inviolable, and unless something interferes with the use of his mind or will, he will also be held accountable for these duties. A man can become a member of a group in society, if he will, and acquire other rights and assume other duties. A horse, on the other hand, lacking the note of rationality, lacks also this ontological personality, and so he has no such rights or duties, and cannot become a member of society, or be said to have a juridic personality. He acts, not according to reason, but by instinct. Thus we do not speak, strictly, of the "rights" of a horse since he is not a person, nor do we talk of an "immoral" horse, because it is only persons who can become the subject of laws and duties in the juridic order.

In the case of Christ, although He was truly a man, with a true human nature, what He did was not attributed to a human person. In the case of Christ, there was no human "person" but only a divine Person, so that we may never speak of what Christ the Man did, but only of what Christ did as Man — that is, in His human nature. The one and the same divine Person was responsible for the acts of Jesus, whether He acted as God or as Man. Thus every time He did *anything,* whether it was to speak or sleep or eat or walk, it was *God* — the Second Person of the Trinity — who got the credit for those actions: who was responsible for them. In that way, it was not just a man, but actually God who spoke or slept or ate or walked. And in that way also, it was *God* who died upon the cross.

God, in His divine nature, of course, cannot die; death implies a material thing, a body, that can wear out and cease to function properly. God, in His divine nature, could have no such body; that would make Him imperfect. In the human nature of Christ, however, there is a body and a soul. That body can wear out, the blood drain from the veins, and the heart stop beating, and there is death, bringing about the separation of that body and soul. Ordinarily when we see a body wasted away, we say that this "man" has died. But Christ never acted in any way so as to get credit, as it were, just as a man; everything He did was attributed to the one only person He possessed: the divine Person. And so we say that God died on the cross, just as it was God whose tiny voice pierced the dark night at Bethlehem, whose sermons moved the crowds of Palestine, whose arms cast out the money-changers from the temple.

WHY THE CROSS?

It was in this way that the Redemption was accomplished. One question remains, however, and that is *why* Christ chose to die upon the cross. Why could He not have come to earth and suffered only as a child: or simply have been scourged and no more; or perhaps have offered only one prayer to the heavenly Father? Any one of these actions would have been sufficient, absolutely speaking, to re-deem mankind, for it would have been an infinite action of God, yet coming from a true member of the human race. Why did the Divine Will demand the death on the cross?

The only answer can be the answer of Christ Himself: it was to be a proof of His great *love* for us. Mankind has generally accepted the opinion that the greatest thing a person can do to show love for someone is to die to save or to protect him. War heroes have always been honored because of that. "Greater love than this no man has, that one lay down his life for his friends."[12] All men knew that, and accepted it, so what Christ was really saying was that "if anyone has loved you by dying, I do not want to leave any possibility for you to think that I have loved you less. No one has loved you more than I, and to prove to you and to keep you from even thinking that someone might have loved you more, I will give up my life for you as a supreme demonstration of love for another. It is not so difficult to give up one's goods, one's property: but one's life — that is hard. Yet since it is the greatest proof of love, I will give just that proof."

It was not the *suffering* of Christ that pleased the Father; it was not the degree of that pain which brought about the redemption

— as though Christ had to suffer more because the sins of all were at stake. *Any* act of Christ, the God-Man, would have been enough, for any act was of infinite worth. It was only in adapting Himself to our human nature and human standards that Christ chose *death* to prove to us His love.

The death on the cross, then, was the climax of the life of Christ; His days on earth looked toward that hour. He lived constantly in the shadow of the cross, and scarcely had He been born when Simeon uttered those words over Him: "Behold, this child is destined for the fall and for the rise of many in Israel, and for a sign that shall be contradicted."[13] He prepared Himself always for that time when His hour might come, when He would rise up from prayer to meet His executioners; when "the world may know that I love the Father, and that I do as the Father has commanded me";[14] when Christ was "obedient to death, even to death on a cross."[15]

THE REDEMPTION

There are two sides to redemption: what we call "objective" redemption and "subjective" redemption. When Christ became Man, He did so to bring mankind back to God — to "redeem" them, that is, to buy back the freedom lost by sin. Christ came to deliver men from the bondage of sin, and to restore them to the life of grace. He did this through His own death on the cross. We know this as *Objective Redemption.* We were bought back at a great price, as the Apostles remind us: "You have been bought at a great price . . . you were redeemed from the vain manner of life handed down from your fathers, not with perishable things, with silver or gold, but with the precious blood of Christ, as of a lamb without blemish and without spot."[16]

Objective Redemption means that Christ died for all. In His own human nature, He contained, in a way, the human nature which He shared with every other human being ever to live. He was the representative of every man for that reason: to atone for the sins of everyone. He became the New Adam: "Therefore as through one man [Adam] sin entered into the world and through sin death, and thus death has passed into all men because all have sinned . . . so from the justice of the one [Christ] the result is unto justification of life to all men."[17] Christ became in this way the *Moral Head* of mankind, and as such He redeemed every single one of us. By mere birth, we are linked to Christ as the Moral Head; in Him and in Him alone is there salvation. He acted on behalf of all mankind, and thus salvation is made possible for us all. This notion of "objective redemption" is what some spoke of when writing of the Mystical Body, understanding it in an applied sense rather than the strict sense.[18]

SUBJECTIVE REDEMPTION AND THE CHURCH

We are not saved merely by the fact of Christ's death, however; for, between Calvary and our salvation, something very important intervenes: our *free will*. The grace of Calvary must be applied to our souls, and in that, we must co-operate freely. This is what we call "subjective redemption," redemption as applied to us as the subjects.

It is here, in the process of saving individual men, that the visible Church, the Mystical Body of Christ, fits into this grand outline of Divine Providence. In this long but beautiful work of linking up mankind, one by one, with the Redeemer, the Church has her own role to perform. As Pius XII writes: "As He hung upon the Cross, Christ Jesus not only appeased the justice of the Eternal Father which had been violated, but He also won for us, His brethren, an ineffable flow of graces. It was possible for Him of Himself to impart these graces to mankind directly; but He willed to do so only *through a visible Church* made up of men, so that *through her all might co-operate with Him* in dispensing the graces of Redemption."[19]

All men became "brothers according to the flesh,"[20] of the only-begotten Son of God through the Incarnation. But more than that, through Objective Redemption, those brothers "receive also the power to become the sons of God";[20] those brothers are to become tabernacles of grace as well. It is the great glory of the Church of Christ to be *the medium* through which Christ applies to the souls of men the grace of Redemption. "As the Word of God willed to make use of our nature, when, in excruciating agony, He would redeem mankind, so in the same way throughout the centuries He makes use of the Church [that is, the human nature of those people who are the Church] that the work begun might endure."[20] The Church is the extension of Christ in time and space; it carries on the life and the work of the Redeemer, and it will continue that labor until the end of time, always going further, incorporating more and more of mankind into the glorious Body of Christ. The Church, by its very nature, cannot be satisfied at any time with the number of those who form her membership, but must go out to preach to all, "recognizing in other men, although they are not yet joined to us in the Body of the Church, our brothers in Christ according to the flesh, called, together with us, to the same eternal salvation"; thus will Christ be able to "make His brothers according to the flesh partakers of the divine nature, through sanctifying grace in this earthly exile, in heaven through the joys of eternal bliss."[21]

In the plan of Christ, it is through the Church that all men are to receive grace. To enable her to perform the task assigned to her, Christ has endowed His Mystical Body with the means of granting grace to mankind. There is, first of all, the Sacrifice of the Mass. Calvary was the greatest and most important moment in the life of the God-Man, Christ; it is also to be the very center of the life of the Mystic Christ. The Mass is nothing more than the Sacrifice of Calvary: one fleeting moment in the life of Christ, cut out and frozen, as it were, to be relived day by day, "from the rising of the sun even to the going down,"[22] until the end of time. Day by day the faithful may return to the hill of Calvary to drink deep of its graces. What Christ once wrought in the world for all through His death on the cross is now effected in the souls of individual men through that same death renewed in the Mass. It is to be the supreme instrument, as it were, whereby the merits won by the divine Redeemer upon the cross are distributed to the faithful. As Pope Pius XII writes in his encyclical *On the Sacred Liturgy:* "[The death of Christ] does not immediately have its full effect; since Christ, after redeeming the world at the lavish cost of His own blood, still must come into complete possession of the souls of men. Wherefore, that the [subjective] redemption and salvation of each person and of future generations unto the end of time may be effectively accomplished, and be acceptable to God, it is necessary that men should individually come into vital contact with the Sacrifice of the Cross, so that the merits which flow from it, should be imparted to them. . . . The august Sacrifice of the altar is, as it were, the supreme instrument whereby the merits won by the Divine Redeemer upon the Cross are distributed to the faithful: 'as often as this commemorative sacrifice is offered, there is wrought the work of our Redemption.' This, however, so far from lessening the dignity of the actual sacrifice on Calvary, rather proclaims and renders more manifest its greatness and its necessity, as the Council of Trent declares. By its daily immolation it reminds us that there is no other means of salvation except in the cross of our Lord Jesus Christ, and that God Himself wishes that there should be a continuation of this sacrifice 'from the rising of the sun till the going down thereof,' so that there may be no cessation of the hymn of praise and thanksgiving which man owes to God, seeing that he requires His help continually, and has need of the blood of the Redeemer to remit sin which challenges God's justice."[23]

THE SEVEN SACRAMENTS

The seven Sacraments are also the God-given means of grace for mankind. Everything men need for their spiritual growth, from the cradle to the grave, is attended to in these rites. Through the waters of Baptism those who are born into this world dead in sin are not only born again through grace, and made members of the Church, but they become able and fit to receive the other Sacraments. By Confirmation, the faithful are given added strength to protect their life of grace and to defend the Church and the faith; in the sacrament of Penance a saving medicine is offered for the members of the Church who have fallen into sin. In the Holy Eucharist they are nourished and strengthened, and united to one another most intimately through their sacramental union with Christ. And finally, like a devoted mother, the Church is at the bedside of those who are sick unto death, and if it be not always God's Will that she restore health to this mortal body, nevertheless she administers spiritual medicine to the wounded soul and sends new citizens to heaven, who will enjoy forever the happiness of God.

For the social needs of the Church, Christ has provided two other Sacraments. Through Matrimony, provision is made for the external and duly regulated increase of Christian society, the birth of children for the Mystical Body; and, what is of greater importance, for the correct religious education of the children, without which this Mystical Body would be in grave danger. Through Holy Orders men are set aside and consecrated to God, to offer the Sacrifice of the Eucharistic Victim, to nourish the flock of the faithful with the Bread of angels and food of doctrine, to guide them in the way of God's commandments and counsels, and to strengthen them with all other supernatural helps.[24]

THE RETURN TO GOD

The final goal, of course, of the entire plan of God for mankind is to draw all men to the eternal happiness of heaven. It is the very purpose for their existence. Thus we see the finish of a grand circular movement out from God and back to God once more: creation, original sin, redemption, restoration to grace through Christ and the Church by means of the Mass and the Sacraments, and finally the full outgrowth of grace: the beatific vision. In it all, the visible Church, the Mystical Body of Christ, has its own important role to play, and it is in that light that the Church appears in her true beauty. She is not a motley group of politicians, of self-seekers, but a family of love, the instrument of Divine Love itself for the salvation of the world. Men come to God through Jesus Christ, and far from standing between Christ and the individual, the Church IS Jesus Christ diffused and communicated in time and space. She desires only to sweep all mankind along in this movement of love returning to God. She labors for the good of all men, drawing them all to herself as did Christ, "for building up the body of Christ, until we all attain to the unity of the faith and of the deep knowledge of the Son of God, to perfect manhood, to the mature measure of the fullness of Christ."[25]

CHAPTER VII

THE CHURCH IS BORN

WHEN we speak of the birth of the Church, we are speaking again in rather poetic fashion. Like the term *Mystical Body,* this notion implies a certain likeness between one thing and another: in this case, a similarity between the birth of a child and the beginning of the Church's life.

We read in the hymn for the Feast of the Sacred Heart that "the Church, united to Christ, was born from His riven heart"[1] upon the cross. It is simply the poetic way of saying that the Church began to exist *as the Church,* the Mystical Body, on Good Friday when Christ died. The Church is a group of people, as we have mentioned so often already, but it is not just an ordinary group: it is rather a living group, living a life all its own — a divinely given life. In this respect, it is more like a living organism than an organization. The very word *mystical* is used to lay emphasis upon that unique life. It is this sustaining power of God which explains the continued existence of the Church, unchanged throughout the centuries, and which sets it off from any other group of men in the world. The Holy Spirit comes upon this group, and unites the members to one another and to Christ in a very special way, so that we compare Him to the soul of a human body and call Him the *Soul* of the Mystical Body. The question then, put in its most simple form, is this: at exactly what time did the Holy Spirit begin to act as the Soul of the Church; when was it that He *first* poured out these special gifts over the members, uniting them to Christ in a special way, making them different from any other grouping of people in the world?

BORN ON THE CROSS

That moment was the very moment when Christ breathed forth His last breath upon the cross. Since the Mystical Body was to be an extension of Christ and His work in time and space — "Another Christ" — it was only fitting that this tremendous work should never cease for a moment. There is perfect continuity between the historic Christ and the mystic Christ. When His mission on earth was completed, at once the Church's began; when Christ had objectively saved mankind, He began at once to apply that redemption to the souls of individual men then living through the Church.

Like many things in Christ's religion, there is something of the mysterious about the origin of the Church itself — mysterious in the sense that the divine element began to be active in that body with no apparent change in the human side. Here, before the death of Christ, we had a group of men, hand picked in certain cases by Christ Himself to perform special duties, but up to this point just an ordinary group. They were a "moral" body, such as was described in Chapter II.[2] They were a group in which the principle of union was nothing else than the common end or purpose, and the common co-operation of all under an authority so as to reach that goal. They were all agreed on following Christ; Christ was their leader. But for all that, they were no different from such organizations today as the American Legion or the Sodality — organizations bound together under a leader for the attainment of a certain, common goal. This group was to form the Church, but it was not as yet the Church. It was the material side, the external; what was lacking was the divine element, that outpouring of the Holy Spirit.

At the moment when Christ died upon the cross, that divine element was supplied, and this group of men became the Church; this "moral" body of men became the "Mystical" Body, joined for all time to its Head, Christ. It was something like the consecration at Mass. Before the priest recites the powerful words which change bread into the Body and Blood of Christ, we can see only a white host, and even after those words, it seems as though that is all that is there. There appears to be no difference, yet there is a vast change. It is not only what appears to be bread which we see; actually it is the body and blood of Christ which lies upon the altar.

Thus, before the death of Christ we saw only a group of men — the followers of Christ; and after His death we see the same group, and apparently there has been no change at all. But there *is* a vast change: that group is now different from all others in the world; it is now the Mystical Body of Christ. It was at that moment that the Church began, that unique organization of men, unlike any other on this earth. It marked the start of a new mingling of the human and divine in life.

AN INFANT CHURCH

It was as yet a rather disorganized Church; it was a very frightened Church. Christ had prepared the way, but He had yet to complete the structure during those days He spent with the infant Church from Easter Sunday until He ascended into heaven forty days later; and then to strengthen it on the day of Pentecost by a special power given from heaven. During those forty days while Christ appeared to them and spoke of the kingdom of God (that is, of the Church, and how they were to guide it), the Apostles grew more and more conscious of what had happened upon Calvary, not only to Christ, but to themselves; they gradually realized they were now a new group, living the life of Christ. And finally on the day of Pentecost, when the Holy Spirit descended upon them, they were ready to begin the "public life" of the Church, and draw others into that intimate union with Christ. Indeed, so zealous were they that they baptized about three thousand souls that first day.

Pope Pius XII points out again, that there is a close similarity between the life of the historic Christ and the life of the mystic Christ. There was the preparation and annunciation, the birth, and finally the public manifestation. These three are nicely summed up in the words of Pope Leo XIII: "The Church which, already conceived, came forth from the side of the second Adam in His sleep on the Cross, first showed Herself before the eyes of men on the great day of Pentecost."[3]

PREPARATION AND ANNUNCIATION

For centuries before the actual coming of Christ, God had prepared the way for Him. Many prophets had come to speak of the Messias, not simply to promise that He would come, but even to tell to a certain extent what He would be like. The day finally came when God took actual steps to bring about the great event by sending the Archangel Gabriel to Mary, to ask her to become the Mother of God. At the very moment when Mary uttered her "Fiat: Be it done to me according to Thy word," the eternal Son became incarnate within her immaculate womb. For nine months the angels waited in hushed expectancy while the all-pure body of the God-Man was fashioned within the womb of His Mother. And Christ was born on Christmas Day.

The Church also had its time of preparation and annunciation, for as Pius XII explains: "The Divine Redeemer began the building of the mystical temple of the Church when by His preaching He made known His precepts; He completed it when He hung glorified on the Cross; and He manifested and proclaimed it when He sent the Holy Ghost as Paraclete in visible form on His disciples."[4]

In a way, the Church had its very first beginning at the moment of Christ's incarnation, for Christ assumed His sacred body, not merely that He might become man, but also that He might be the Head of the Church. Even within His Mother's womb, Christ bore the exalted title of Head of the Church.

From the beginning of His public life, however, our Lord actually set about organizing His Mystical Body; it was the time of preparation and annunciation. He promised it and spoke about it many times, telling His disciples what the purpose of the Church would be, what their tasks would be; how one might become a member of the Church, and how one should live as a member of this Body. The day finally came when Christ took the biggest step toward forming that Church — when He told Peter that he was to become the prince of the Apostles, the visible head of that group on this earth. And the night before He died He instituted the Sacrifice and Sacrament of the Eucharist as *the* prayer of worship for His Church. This group was sufficiently formed now to be born into the world: born as an infant Church, not as a strong, fully grown Church; but it was ready for that outpouring of the Holy Spirit which would mark its origin, its beginning as a unique group, different from all others in the world.

THE BIRTH

The birth of the Christ Child was a beautiful scene of solemn simplicity, for although there were sufferings and hardships, there was still much love, for the angels sang above the humble cave of Bethlehem as Mary and Joseph watched over the Infant; and the bright star of Christ shone gloriously, while the shepherds bowed down in lowly adoration. It is a scene which will speak for all time to come of love — Love Incarnate.

The birthday of the Church was quite a different scene. This occurred in suffering and pain and anguish upon the gibbet of the cross, amid the cries of those who hated Christ, and who were soon to turn their hatred upon this newborn Church as well. It was a fitting place for its birth, however, for the pain and suffering in which it was born are to be its lot for all time. Indeed, it is clear, as Pius XII remarks, how closely "this Church which Christ purchased with His own Blood, and whose members glory in a thorn-crowned Head . . . resembles its divine Founder who was persecuted, calumniated and tortured by those very men whom He had undertaken to save."[5] This was to be the lot of the Church among men, and it could not be otherwise, for such was the promise of Christ: "If they have persecuted me, they will persecute you also."[6]

At that very moment of its birth, the Mystical Christ was given all the graces and powers from God that this Body would need to perform its work in the world. For *"just as* at the first moment of the Incarnation the Son of the Eternal Father adorned, with the fulness of the Holy Spirit, the *human nature* which was substantially united to Him, that it might be a fitting instrument of the Divinity in the sanguinary work of the Redemption; *so* at the hour of His precious death He willed that *His Church* should be enriched with the abundant gifts of the Paraclete in order that in dispensing the divine fruits of the Redemption she might be, for the Incarnate Word, a powerful instrument that would never fail."[7]

Christ did not begin His public life immediately after birth, however. He was yet in His infancy, and was kept from the world and from those who would destroy Him; He lived His hidden life for a time in Egypt, and then in the little village of Nazareth. Similarly, the Church was still very much an infant when it was born; its members were scattered and frightened of those who would destroy them. Thus, for some fifty days the Mystic Christ was to live a hidden life before it stepped out boldly to announce the good tidings of Christ to the world. Under the careful tutelage of the divine Head Himself, the infant Church developed, for, as Pius II wrote many years ago, "suffering upon the cross, Christ came into possession of His Church through His own blood, and He personally ruled over it until the day of the Ascension, and like a true leader and ruler, directed all things in the proper way."[8]

When Christ was taken up into heaven, the Church returned to make its last retreat before entering upon its public life, somewhat as Christ prayed for forty days in the desert before beginning His life of preaching. In obedience to the command of Christ "not to depart from Jerusalem," the members of the Church returned to the upper room "and continued steadfastly in prayer," waiting for the coming of the Paraclete as promised: "But you shall be baptized with the Holy Spirit not many days hence."[9] Under the leadership of Peter, the vicar of Christ, they chose Matthias to take the place of the traitor Judas, so that their number might be again complete. The Mystical Christ was about to speak to the world.

PUBLIC MANIFESTATION

When Christ entered upon His public ministry, He willed that that beginning should be marked by a wonderful event, something which would point Him out to the people, as it were, and testify to the divine nature of His mission. It was His baptism by John in the River Jordan. His cousin John had been baptizing people as a sign of repentance; it was not the Christian baptism which we know today.

John knew that he was simply preparing the way for Christ, and he told this to the Jews: "I indeed baptize you with water, for repentance. But he who is coming after me is mightier than I, and his sandals I am not worthy to bear. He will baptize you with the Holy Spirit and with fire."[10]

Realizing this, then, John was overcome with true humility when Christ approached him and asked to be baptized by him. "It is I who ought to be baptized by thee, and dost thou come to me?"[11] he asked. Many people were standing about, those whom John had just been baptizing, and they heard what Christ and John were saying. But Christ insisted, answering, "Let it be so now, for so it becomes us to fulfill all justice"; and as the people watched, Christ and John descended into the waters. It was a peaceful scene: the people watched silently as John performed the rite of his baptism over this unknown man who had just come from Galilee. And as they watched, wondering perhaps why the great John had appeared so humbled in the presence of this stranger, the wonderful event occurred. The heavens were opened, and the Holy Spirit descended in the form of a dove and rested over the head of Christ; and a voice from the heavens shattered the silence, saying, "This is my beloved Son, in whom I am well pleased."[12]

This marked the beginning of the public life of Christ. Until this time He had remained hidden in the quiet life of Nazareth. It was immediately after this that He went out to prepare Himself by fasting forty days in the desert; after this He began to preach and to choose His disciples. From now on He was to remain constantly in the public eye, His name known throughout the land. This incident marked Him as someone of divine favor; the authority of God was with Him.

So also with the Church. When it was about to enter into its public life, only some fifty days after birth, a noteworthy incident occurred, calling the attention of thousands to the divine favor overshadowing this group. "For just as He Himself, when He began to preach, was made known by His Eternal Father through the Holy Spirit descending and remaining on Him in the form of a dove, so likewise, as the Apostles were about to enter upon their ministry of preaching,

Christ our Lord sent the Holy Spirit down from Heaven, to touch them with tongues of fire and to point out, as by the finger of God, the supernatural mission and office of the Church."[13]

The first Pentecost was a memorable day. It was a quiet Sunday morning and the Jewish feast of Pentecost, begun at sunset the previous day, was drawing to a close. There were thousands of visitors in Jerusalem, come there to celebrate the feast, which is one of the great feasts of the year. It was a day of thanksgiving, known also as the Feast of the Harvest; according to some it commemorated the day when the Law was given to Moses on Mount Sinai. The infant Church, however, at this time was gathered together in prayer in an upper room — hidden from the others, unknown to many. But suddenly the great sign appeared, like trumpets announcing the entrance of a great and noble personage. As the crash of thunder and the sound of the trumpet had announced the giving of the Law of the Old Testament to Moses,[14] so now, as the Church of the New Testament was about to step out to replace the old, "there came a sound from heaven, as of a violent wind coming, and it filled the whole house where they were sitting; and there appeared to them parted tongues of fire, which settled upon each of them."[15]

It was in this way that God marked the beginning of the Church's public life, and called attention to the importance of her mission. As with the historic Christ, so with the Mystic Christ, this was done with a sound from heaven and the visible coming of the Holy Spirit. This was what Christ had promised. Having already solemnly installed Peter as His vicar in the Church, as He had previously told him He would do, He ascended into heaven; and now, sitting at the right hand of the Father, He wished to make His Church known, and proclaim it to all the people.

As soon as the sound of this roaring wind was heard, crowds hastened to the building where the Apostles were gathered, hoping to discover the meaning of it. The disciples then threw open the doors and rushed out to begin their glorious work of preaching, and, as Peter spoke, the hearts of about three thousand souls were moved to receive his words, and they were baptized.

The Mystical Body entered upon its public life, to remain constantly from then on in the public eye; it was to go to the ends of the earth, ever drawing more and more into this loving union with Christ. Men could no longer ignore it, no more than mankind could long ignore Christ. He was not just another philosopher. As even the impious Voltaire has remarked: "No wise man or thinker has had the least influence upon the manners or morals of the street on which he lives; but Jesus Christ has had an influence upon the entire world."[16]

And since the Church is Christ, the same may be said of her. She will always seek to influence the entire world; she will continue ceaselessly to speak to all of mankind, offering them the love of Christ. And it is left to every man to decide whether he will accept or reject that love, and the Church which leads us to it.

CHAPTER VIII

THE CHURCH IS A VISIBLE BODY

It has been said often enough now that when we call the Church the Mystical Body we are using a figure of speech, but yet that phrase refers to a reality: a group of people who are intimately united to Christ in a special way. This group is also a well-determined, visible group; one need have no hesitancy about stating just which people go to make up that group and which do not.

Pius XII has very clearly pointed out the requirements for membership in the Mystical Body. "Actually only those are to be included as members of the Church," he writes, "who have been baptized and profess the true faith, and who have not been so unfortunate as to separate themselves from the unity of the Body, or been excluded by legitimate authority for grave faults committed."[1] In other words, all members of the Roman Catholic Church and only members of the Roman Catholic Church are to be considered members of the Mystical Body on this earth.

A QUESTION

Before going too far it will be well to pause and answer a question which might arise here. "I had read in a book that if a person had sanctifying grace he was united to Christ and was thus a member of the Mystical Body; why limit such membership now to Roman Catholics — surely many outside the Church are in the state of grace?"

The answer involves making a few clear-cut but simple distinctions.

There are, it must be admitted, many books and pamphlets which speak of sanctifying grace as being the one requirement for membership in the Mystical Body. Some of them even distinguish between the Church and the Mystical Body (as one would have to in this case), and state that there are many who are members of the Mystical Body — that is, who are in the state of grace — but who are not members of the Catholic Church. What they have in mind, however, is an *applied notion* of the Body of Christ, and not the primary concept found in Scripture. As was explained in Chapter IV, St. Thomas Aquinas in particular spoke of the Mystical Body in terms of grace, and his influence in modern Catholic thought has been very great, so that many, following him, have written on this subject along similar lines.

When Pope Pius XII speaks, however, he has in mind this basic concept of Sacred Scripture in which the Mystical Body and the Catholic Church on this earth are exactly the same thing. The union with Christ which a person has in the state of grace is a very real union, but it is *not* the union with Him in the Mystical Body. There are many outside the Church who do have grace, no doubt; there are also many members of the Mystical Body who lack sanctifying grace, for as the encyclical reminds us: "One must not imagine that the Body of the Church, just because it bears the name of Christ, is made up during the days of its earthly pilgrimage only of members conspicuous for their holiness, or that it consists only of those whom God has predestined to eternal happiness."[2] Membership in the Body of Christ, then, is determined by something else. We refer to it as the *Triple Bond*.

THE TRIPLE BOND

The Holy Father points out just what this Triple Bond is in the quotation given above. It is: (1) Baptism, (2) profession of the true faith, and (3) submission to the Roman Pontiff. All of these are *visible* things in some respect, so that there can be no doubt about whether one actually belongs to the Church. The Body of Christ is above all a visible body, and so also must be its requirements for membership. The possession of sanctifying grace is not something visible; it is something essentially invisible, and if it were to be the requirement for membership, no one could ever be sure who were the members of the Church and who were not.

If we look at the three points of the Triple Bond, all of this should become a bit clearer. First of all, there is Baptism. By this is meant the valid reception of the Sacrament of Baptism, *baptism of water*. At times we hear people speak about "baptism of blood" or "baptism of desire." These are not Sacraments, but rather means by which the effects of Baptism can be supplied for those who cannot receive the Sacrament of Baptism. By the valid reception of baptism of water, a person receives a *sacramental seal* or *mark* upon his soul; it is this which makes one a member of the Mystical Body. This sacramental seal is the *basic bond* of union. In the case of an infant, it alone suffices to make one a member of the Church. It will also have this same effect for an adult, provided no obstacle is placed hindering that effect. Such an obstacle would be either a refusal to accept the true faith or to adhere to the rule of the Pope. This spiritual seal remains, however, even if one should commit a mortal sin. Thus, unless that mortal sin is a sin against faith or a refusal to adhere to the rule of the Holy Father, the sinner is still a member of the Church.

In the case of baptism, then, there can be no doubt as to the visibility. When the priest (or in case of need, a layman) pours the water and recites the words of baptism, the sacramental seal is immediately produced upon the soul of the person. The pouring of the water and the recitation of the words are things which we can see and hear, and because of the promise of Christ, we know that this effect will always follow upon the valid administration of the Sacrament; the connection is so intimate that it will never fail. Thus we can know for certain that a person is a member of the Church through Baptism.

In the case of an infant, this Baptism is all that is needed. For an adult, however, there are these two obstacles which could stand in the way and keep that person from being a true member of the Church. The adult, unlike the child, has the use of his reason and free will, and so God demands the proper use of each of them in acquiring membership in His Church.

FAITH

The first obstacle which a man could place to the effect of his Baptism would be the refusal to submit his mind to the Mind of God; the refusal of the human intellect to accept the revelations of the Divine Intellect. Thus, for the adult, there is the requirement of *faith*. Again, what is required is a visible adherence to the revealed truths taught by the Church of Christ. If a person were to reject publicly these truths, even though through no fault of his own, he would thereby lose membership in the Body of Christ. This is the actual case in the life of an infant baptized validly in an heretical sect. By that valid baptism of water, he becomes a member of the Roman Catholic Church, even though he be baptized in the Lutheran Church, let us say. When he reaches the age of reason, however, and freely adheres to the Lutheran beliefs, he has placed the first obstacle to his membership in the true Church, and is no longer numbered among those who "profess the true faith." If an adult were baptized in an heretical sect, the obstacle would be present at once. Such individuals may reject these truths unknowingly, and may be entirely guiltless in this regard; and they may surely remain in the state of grace. They are actually failing, however, to accept the truths as revealed by God. We see again that there is a great difference between the union of grace and the union of the Triple Bond.

It is for this reason that all heretics — those who deny some truth of faith — are excluded from membership in the Mystical Body. By failing to accept the true faith, they place an obstacle to the first effect of their Baptism — that is, of making them members of the Church. Those, on the other hand, who do accept the true faith, and show it publicly in their profession, in their prayers, in their actions, remain members of this Body. That will be those, in other words, who accept and profess the beliefs of the Roman Catholic Church.

The same thing is true of the apostate — the Catholic, that is, who abandons his faith completely, even though he does not join an heretical sect. He loses his membership because of his sin of apostasy, which is really a sin of heresy: a denial of revealed truth. This means more than simply "not practicing" his religion, of course — not attending Mass or receiving the Sacraments. It involves giving up the very beliefs themselves. When a man casts aside his Christian faith like that, he breaks the bond of union, and since he can hardly help but realize what he is doing, the spiritual state of his soul is sad indeed.

SUBMISSION TO THE ROMAN PONTIFF

There is one other obstacle which might hinder the adult from union with Christ in His Church; it would be the refusal to submit one's will to the Will of God; the refusal of the human will to accept the yoke of obedience demanded by God toward His official representative on this earth, the Roman Pontiff.

In this way, all schismatics are excluded from membership in the Mystical Body. A heretic is one who refuses to accept the beliefs of the Catholic Church; a schismatic is one who refuses to accept the ruling authority of the Church. Practically speaking today it is impossible for any group to remain, for any time, merely schismatical, or "cut off" from the Pope as the word means, without at the same time becoming heretical; for, in refusing to listen to the Pope, a man would also be led to deny the dogma of the infallibility of the Pope, and this denial would make him a heretic.

This requirement for membership is also something visible. We can easily enough see who are the people who listen to the words of the Supreme Pontiff, and who guide their lives according to his directions. It brings us back once again to the conclusion that the Mystical Body is a visible body and thus its members can easily be known.

Besides the schismatic, there is one other type of person who would lose membership by refusing to listen to the Pope: the *excommunicatus vitandus,* that is, a person who has been put out of the Church by the lawful authorities in an altogether special manner. The phrase means "an excommunicated person who must be avoided." He is considered so dangerous that the faithful are directed to avoid all communication with him; he is considered as having lost membership in the Church entirely. Others who are excommunicated for different offenses, such as marrying outside the Church, are deprived of all their *rights* in the Church (for example, the right to receive the Sacraments, to act as godparents, the right to be buried from the Church), but they retain their membership in the Body. Such is not the case with the *excommunicatus vitandus:* the excommunicated person who must be avoided. He has been excommunicated in a special manner and has lost even his membership. In actual practice, this type of excommunication is always imposed by name on the individual, and such a person is almost always either a heretic or schismatic on some other point long before this most serious penalty is levied against him.

To sum this up, then, in the words of Pius XII, we find that valid baptism of itself will make one a member of the Mystical Body by virtue of the sacramental seal which it confers. In the adult, two other things are required so that this effect may take place: profession of the true faith and submission to the Roman Pontiff. If a man possesses all of these, he is truly a member of the Mystical Body.

Pius XII writes that "actually" only those are to be included as members who fulfill these requirements. He says that because "potentially" all men are members; all mankind is destined to enjoy this union with Christ in the Church. Actually, however, many do not because of a failure to fulfill the requirements of this Triple Bond. "Only those," he says, "who have been baptized" (by baptism of water), "and profess the true faith" (thus excluding all heretics), "and who have not been so unfortunate as to separate themselves from the unity of the Body" (schismatics) "or been excluded by legitimate authority for grave faults committed" (*excommunicatus vitandus*) "are to be included as members of the church."[3]

MEMBERS AND SUBJECTS

The force of the baptismal seal is seen also in the attitude of the Church toward those outside the fold. This spiritual mark is really a power given to the soul, enabling it to perform certain Christian acts in union with Christ and giving it the right to receive the other Sacraments of the Church. It sets up a relationship between Christ and the person, and between Christ's Church and the person, which endures as long as the seal remains — hence, a permanent relationship. It involves a change in the very soul of the individual, for while all the Sacraments give a likeness to Christ in *being* (that is, through the life of grace), Baptism, Confirmation, and Holy Orders also give a likeness to Christ in *function* (that is, by imparting this new power or office, this indelible mark or seal). It is because of the permanency of this sacramental seal that these three Sacraments can be received but once.

This permanent nature of the sacramental seal holds even in those excluded from membership in the Mystical Body because of heresy, schism, or excommunication. Thus we have a distinction between those adults who are "members" of the Church and those who are "subjects" of the Church. The term "subject" is more inclusive than the term "member," for among adults the relationship of *subject* is based upon the sacramental character alone, while to be a *member* faith and submission to the Pope are required besides. The laws of the Church thus bind all baptized persons, and the Church manifests her knowledge that she has jurisdiction over all the baptized, even those who are not actually her members, when (as in the Code of Canon Law) she takes care to exempt some from part of her matrimonial legislation.[4] Thus a baptized person who becomes a rebellious Christian, whether in good faith or not, has still a certain relationship to the Church.

This does not mean, of course, that such people sin by not obeying the laws, for their ignorance of those obligations excuses them where they are not expressly exempt. This distinction between a member and a subject does, however, emphasize the importance and far-reaching effects of the baptismal seal. In practice, baptized non-Catholics are excused from observance of the Church's laws. This is not true of anyone who would leave the Church after having been raised in the true faith or converted to it. Such a person would remain subject to all the laws of the Church in the strictest sense, even though he would join another sect. A Catholic cannot cast off this yoke at will, and though he may lose his membership through heresy or schism, he still remains a subject of the Church and all of her laws by virtue of the character indelibly impressed upon his soul by Baptism.

We can see, then, the attitude of the Church toward all those outside her membership, whether they have sinfully abandoned their faith, or whether they remain outside through ill will or inculpable ignorance. The Church is their true home. All those who are not baptized at all will find in the Church of Christ the home which the divine Redeemer established for them, and which He desires them to enter; and those who have been baptized will be enabled to discover the full meaning of that Baptism in the Catholic faith.

With these things in mind, we can better understand the meaning of the Holy Father's paternal words concerning those who are not Catholics: "Persevering in prayer to the Spirit of love and truth, We wait for them with open and outstretched arms to come not to a stranger's house, but to their own, their father's home."[5]

IMPORTANCE OF ENCYCLICAL

Pius XII intended to settle all disputes in the question of how we are to understand the doctrine of the Mystical Body. Some failed to see that as they ought, however, and so he repeated what he had said when he wrote his later encyclical on modern errors in the field of philosophy and theology, *Humani Generis,* of August 12, 1950.

"If the Supreme Pontiffs in their official documents purposely pass judgment on a matter up to that time under dispute," he writes, "it is obvious that the matter, according to mind and will of the same Pontiffs, cannot be any longer considered a question open to discussion among theologians."[6]

His Holiness then refers to the teaching on the Mystical Body in particular: "Some say they are not bound by the doctrine, explained in Our Encyclical Letter of a few years ago, and based on the sources of Revelation, which teaches that the Mystical Body of Christ and the Roman Catholic Church are one and the same thing. Some reduce to a meaningless formula the necessity of belonging to the True Church in order to gain eternal salvation. Others finally belittle the reasonable character of the credibility of Christian faith. These and like errors, it is clear, have crept in among certain of our sons who are deceived by imprudent zeal for souls or by false science. To them We are compelled with grief to repeat once again truths already well known, and to point out with solicitude clear errors and dangers of error."[7]

THE "SOUL" OF THE CHURCH

There has been a good deal of writing also in which the phrase "soul of the Church" has been used in a somewhat unorthodox fashion. The encyclical on the Mystical Body has once and for all rejected such an interpretation of the soul of the Church. The explanation at times left the impression that it was less important to belong to the visible Church than to be united to Christ by grace. To make this clearer, a distinction was made between the "body" of the Church and the "soul." Those who belong to the visible Church were said to belong to the body; those who, although claiming no relationship to the visible organization, yet lived in the state of grace, were said to belong to the "soul" of the Church. In this way, the notion came about that the "soul of the Church" was an invisible organization of some sort, and that God primarily intended this invisible grouping of the followers of Christ, thus uniting them to Him; and, further, that it was far more important to belong to this group than it was to belong to the visible Church.

This was an easy solution to certain problems; especially so, as an explanation for the axiom "Outside the Church there is no salvation," which was supposedly to be understood in the sense of "outside the *soul* of the Church, at least, there is no salvation." It was a distinction laden with dangers, however, and Pius XII emphasizes over and over again that there is no such invisible organization, and that "they err in a matter of divine truth, who imagine the Church to be invisible, intangible, a something merely 'pneumatological' as they say, by which many Christian communities, though they differ from each other in their profession of faith, are united by an invisible bond."[8] Grace would be just such an invisible bond, and it would be the bond of union in this unorthodox explanation of the "soul of the Church."

Although the teaching on the "soul" of the Church did not intend to state these things in so blunt a manner, and to place the visible Church in a less important light, yet drawn to its logical conclusion, it could not do otherwise. Since the appearance of the encyclical on the Mystical Body, then, this terminology has been abandoned, although it is still to be found in works published prior to the Encyclical in 1943. These are, generally speaking, the works which distinguished between the Church and the Mystical Body. The Catholic Church would tend to be identified more with the "body" of the Church; the Mystical Body would indicate, on the other hand, that invisible group, referred to by others as the "soul" of the Church.

We might read, for example, a statement such as the one cited in Chapter IV, taken from an older work on the subject: "Therefore, as far as its mission is concerned, the mystical body of Christ is not limited to the visible Church, but embraces potentially all those who are predestined to salvation — namely, all mankind. Neither can one say that the mystical body is limited, in an actual sense, to those who belong visibly to the Church. . . . His members may be called those who live in inner, vital union with Him. This body of Christ extends beyond the boundaries of the visible Church, which is universal and includes an incalculable multitude from all nations and ages and religions, 'baptized and unbaptized, circumcised and uncircumcised, all those whose intentions are good and who maintain an inner communion with God and Christ.' They are, in their entirety, the real members of the one mystical body, of the new race in Christ."[9]

Such a statement could not be brought into accord with the teaching of the *Mystici Corporis*. It could be explained, were one to accept one of the applied notions of the Mystical Body, but in the primary notion, presented for our acceptance by Pius XII, the Catholic Church and the Mystical Body are exactly coextensive: whoever is a member of one is a member of the other. There is no difference whatsoever. As Monsignor Fenton wrote at the time: "Once and for all, the *Mystici Corporis* has stigmatized such an hypothesis as erroneous. There is no Church of God in this world in any way distinct from the one visible society which Jesus Christ instituted. . . . The men and women in whom the Holy Ghost dwells through sanctifying grace do not constitute any social organization by themselves in this world."[10] Thus, all other similar statements must be explained in this fashion also. There is no invisible organization that serves as a way to heaven, and as we shall see in Chapter XIV, the Soul of the Church is a Person, the Holy Spirit Himself, and not a separate organization.

CHAPTER IX

THE CHURCH AND SALVATION

WHEN we speak about the necessity of the Church for salvation, we are in a position to see just how closely Christ has united Himself to His Mystical Body. On the road to heaven, a man can no more bypass the Church than he can bypass Christ. This has been the constant teaching of the Church throughout the centuries. This oneness between Christ and His Mystical Body extends to the very work of saving mankind; He shares both His life and His redemptive work with His mystic members.

This doctrine will never shock those who realize what the Church on earth actually is — the living Body of Christ. As He willed it, His Church upon earth is to be a continuation of Himself: "Jesus Christ prolonged in space and time, and communicated to men."[1] This living Body, then, could hardly be considered a useless adjunct in the work of redemption. If we are to do anything more than speak in poetic imagery when we talk about the Mystical Body, we must recognize that the Church plays a most important role in *applying* the graces of Calvary to the souls of men. And this is its work. The Church does not redeem mankind by any essential, objective action of its own. This work of "Objective Redemption," as we noted above,[2] was accomplished by Christ alone, as Pius XII reminds us: "Dying on the Cross, He left to His Church the immense treasury of the Redemption, towards which she contributed nothing."[3] In this work of Objective Redemption, the members of the Mystical Body had no part to play whatsoever. Salvation is from Christ alone.

SUBJECTIVE REDEMPTION

This grace of Christ must, however, be applied to the souls of individual men. They must become the actual *subjects* of grace, men and women whose souls are actually bathed in the redeeming grace won for them upon Calvary. This is "Subjective Redemption," and it is only in this continuation of the work of redemption that the Mystical Body shares: "When those graces [won on Calvary] come to be distributed," Pius XII continues, "not only does Christ share this work of sanctification with His Church, but He wills that in some way it be *due to her action*."[4] This is the mystery of the Church, the very heart of its necessity. Man, a social being by nature, is not to be less so when elevated to the supernatural level. Even salvation is to be due, in a very real way, to the social, communal labors of an entire, God-directed group of men. These people, under Christ, will help one another on the road to their common and eternal goal of life.

Naturally we should immediately conclude from this truth that no one would be able to get to heaven apart from this Church of Christ. If the Church is the continuation of Christ, it is also something essential to the plan of salvation. Some men, of course, will at once object to that conclusion: "God is not so weak and powerless that He must tie Himself to a group of men, and seek their help in saving mankind!" And that statement is 100 per cent correct. To say anything else would be to deny the very nature of an omnipotent God. God is not weak and powerless; He does not need the Church. But it is not a matter of whether God needs the Church absolutely, but of whether He *freely willed* to make it something necessary for salvation. If we attempt to pass over the Church by saying that "God does not need it," we are merely side-stepping the real issue.

OUTSIDE THE CHURCH NO SALVATION

This entire teaching on the intimate union between Christ and His Mystical Body is summed up in the axiom: "Outside the Church there is no salvation." It is a doctrine that has always been officially proposed by the Church throughout the centuries.[5] We have the most recent and most exact statement of this truth, however, in the important Letter of the Holy Office, written to Archbishop Cushing of Boston in 1949, in regard to the Feeney controversy: "Among those things which the Church has always preached and will never cease to preach is contained also that infallible statement by which we are taught that there is no salvation outside the Church. . . . Not only did the Saviour command that all nations enter the Church, but He also decreed the Church to be a means of salvation, *without which no one* can enter the kingdom of eternal glory."[6]

As a glance at the past will indicate, however, theologians have not always explained this axiom in the same way. What it aims at expressing primarily is the central importance of the Church in bestowing grace upon men. Yet theologians have regarded the axiom in different ways in attempting to interpret it. Not all of their explanations were well chosen. At times some men explained the axiom in a manner that would "reduce to a meaningless formula the necessity of belonging to the true Church in order to gain eternal salvation," as Pius XII said in condemning such explanations.[7] For this reason, the Holy Office emphasizes a particularly important point: "This dogma must be understood in that sense in which the *Church herself understands it.* For, it was not to private judgments that Our Saviour gave for explanation those things that are contained in the deposit of faith, but to the teaching authority of the Church."[8]

ACTUAL MEMBERSHIP NOT NECESSARY

Like all axioms, the phrase is a brief wording of an established truth. It does not claim to express in four Latin words the entire content of this doctrine. Thus it is entirely possible for men to get many different meanings out of those words, depending upon what they might read into them. But we cannot argue on the basis of personal opinions about what the axiom could or could not mean.

The Letter of the Holy Office, then, absolutely and explicitly sets forth this truth: "That one may obtain eternal salvation, it is *not always required* that he be incorporated into the Church actually as a *member.*"[9] We do not, in other words, have to give an explanation that will somehow or other get all of those people to be saved "inside" the Church. This does not mean, of course, that those people can be saved *apart* from the Church, or *independently* of the Church. They can no more bypass the Mystical Body on the road to heaven than they can bypass Christ. Thus, as the Holy Office adds: "That one may obtain eternal salvation, it is necessary that at least he be united to her by *desire* and *longing*."[10] This will become clearer as we go along.

The chief difficulty with most of the unacceptable explanations was that they sought to get everyone "in" the Church somehow or other. They felt that, by some means, they had to present an explanation that would make everyone saved a *member* of the Church. One of these solutions unfortunately became very widespread, and it must still be rooted out of certain minds. It explained salvation by making a distinction between the "Body" of the Church, and its "Soul." The members of the *visible* Church were said to belong to the *Body;* and those outside the Church who lived good lives and possessed sanctifying grace, were said to belong to the *Soul* of the Church. Since the encyclical of Pius XII on the Church, such a notion must be rejected absolutely, as we noted in the previous chapter.

OTHER EXPLANATIONS

Some men explained the salvation of those who were not members of the Church by referring to them as "exceptions" to God's ideal plan; they were saved, they said, through extraordinary means of salvation, rather than the ordinary means — that is, the Church. This explanation, however, made the Church seem very unessential. These people not only could, but actually would, bypass the Mystical Body on the road to heaven. It would give to the axiom nothing more than a very limited meaning. The statement would be true for many, but not for the "exceptions"; and these would naturally be very numerous, since the number of actual members of the Church would most often be less than the number of nonmembers.

Others approached more closely to the acceptable explanation, but their use of words brought them to an unacceptable position. They spoke of those who were *"actually members* of the Church" (*in re*), and those who were *"members* of the Church *in desire"* (*in voto*). Or they spoke of those who belonged to the Church either actually or in desire. This gave the impression of explaining the axiom away. Thus they would say that it is necessary to *belong* to the Church, or to be a *member* of the Church in order to be saved, and people would understand them according to the accepted meaning of the terms. A member, according to the actual terminology in use the past few centuries, is an actual part of an organization, one of the men composing a visible society such as the Church. With this explanation, however, they would introduce a new meaning to the word "member." It almost gave the impression that these theologians were drawing forth a rather subtle distinction from somewhere up their sleeve. "Ah," they would say: "You misunderstand us. There are *two* kinds of members: those who actually belong, and those who belong in desire. You *must* be a *member* of the Church to be saved, but *either kind* of membership will do."

Little wonder that this explanation seldom managed to convince. It sounded a bit too much like theological double talk. The very term "member in desire" is liable to the criticism of being bad English and clumsy theology. Desire is the tendency to an *absent* good, and one can only desire or long for membership in the Church if he does not possess such membership. The individual who is said to *pertain* to the Church in desire is not a member, although whether he knows it or not, he really wants to become one.

RELATIONSHIP TO THE CHURCH

We may note, therefore, that phrases which state that a person must "belong" to the Church in order to be saved; or those which state a man cannot be saved "outside" the Church do not mean, as the Church herself understands them, that a man must be a *member* of the Church. This does present a problem. The very word "belong," as we use it today, certainly carries with it the notion of being a member, of being what people always understand the word to signify — an actual part of a visible organization. We cannot hope to succeed very well in giving new meanings to old words in order to discuss our theological problems. In order to avoid confusion, we might be well advised to phrase our teaching a bit more precisely.

The official documents of the Church seem to give a hint in this regard. In the encyclical on the Mystical Body, we find the distinction between those "who *belong* to the Church" and "who are *members* of the Church," on the one hand; and, on the other, those "who have a certain *relationship* to the Church," or "who are *related* to it in *desire*."[11] Similarly, in the Letter of the Holy Office, we note the difference between those "who are actually *incorporated* into the Church as *members*," and those "who are *united* to the Church only by *desire*" — or "who *adhere* to the Church," as the Latin verb expresses it (*adhaereat*).[12] The verb carries with it the notion of hanging on to something — like adhesive tape; or of keeping close at hand, nearby. It expresses the same thing as the phrase "to have a certain relationship with the Church."

We might possibly translate certain of these phrases by something closer to the phrase "belong in desire," but it does tend to confuse the ordinary person. And quite apart from the confusion it might create, we might also slight the real value of the Church by giving the false impression that there are two kinds of equally good members in the Church: those who belong actually, and those who belong in desire. For practical purposes, this terminology is scarcely a breath away from the old "body" and "soul" explanation. In fact, in former years, the two were frequently combined. The "Body" of the Church was to be those who were actually members; the "Soul" consisted of those who belonged "in desire," as they said.

For the same reason, such a manner of using the term "member" is liable to obscure the benefits which only those who actually belong to the Mystical Body can possess. If we look upon both kinds of "membership" as equally good, we are not going to see quite so easily just how secure one type is, and how insecure this supposed "member by desire" still remains. But we will return to this in a moment.

THE VISIBLE CHURCH

In all of this, it is obvious that the visible Church has a most important role to play in the redemption of mankind. Since that Church is a group of people, united to Christ, it is also evident that any man who comes to believe in Christ ought to associate himself with that group officially. This was the very command given by Christ to His Apostles. Should a man knowingly reject this Church which is so intimately joined to Christ as to be His Mystical Body, he would thereby reject Christ also. We cannot separate Christ and His Mystical Body, as Christ Himself said, speaking to those disciples who were to form His Church: "He who hears you, hears me; and he who rejects you, rejects me; and he who rejects me, rejects him who sent me."[13] The reality of the Mystical Body is that intimate.

Yet what may be said of those many others who, through no fault of their own, actually do not become members of this visible Church? In some instances, it might be due to the physical impossibility of preaching the Gospel to a yet unknown continent; or at times the failure to attain membership might be due to the neglect of those already members of the Mystical Body to labor as they ought to lead others to the truth.

Pope Pius IX explained this situation very clearly in his *Allocution on Indifferentism* in 1854: "We must, indeed, hold on faith that no one can be saved outside the Apostolic Roman Church, that she is the only ark of salvation, that whoever shall not have entered her will perish in the flood"; yet he adds: "We must equally hold for certain that those who labor under ignorance of the true religion, if such ignorance be invincible, are not held guilty in that regard before the eyes of the Lord."[14]

INVINCIBLE IGNORANCE

They will not be condemned because they are ignorant of the true religion, through no fault of their own (invincible ignorance). These men will be saved, if they serve God as well as they can according to the information they possess. Thus the pagan in darkest Africa can be saved through the grace of God if he lives a life in accordance with his particular knowledge of God; so also the non-Catholic of good faith who adheres to some other religious group, provided he strives to live a life of virtue according to his lights.

But in *neither* of these instances will these men be saved *apart* from the true Church. The salvation that will come to them, either in darkest Africa or in the center of New York City, will come to them only *through* the Church of Christ, the Mystical Body of the Redeemer. They must possess some relationship to that Church. They cannot be saved through their "own" church, nor their "own" religion. It has been the constant teaching of the Church that a man is not saved *through* the Lutheran Church, let us say, or the Methodist, or *because* he believes in the teachings of Mohammed or Confucius. To say that they are, indeed, is to be guilty of the heresy of *Indifferentism,* condemned repeatedly by the Church during these past centuries. These men are saved only through the one true Church of Christ on earth, this visible organization, His Mystical Body. Even more, their salvation is *due* in some way to her action.

It means, in other words, that, as the Letter of the Holy Office explains: "In His infinite mercy, God has willed that the *effects,* necessary for one to be saved, of those helps to salvation which are directed towards man's final end, not by intrinsic necessity [Absolute Necessity of Means], but only by divine institution [Relative Necessity of Means], can also be obtained in certain circumstances when those helps are used only in *desire* and *longing*."[15] This is true of both Baptism and membership in the Church. Some (not all) of the graces which God would grant to the members of His Mystical Body can be obtained by those outside the Church in certain instances. Their relationship to the Church involves a relationship to these other means of grace which only the Church possesses — chiefly the Sacraments and the Mass. In view of all this, God grants to them the *effects* (graces) necessary to salvation, although they do not make actual use of the means of obtaining these graces.

WHY THIS CAN BE SO

Such a solution is possible because of the *manner* in which membership in the Body of Christ is necessary. There are different ways in which a thing is necessary, as the Fathers at the Vatican Council pointed out in their *schema* on the Church.

There is first of all the Necessity of Precept. This makes a thing necessary because of a command, but nothing more. There is, second, the Necessity of Means. This makes a thing necessary in a far more profound manner: it becomes necessary *as a means to an end*. This type in turn is divided into the two kinds of necessity of *means:* (1) that which comes from the very nature of the situation (*Absolute*), and (2) that which has become the means to an end by virtue of the free will of God (*Relative*). We might summarize this in the following schema:

$$\left\{ \begin{array}{l} \text{Necessity of Precept} \\[1em] \text{Necessity of Means} \left\{ \begin{array}{l} \text{Absolute: from the very nature of things} \\[0.5em] \text{Relative: from the free will of God} \end{array} \right. \end{array} \right.$$

It is stated that the axiom "Outside the Church there is no salvation" is to be understood as expressing a *necessity of means,* but one which has become so *by virtue of the free will of God*. In other words, it is a *relative* necessity of means.

WHAT THIS IMPLIES

Membership in Christ's Church thus involves something far more profound than a mere precept. Christ really intended to make His Church the *one means* for getting to heaven, and it will always remain that. There are no exceptions. But since its necessity does come from the free will of God, it is a relative necessity of means. It can happen that those who cannot actually make use of that means by becoming members of the Mystical Body may still reach heaven provided they retain *some* relationship to that Church. God may permit certain dispositions of soul to supply or take the place of actual membership; He may grant the grace of salvation to the individual because of the relationship to the Church which arises from those dispositions. This He actually does.

When it comes to sanctifying grace and charity and faith, we have an example of things involving an *absolute* necessity of means. Their necessity comes from the very nature of things. A man must have sanctifying grace actually in order to enter into the beatific vision, not because God made that so, but because the very nature of God and the heavenly vision demand it. There is no other possibility. God Himself could not allow one to enter the happiness of heaven without possessing sanctifying grace. Such a man would be incapable of seeing God in the beatific vision. Further, God is all-holy, and once He has decided to admit man to the beatific vision at all, He must demand that the person be turned toward Him through sanctifying grace. To allow one who has turned from Him in hatred and sin, and died in that state unrepentant, to see Him face to face, would go contrary to the essential holiness of God.

FAITH AND CHARITY

The same thing is true of faith and charity. These things are *absolutely* necessary means to salvation. A man may not merely "desire" them, and still attain heaven; he must actually possess them. The Letter of the Holy Office emphasizes this fact: "It must not be thought that any kind of desire of entering the Church suffices that one may be saved. It is necessary that the desire by which one is related to the Church be animated by *perfect charity*. Nor can an implicit desire produce its effect, unless a person has *supernatural* faith."[16]

Usually we say that the disposition of soul required in a man in order that he might receive grace outside the Church is that disposition proper to an act of perfect love or perfect contrition. That would be, then, an act of love by which we love God above all else *because* He is so infinitely good *in Himself;* or an act of contrition which is prompted by the motive of perfect love. God does will the salvation of all men, so that all men will be given the opportunity of receiving grace. If, through no fault of their own, actual incorporation into the Church is impossible for some men, God can accept these dispositions of love and sorrow as means by which this needed relationship to the Church is established. These dispositions do not, however, make those men members of the Church in any way.

When we say this, we mean, more precisely, that a man must possess true charity — the infused, supernatural virtue of charity. This is always found with sanctifying grace, and is always lost along with it. No man, however, will reach heaven simply because he is a "good fellow." No amount of naturally good qualities can make up for the lack of supernatural gifts. Thus any desire to belong to the Church (whether it is explicit or implicit) must be joined to sanctifying grace and charity in order to bring about the man's salvation.

The same thing is also true of supernatural faith. This is, however, a separate problem; it is not the question we are discussing at present. Our concern right now is only the necessity of the *Church* for salvation. Yet we must not slight these other things which are also so necessary. We might especially misunderstand this point in regard to faith. We do not mean that a man can reach heaven because of any false belief he might have; nor can he attain heaven because of any feeling of trust he might have that assures him he is saved, even though he calls this "faith." The faith we are speaking of is that defined by the Vatican Council — an infused, supernatural virtue by which we believe, with the help of God, those truths which He has revealed.[17] We accept these truths, which surpass our human understanding, on the authority of God alone.

This means two things: we must have this infused *virtue* of faith, and (in the case of adults) we must also make an *explicit act* of faith. Theology discusses just what are the minimum truths in which a man must exercise this faith in order to be saved, no matter who he is — whether an actual member of the Church, or a man only united to it in desire. At the very least, he must recognize that God exists, and that He is the eternal Rewarder of good and the Punisher of evil. He must see these truths as revealed truths, and this involves, therefore, at least some realization that God has entered into a special relationship with mankind, over and above that which is demanded by human nature alone.

It is not enough to say that the pagan in Africa will get to heaven somehow. He might possibly achieve some such notion (vague but adequate) of God and a supernatural order, but "faith depends on hearing," as St. Paul says.[18] Apart from a private revelation, the man who has not heard the Gospel preached to him *might never* express his faith in any way. The urgency is even more apparent when we consider that some theologians affirm that two other truths must also be professed explicitly in order to be saved: a belief in Christ the Redeemer, and — the truth intimately joined to that one — in the Trinity. But in any event, to make the way more secure for men throughout the entire world, the missionary work of the Church can never cease until the dawn of eternity.

EXPLICIT AND IMPLICIT

The important fact right now is that the Church is the one, sole means to our supernatural end. It is the City of God, raised up against the powers of evil. Anyone who reaches heaven without being a faithful member of this Church is like a man who stumbles along in the darkness, alone and without the helps which only the Church possesses. He may bask in the reflected light of this City, and it will thus help him to reach heaven. He may not even know what it is he is following, and he is certainly far worse off than he would be were he safely within the gates of that City. But it is only through the light of that Church, however dimly he perceives it, that he finds his way to heaven.

Theologians teach that this relationship to the visible Catholic Church, at least by *implicit desire,* is a requisite condition for salvation for those outside the visible body. "Implicit" comes from the word "imply." It refers to one thing that is *implied* in another. There is at times a bit of confusion, however, about what an "implicit" desire for membership would be in a man's mind. Everyone realizes that a man who really and expressly desires to join the Church is conscious of such a desire. A man who is taking instructions to prepare for reception into the Church has an *explicit* desire for membership. It is easy, also, to see how, if, through no fault of his own, he could not actually attain to membership in the Church, he would be saved. He is sincerely trying to do exactly and completely all that God wants of him for salvation. He could possess grace, and should he die before baptism, he could reach the happiness of heaven.

At the other extreme, there is the man who explicitly *refuses* to join the Church of Christ, fully realizing that it is the required means for salvation. He also is aware of what he is doing, and is fully conscious of the consequences when he openly rejects membership. For him there can be no question of grace, for by clearly refusing the Church as the one means of grace, he loses grace as well.

Between these two types, however, there is another person who is not a member of the visible Body, but who neither explicitly desires to become a member, nor knowingly rejects the faith. This may be, of course, due to a completely irreligious state of mind. God has no place in his life whatsoever. He has no desire to serve God at all, even insofar as he knows Him. It is simple to see how he could not be saved, since no one, in or out of the Church, is saved unless he strives to serve God faithfully.

However, this lack of membership or of explicit desire for it might also be due to other causes. The man may never even have heard of Christ's religion, although he does try to live a good life and obey the will of God insofar as he knows it. Such would be the case, for example, of the good pagan in some missionary country who had never heard the Gospel preached; or the case of some good non-Catholic who might have heard of the Catholic religion, but does not grasp its importance and is not moved to make a deeper study of it. Persons of this second type (the good pagan or non-Catholic) are then said to be in *good faith* — another meaning of the word "faith." They do not boast of an irreligious state of mind; quite the contrary, they sincerely try to live a good life and serve God as well as they can with the knowledge they possess of Him.

WHAT IS DESIRED?

The difficulty arises at this point because actually, when we use the term "desire" in ordinary conversation, we think only of an *explicit* desire. We associate the word "desire" with something we explicitly long for, something of which we ourselves are conscious. We have in mind a person who knows that he wants something special, some particular object. As we shall see, however, when theologians use the term "implicit desire," they have something quite different in mind. We must guard our thinking if we are to understand them correctly.

When we speak of an "implicit desire for membership in the Church," we use the word "desire" in a peculiar way, as far as

"Church" is concerned. The Church is not the particular, explicit object sought after. The person is not psychologically conscious of any desire for membership in the Church. We could not detect evidences of it directly in anything he would say or do. It is only indirectly that it is formed. We might think of this in terms of two circles, a smaller one contained within a larger one. The man directly desires some more general object (circle A) which contains in itself a more partic- ular, more specific object (circle B), even though he does not realize that himself. He must desire *something* directly: without an object there can be no desire. In this case, then, what the man *explicitly* desires (A) is something more general: *to do all that is necessary for salvation.* This does imply the necessity of belonging to the visible Church (B), but the man does not realize that. Hence he has only an implicit desire for such membership.

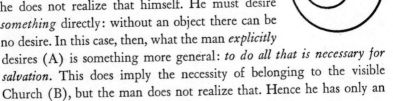

With this attitude, then, such a man can receive grace, and pro- vided he keeps the commandments of God insofar as they are known to him, he can attain eternal life. The visible Church is *the* means of salvation for men in this world, however. If there is not at least this implicit desire for membership in that Body, there can be no question of grace.

FAILURE TO COMPLY

There are two additional points to consider in the lives of all these individuals, however. First, while it is true that they may please God by remaining in the state of grace, yet it is also true that they would be far *more* pleasing to God if they were actually joined to the Body. As the Holy Father writes, "The Church exists both for the good of the faithful *and* for the *glory of God* and of Jesus Christ whom He sent."[19] God is perfect and changeless in Himself; we can neither add to nor take away from His inner glory. There is, how- ever, the external glory of God; and the Church, along with all of mankind, has the responsibility of contributing to the increase of that glory. In the words of St. Paul: "We [Christians] also have been called by a special choice, having been predestined in the purpose of him who works all things according to the counsel of his will, to contribute to the *praise of His glory* — we who before hoped in Christ."[20]

One who is outside the Church, then, is actually failing to comply with the will of God, and, in failing to do so, he is retarding the "building up the body of Christ," and is keeping the Church from attaining "to perfect manhood, to the mature measure of the fullness of Christ."[21] The external glory of God, therefore, is less than that which should be given to Him. Such a man, even though not complying with the will of God, does not commit a formal sin; he is not held guilty before the eyes of God. But he does commit a material sin. A *formal* sin is one that is committed knowingly and freely; the result is the loss of sanctifying grace if it be a mortal sin. A *material* sin is the performance of a forbidden action by one who is not conscious that it is wrong and therefore does not freely will the sin. If a Catholic eats meat on Friday, thinking that it is Thursday, he commits no formal sin, but he does commit a material sin. He does not lose sanctifying grace, but he has done something wrong. The same is true of membership in the Church. One who is not a member may not lose sanctifying grace if he does not realize his obligation; but he is doing something wrong, and would be more pleasing to God if he were incorporated into the Body of Christ where he might contribute to that glory of God which is one of the reasons for the Church's existence.

As Archbishop Myers has explained in his book on the Mystical Body: "The continual stressing of the 'good faith' of those who are unfortunately out of visible communion with us, does seem to undermine the traditional horror of heresy and of heretics, replacing it by a horror of 'heresiarchs' [that is, the originators and leaders of heretical sects]; it seems to put a premium on muddleheadedness, and to reserve the stigma of heresy for the clearheaded ones. After all, the malice of heresy lies in the rending of the Body of Christ: what our Lord meant to be one, heretics, even material heretics, divide. They may be in good faith — and that good faith will at some moment lead them to see what they had not seen before — but the fact remains that their error or ignorance, however inculpable, retards the edification of the Body of Christ. Even the claims of Charity should not blind us to the importance of growth in the knowledge of objective truth, as contrasted with the limitations of error, however well-meaning it may be."[22]

DEPRIVED OF HELPS

Then, secondly, it is good to recall to mind that those outside the Church also lack very many God-given helps which He intended to form an integral part of life in the Mystical Body. Their remaining in this state is a fact of very far-reaching importance. As our Holy Father explains in speaking of those who do not belong to the visible Body of the Catholic Church: "From a heart overflowing with love, We ask each and every one of them to correspond to the interior movements of grace, and to seek to withdraw from that state in which they cannot be sure of their salvation. For even though by an unconscious desire and longing they have a certain relationship with the Mystical Body of the Redeemer, they *still remain deprived* of those many heavenly *gifts* and *helps* which can only be enjoyed in the Catholic Church."[23]

We must always remember that it is easier to save one's soul in the Catholic Church, provided, of course, that a man makes use of the helps at his disposal. That is one of the glories of being a Catholic, and one of the best answers to the false assertion that "one religion is as good as another." If it is difficult for Catholics to live good lives and to avoid mortal sin, it is surely more difficult for those outside the Church, who lack all these gifts. If we deny that, our only alternative is to say that all the helps which the Church offers — the Mass, the Eucharist, the Sacrament of Penance, Confirmation — are of no avail. These are those helps which can only be enjoyed in the Catholic Church. If we did not admit this, we would have to say that the position of the Catholic is no different from that of one who does not even know that these gifts and helps exist. But the Catholic who has ever known the consolation, the strength to be won from his faith could never bring himself to admit that. The man who has risen from the confessional with the heavy load of sin lifted from his shoulders; the man who has knelt before the Eucharistic Christ, and has known the incomparable joy of receiving Him into his heart and conversing with Him, could not accept that position. One who has felt the grace of the Sacraments of Baptism and Confirmation surge forth to illumine his darkened mind and strengthen his faltering will; who has learned to see Christ in His ordained priests, and has grasped the beauty and sanctity of Christian marriage, or has seen the peace and quiet of eternity descend upon a dying soul as he receives the Sacrament of Extreme Unction — surely such a person could not bring himself to say that he is no better off than those who have no Sacraments at all, or Baptism and Matrimony at most, and who have never viewed a single Mass with the eyes of faith. For him, there is no comparison between his life and the life of one outside the Church.

THE REASON FOR GRANTING GRACE

If we look more closely at this bestowal of grace, we can note the importance of the Church even more. Thus far we have looked at the question mostly from the bottom up, as it were — that is, considering how a man feels and what it is he desires. Looking at it now from the *top down,* from *God's* point of view, we can see that grace is never given apart from the Church. Even the actual graces which are given to draw men to God are given also to draw them to the Church of Christ, at least by the unconscious desire and longing we have talked about.

We say that a man outside the Church can be saved by making an act of perfect love or perfect contrition. If we were to take that act of love apart, however, from God's point of view, we would find that one of the essential requirements for the bestowal of sanctifying grace would be the presence, in that act, of at least an implicit desire for the Church. It is this implicit desire that *God sees* in the act of perfect love on the part of a man outside the Church. While the man himself is not conscious of its presence at all, God is conscious of it, and grants him grace because of the Church, and through the Church. If this desire (called the *votum* by theologians) were explicitly and culpably excluded, God would not grant the grace. Once God established the Church as *the* means of grace for mankind, that channel is never completely excluded from the mind of God in the bestowal of grace. This *votum,* however, implies a real intention on the part of the individual. A vague, ineffective notion that "I'd like to be good and serve God as I ought" is not enough. This would be merely a velleity and no real intention at all. The explicit desire to do all that is necessary for salvation must be an effectual intention.

As God looks down upon the earth today, He sees a group of people, spread out across the face of the earth, united under the Headship of His Son. He is certainly pleased with the inner life of that group, and when it comes to conferring sanctifying grace upon the people in the world, it is given always because of that group. Though God could impart graces to mankind directly, He willed to do so only through a visible Church, and once He so willed He does not grant grace independently of that Church. As Father Henri de Lubac has expressed it: "God, desiring that all men should be saved, but not allowing in practice that all should be visibly in the Church, wills nevertheless that all those who answer his call should in the last resort be saved through his Church. *Sola Ecclesiae gratia, qua redimimur* . . . and if it is thought that in spite of all these considerations the formula 'outside the Church, no salvation' has still an ugly sound, there is no reason why it should not be put in a positive form and read, appealing to all men of good will, not 'outside the Church you are damned,' but 'it is by the Church and by the Church alone that you will be saved.' For it is through the Church that salvation will come, that it is already coming to mankind."[24]

It is interesting to consider the role of this group of people in bringing grace to mankind. Imagine the importance of the Church on the day of Pentecost. As God looked down on the earth, He saw a tiny group of men and women gathered in an upper room in Jerusalem: the *Church.* And yet it was because of that tiny, seemingly insignificant group that any grace at all was then conferred on any of the seven continents. The same is true today, true throughout the entire era of the New Testament. If the world receives grace today, it is *through* this group of people under Christ, and even, in a very real way, *because* of them. Whenever through the centuries this group has gathered to pray in its most official act, it was united most intimately with Christ, for Calvary and their prayer are identical: it is the Mass. The Mass is not the prayer of all, but only of the Church. "The sacrifice of the cross belongs to the whole world," writes Dom Vonier, "but the Eucharistic sacrifice belongs to the Church only . . . [yet] if the Eucharistic sacrifice is a power in this world that affects even those who are not in the body of the Church, it is still through the body of the Church that the power is exerted. The Eucharistic sacrifice reaches the infidel, not directly, but through the Church."[25]

From God's point of view, the Church is of tremendous importance upon this earth. He desires every man to enter into actual union with Christ in this visible body. No one is safe and secure in the way of salvation until he does enter into that union. Thus the condition of a man who is united to the Church by an implicit desire still remains far inferior to the condition of an actual member. As long as he remains outside this social Body of Christ, he is adrift by himself in a rather leaky skiff while others remain secure within the living ark of Noe. He remains deprived of all that strength and help which he can receive only in the bark of Peter, the Roman Catholic Church.

To explain how people can be saved outside the Church is not to state an ideal. The halfhearted attitude that "God will take care of those outside the unity of the Mystical Body" tends to forget that the great dignity of the Church in the plan of salvation carries with it equally heavy obligations — obligations which rest upon every single member of Christ's Mystical Body. We can certainly put no limit on the mercy of God, but if it is necessary to explain how great numbers can be saved by that divine mercy outside the Church, it is good to remember that there would be considerably fewer numbers involved if every member of Christ's Church labored as he ought toward bringing others to the truth and safety of that Mystic Body; if every member labored as he ought "for building up the body of Christ, until we *all* attain to the unity of the faith and of the deep knowledge of the Son of God, to perfect manhood, to the mature measure of the fullness of Christ."[26]

CHAPTER X

THE CHURCH IS A LIVING BODY

AFTER having pointed out just who is to be considered a member of the Mystical Body, it might be well to go on to look at the inner life of that body in more detail; for there are always to be considered the outer and the inner sides, the human and the divine elements. If the requirements of the "Triple Bond" make membership in the Body of Christ appear as a rather harsh, juridical affair, it is only in viewing the inner spirit of that grouping that we shall see the real meaning of that membership.

Assuredly the Church is people: people who have been baptized, who hold fast to the true faith and submit to the rule of the Holy Father. But it is not a mob, a disorganized mass of people. Quite the contrary, its organization is so strong, so unique, so all-inclusive that it justifies all the more the use of the term "body." The human body is a beautiful, though intricate, example of unity; or perhaps beautiful because it is so intricate in its simplicity. There is not a single part of the body which does not have its own particular role to play, and as far as that particular job is concerned, it is all-important for a perfect human body. No matter how small, how delicate, every organ in our body fits in perfectly with the entire picture. The progress of modern science has only served to reveal to us all the more this wonder of God's creation. Even the tiniest cells, invisible to the eye, become objects of amazement beneath a microscope. We speak of this whole unit by using a special term: we call it an *organism*. It is a word which expresses much.

THE CHURCH AN ORGANISM

An organism is a *living,* vital, closely knit unit, so constituted that all the different parts of the organism (called organs) are mutually related and dependent. It is this inner spark of life which distinguishes an organism from other bodies. A stone, for example, is not an organism, for it is lifeless. And it is for this reason that we can truly say that the Church is more like an "organism" than an "organization." Of all the groups of people in the world, the Church stands out unique, in that it is fired with a divine spark of life. There is something within the members of that group itself which binds them intimately to Christ and to one another. They live a new and special life, and this life of grace is not lived merely within themselves, but it is also a *social life* in grace, united to all others in the Church. We speak of this spark of life which vivifies the Church as the "Soul" of the Mystical Body: the Holy Spirit.

Other groups of people, of course, are spoken of as "bodies," as mentioned previously; the legislative body, for example. But the value of the word *mystical* as applied to the Church is that it calls our attention to this important difference between other groups of people and the "Mystical" Body; it *reminds us* of this inner life possessed by the Church, which makes her resemble an organism more nearly than a mere organization of people.

UNDERSTOOD PROPERLY

The Church is not to be understood as an organism without any qualification. First of all, its life comes from a *supernatural* source. It is entirely unique; there is nothing like it upon this earth. This is tremendously important, and should at once put us on our guard against pushing the comparison too far. Second, as Pope Pius XII points out,[1] in a *natural* body, the parts are united in such a way that they exist only for the good of the whole body; apart from that they have no existence, they are nothing. In the Mystical Body, on the contrary, this mutual union between the members, although it is based on something intrinsic in each and very intimate, still leaves to the members their individual lives: they have their own individual personalities. Thus while their life in the Church is directed to the good of all the members, it is *not* directed toward that purpose *alone*. They are not so wrapped up in Christ, as it were, that they lose their own independence. Every individual is important in himself; each has his own goal in life and his own soul to save. The Church exists both for the good of the faithful, taken altogether and separately, and for the glory of God and of Jesus Christ whom He sent. Some have actually exaggerated the place of the glory of God, falsely claiming that one could become so eager for the glory of God that he would be completely indifferent to his own salvation; others have failed to understand the nature of this union properly, and have thus arrived at a distorted idea of unity. "They make the Divine Redeemer and the members of the Church coalesce in one *physical* person, and while they bestow divine attributes on man, they make Christ our Lord subject to error and to human inclination to evil. But Catholic faith and the writings of the holy Fathers reject such false teaching as impious and sacrilegious; and to the mind of the Apostle of the Gentiles, it is equally abhorrent, for although he brings Christ and His Mystical Body into a wonderfully intimate union, he nevertheless distinguishes one from the other as Bridegroom from Bride."[2]

With these differences noted, we may speak of the Church as a "living organism." It is a very striking phrase. This "organic" structure and development of the Church can be seen in all of her existence. It can be seen in her arrangement of members and offices, in the lives of individuals and in the life of the Church as a whole. We can see it in the organic growth of the Church: always acting and living as a unit, as one single body that remains always the same, despite nonessential changes throughout the years. The Body of Christ, the Church, "because she is a body," writes Cardinal Suhard, "does not remain stationary. She develops, changes, grows. The parable of the mustard seed applies literally to her. 'It is the least of all seeds, but when it is grown up, it becomes a tree, so that the birds of the air come and dwell in the branches thereof.' "[3]

As Cardinal Suhard adds by way of explanation concerning the

Church: "Incarnate like Christ she is passible like Him. She knows in turn persecution and triumph. She repeats His joyous, glorious and sorrowful mysteries, Thabor and Calvary. Why should we be surprised that she is ceaselessly fought, often humiliated, always suffering in some part when we remember that her terrestrial becoming renews the suffering life of the Redeemer. . . .

"What a sublime mystery the Church is! Each instant she must both be and she must become. She must 'be' without change, in her invisible reality, 'become,' century by century in her visible reality. 'Because the Church is a body,' explains Leo XIII, 'she is visible to the eye; because she is the Body of Christ she is a living body, active, full of vitality, maintained and animated as it is by Jesus Christ who permeates her with His virtues almost like the trunk of the vine nourishes and makes fertile the branches united to it. In living beings, the vital principle is invisible and hidden in the very depths of the being, but it betrays and manifests itself by the movement and action of the members; in this way the principle of supernatural life, which animates the Church, appears to all eyes by the acts it produces.' . . .

"History gives these doctrinal views the precious confirmation of its facts. In appealing to it we have no intention of sketching even briefly the history of the Church but simply to show that in all periods the Church appears simultaneously with its twofold element: incarnate, she assumes all the social and cultural forms of the peoples she reaches; timeless and transcendent she 'is' and never ceases to be herself in the civilizations she passes through. In this process she is eternally young because, she has never bound herself to the structures she assumes only to sanctify. . . . Years pass, doctrines [of the world] wane and are replaced. Adversaries become tired or disarmed. One has just fallen with a crash. The Church remains."[4]

COMPARISON OF ST. PAUL

St. Paul spoke of the Church in this organic way, showing us the very close dependence of the members upon one another. As was mentioned in Chapter II, Paul thought that there was a striking similarity between the make-up of the human body and the make-up of the Church. The human body is not a hodgepodge of organs, but rather a perfectly grouped and organized whole. Each particular part of that body has its own job to do: the hands, the feet, the heart, the tiny ducts, and the blood cells. They act and react upon one another. The eye sees what the hands reach out for; the feet take the individual to the place he wants to go. The different parts work hand in hand, as it were, helping one another to obtain the very best good for the individual concerned. And they react on each other also. If a man has a toothache, he is liable to get a headache as well, and his stomach may become unsettled. It is always the individual who is either sick or well, happy or sad; and the entire body seems to reflect that mood, whatever it may be.

Paul saw this, and he transferred the idea to the notion of the Church. The Church of Christ is *like* a human body in certain respects. The Church is a *social* body; a group of people united through Christ, and for that reason intensely interested in one another. One who does not become conscious of this *social-minded* attitude required of a member of the Church, does not understand the Church. To be a member of the Mystical Body means to have certain obligations as well as certain privileges, for as the Holy Father remarks: "As in the [physical] body when one member suffers, all the other members share its pain, and the healthy members come to the assistance of the ailing, *so in the Church* the individual members do not live for themselves alone, but also help their fellows, and all work in mutual collaboration for the common comfort and for the more perfect building up of the whole Body."[5]

Again, just as the human body has definite arrangement and organization, so in the Church different people have different offices to perform — all depending upon one another but each with a different job to perform. St. Paul expressed it in these words: "As in one [physical] body we have many members, yet all the members have not the same function, so we, the many, are one body in Christ, but severally members one of another. But we have gifts differing according to the grace that has been given us. . . ."[6]

It is important, as well, to remember that the Church is not made up solely of those who have the "higher" offices, any more than the human body consists only of the head or the hands. To view the Mystical Body as it is we must take into consideration the Pope, the bishops, the priests; but also the religious, the mothers and fathers of families; the adults and the children alike. All of them are members of Christ; all of them have some special role to play in the Church.

If we look at some of the longer sections of the Pauline Epistles, we can see how completely the Apostle has worked out this notion. When Paul wrote these letters, he always took it for granted that the people already understood the basic doctrine of the Mystical Body, and that they were to a certain extent conscious of the unity among them. He is not giving an explanation for beginners; he is rather applying to different problems the basic truths which they had already learned.

EPHESIANS

The people of Ephesus, for example, needed additional instruction on the point of the universality of Christ's Church: it was to be open to both Jew and Gentile. These people were for the most part converted Gentiles, and Paul wanted to emphasize on their minds that the New Testament, unlike the Old, did not exclude the Gentiles, and that all the truths of God were now revealed to them. He speaks therefore of the unity of all men in the Mystical Body: "The Law of the commandments expressed in decrees he [Christ] has made void, that of the two [people: Jew and Gentile] he might create in himself one new man [the Mystical Christ], and make peace and reconcile both in one body [the Mystical Body: the Church] to God by the cross, having slain the enmity in himself."[7] And the conclusion for these Gentile converts is that they are to rejoice, for they are "now no longer strangers and foreigners, but . . . are citizens with the saints and members of God's household."[8]

Again, in the same letter, St. Paul uses their knowledge of the doctrine of the Mystical Body to emphasize the unity which should exist between a Catholic husband and wife. He makes use of this basic teaching to treat of another doctrine: the beauty of Christian marriage. "Let wives be subject to their husbands as to the Lord;

because a husband is head of the wife, just as Christ is head of the
Church, being himself saviour of the body. . . . Husbands, love your
wives, just as Christ also loved the Church, and delivered himself up
for her. . . ."[9] Paul would hardly expect these people to arrive at a
profound view of the beauty of marriage unless they *already* understood the intimate nature of the union with Christ in the Mystical
Body which he was using as an example.

FIRST CORINTHIANS

It is in the First Epistle to the Corinthians, however, that we find
the best known and the most extended treatment of the resemblance
of the Church to a human body. In one instance, St. Paul made
use of the doctrine to bring home the great need of purity and
chastity for one who is so intimately united to Christ in the Church.
"Do you not know that your bodies are members of Christ?" he
asks them. It is people, with their bodies as well as their souls — the
whole person — who make up the Mystical Body, and are thus members of Christ, just as He is their Head. "Shall I then take the members of Christ and make them members of a harlot? By no means!"[10]
What a great indignity to give their bodies — the members of Christ
— over to lust. Again we have an example of how Paul made use
of this more basic doctrine in applying it to other problems. If these
people were not especially conscious of their union with Christ in
the Church, the argument would seem to have but little meaning to
them, and Paul was striving to make a strong effect. He had wished
them to become overwhelmingly conscious of their absolute oneness
with Christ, not simply in their souls, but extending to their very
bodies. In their whole being they are "Christ." Let the consciousness
of that oneness and the consecration of their bodies to Christ which
it involves, be their motive for refusing to give way to the desires
of the flesh through sin. Let men truly "glorify God and bear him
in your body."[11]

In this First Letter to the Corinthians, however, Paul gives another
longer application of the doctrine of the Mystical Body. He speaks in
this passage of the very unity itself, not only between the people and

Christ, but among themselves; he treats of the order and organization between them.

The Corinthians were disputing among themselves about a rather peculiar thing. The early Church was blessed with a number of unusual gifts, given to different people not for their own good, but for the welfare of the Church. To enable her to accomplish the difficult task of converting many people and thus establishing itself in a short time, God deemed these gifts necessary. They are known as the "charismata" or "charismatic gifts"; they may be defined as gratuitous, supernatural, and transitory gifts, conferred for the sake of the general good and for the building up of the Mystical Body of Christ. Thus, one person was given the gift of understanding and explaining in an especially clear manner the mysteries of faith; to another, the power of working miracles or of healing or of prophesying or of speaking or understanding various languages which that person had never studied. These were special gifts, given for a special purpose at that time. There were, of course, the usual offices of the Church as well: the bishops and priests, their helpers, and the laity.

THE DIFFICULTY

The point of dispute among the Corinthians was whether it was better to be given one gift or office rather than another. Pride or envy was the basis of this problem; it was for this reason that Paul wrote his beautiful digression on charity in Chapter XIII. Some would argue therefore, that it was better to be able to work miracles than to have the gift of tongues; or that it was more important to have the gift of understanding than to be able to heal. To show the foolishness of such arguments, Paul calls to mind again the close resemblance between the Church as the Body of Christ, and the human body. He explains first of all that God has given all these gifts, and no one need feel proud about what he possesses. "No one can [even] say 'Jesus is Lord,' except in the Holy Spirit";[12] that is, unless He gives him the grace to do so. Paul then enumerates the various gifts, all coming from the Holy Spirit.

> Now there are varieties of gifts,
>   but the same Spirit;
> And there are varieties of ministries,
>   but the same Lord;
> And there are varieties of workings,
>   but the same God,
>   who works all things in all.
> Now the manifestation of the Spirit
>   is given to everyone for profit.
>   To one through the Spirit is given the utterance of wisdom;
>   And to another the utterance of knowledge,
>   according to the same Spirit;
>   To another faith, in the same Spirit;
>   To another the gift of healing, in the one Spirit;
>   To another the working of miracles;
>   To another prophecy;
>   To another the distinguishing of spirits;
>   To another various kinds of tongues;
>   To another interpretation of tongues.
> But all these things are the work of one and the same Spirit,
>   who divides to everyone
>   according as he will.[13]

When he finishes recalling these truths, the Apostle goes on to make comparison of the Church with the human body:

> For as the [human] body is one
>   and has many members,
> And all the members of the body,
>   many as they are,
>   form one body,
> So also is it with [the Church].[14]

Actually Paul does not say "the Church"; what he writes is: "So also is it with *Christ.*" It gives us a good example of Paul's mentality. For twelve verses he had been speaking about the Church, the various gifts possessed by those people who made up the Church. Now with seeming abruptness, he suddenly begins to speak about Christ. The explanation is that for Paul there was so intimate a union between Christ and the Church that together they form a new man, a new "Christ," so that actually we can speak just simply of Christ, and include the Church as well. Today we refer to this notion as the

"Whole Christ," or the "Mystical Christ": Christ in His fullness, the God-Man Himself being the Head of the Whole Christ, and the Roman Catholic Church the Body — the Mystical Body. Paul wanted, however, to continue emphasizing the unity found in the Church, so he said simply, "So also is it with Christ"; but in the very next sentence he indicates he meant the Church, for he continues to speak about it, just as he had for the first twelve verses: "For in one Spirit we were all baptized into one body [the Church], whether Jews or Gentiles, whether slaves or free; and we were all given to drink of one Spirit."[15]

Paul then goes on to speak of the organization of the Church, telling the people that each one has his particular role to play, just as do the different members of the human body.

> For the [physical] body is not one member, but many.
>   If the foot says,
>   'Because I am not a hand, I am not of the body,'
>   is it therefore not of the body?
>   And if the ear says,
>   'Because I am not an eye, I am not of the body,'
>   is it therefore not of the body?[16]

The impression he wants to leave with them is the foolishness of some member of the Church in saying, "Oh, that's no concern of mine; I'm not the priest." Such a person is still a member of the body of Christ, and to say that he has not the work of the priest to do may be true, but it does not alter the fact that he *is* obliged to certain things himself. Such a distinction of labor is necessary for the well-being of the whole body. St. Paul continues therefore:

> If the whole body were an eye,
>   where would be the hearing?
> If the whole body were hearing,
>   where would be the smelling?
> But as it is, God has set the members, each of them,
>   in the body as he willed.
> Now if they were all one member,
>   where would the body be?
> But as it is, there are indeed many members,
>   yet but one body.[17]

EVERYONE IS IMPORTANT

So with the Church. If there were only priests, and nothing else, we would destroy the notion of the Mystical Body; or if there were only lay men and women, and no priests, the same result would occur. Surely the positions of the Holy Father, the bishops, and priests make them the first and chief members of the Mystical Body, but by no means the only members. As Pius XII writes: "One must not think that this ordered or 'organic' structure of the body of the Church contains only hierarchical elements [that is, bishops] and with them is complete. . . . When the Fathers of the Church sing the praises of this Mystical Body of Christ, with its ministries, its variety of ranks, its offices, its conditions, its orders, its duties, they are thinking not only of those who have received Holy Orders, but of all those too, who, following the evangelical counsels, pass their lives either actively among men, or hidden in the silence of the cloister, or who aim at combining the active and contemplative life according to their Institute; as also of those who, though living in the world, consecrate themselves wholeheartedly to spiritual or corporal works of mercy, and of those who live in the state of holy matrimony. Indeed, let this be clearly understood, especially in these our days: fathers and mothers of families, those who are godparents through Baptism, and in particular those members of the laity who collaborate with the ecclesiastical hierarchy in spreading the Kingdom of the Divine Redeemer occupy an honourable, if often a lowly, place in the Christian community, and even they under the impulse of God and with His help, can reach the heights of supreme holiness, which, Jesus Christ has promised, will never be wanting to the Church."[18]

The help of every member of the Body is required; the people depend upon the priests, but the priests also look to the laity for assistance in performing the work of Christ. The world is to be saved through the work of all. St. Paul brings this out in his own manner in the Epistle to the Corinthians:

> And the eye cannot say to the hand,
> 'I do not need thy help';

Nor again the head to the feet,
  'I have no need of you.'
Nay, much rather, those that seem the more feeble
  members of the [physical] body
    are more necessary;
And those that we think the less honorable members
    of the body,
  we surround with more abundant honor,
And our uncomely parts receive a more abundant comeliness,
  whereas our comely parts have no need of it.
But God has so tempered the [physical] body together
    in due portion
  as to give more abundant honor where it was lacking;
That there may be no disunion in the body,
  but that the members may have care for one another.[19]

And he adds the thought of how the body acts and reacts upon
its different parts; how a toothache, for example, might cause also
a headache and an upset stomach; or how joy pervades the entire
person:

And if one member suffers anything,
  all the members suffer with it,
Or if one member glories,
  all the members rejoice with it.[20]

Finally St. Paul draws the comparison for the Corinthians. He
had spoken to them first of the Church; then he spoke of the
human body; he now points out the great similarity between the two.

Now you [people] are the body of Christ,
  member for member.
And God indeed has placed some in the Church,
  first apostles, secondly prophets, thirdly teachers;
    after that, miracles, then gifts of healing,
  services of help, power of administration,
    and the speaking of various tongues.
Are all Apostles?
  Are all prophets?
Are all teachers?
  Are all workers of miracles?
Do all have the gift of healing?

Do all speak with tongues?
Do all interpret?
Yet strive after the greater gifts.[21]

Paul leaves the question without an answer, as if an answer were unnecessary. He says to them in effect: "You all know that these things are true in the human body; they are just as true in the Church. So stop quarreling about whether it is better to have one office rather than another, or one gift instead of another. We must each perform the task assigned to us, like the eye which is supposed to see and not to walk. It is only in that way that the Body of Christ will flourish. It is foolishness and pride to speak as you have been speaking, and to quarrel over the gifts of God. There are more important things to think about; yet strive after the greater gifts." He begins then to speak on the love of God and our neighbor; it is for that that they should be far more anxious.

THE UNION OF LOVE

St. Paul emphasizes to the Romans also the necessity of having great love for one another, regardless of the position of each individual in the community. The beautiful passage deserves to be read in full.

By the grace that has been given to me,
    I say to each one among you:
Let no one rate himself more than he ought,
    but let him rate himself according to moderation,
        and according as God has apportioned to each one
    the measure of faith.

For just as in one body we have many members,
    yet all the members have not the same function,
So we, the many, are one body in Christ,
    but severally members one of another.

But we have gifts differing according to the grace
    that has been given us,
        such as prophecy to be used according to the proportion
        of faith;
        or ministry, in ministering;
        or he who teaches, in teaching;

> he who exhorts, in exhorting;
> he who gives, in simplicity;
>   he who presides, with carefulness;
>   he who shows mercy, with cheerfulness.[22]

Here, once again, we see Paul recalling the image of the human body to his readers, to prepare them for an application of this doctrine to their individual lives. In this case, he intends to speak of the fraternal charity and love that should mark the members of Christ on this earth. Because they actually *are* one in the Mystical Body, they must learn to live accordingly. He relates to the Romans in detail, then, some of the ways in which their Christian love should be expressed:

> Let love be without pretense.
>   Hate what is evil, hold to what is good.
> Love one another with fraternal charity,
>   anticipating one another with honor.
> Be not slothful in zeal;
>   be fervent in spirit, serving the Lord,
>   rejoicing in hope.
> Be patient in tribulation,
>   persevering in prayer.
> Share the needs of the saints, practising hospitality.
>   Bless those who persecute you;
>   bless and do not curse.
> Rejoice with those who rejoice;
>   weep with those who weep.
> Be of one mind towards one another.
>   Do not set your mind on high things
>   but condescend to the lowly.
> Be not wise in your own conceits.
>   To no man render evil for evil,
>   but provide good things not only in the sight of God,
>   but also in the sight of all men.
> If it be possible, as far as in you lies,
>   be at peace with all men.
> Do not avenge yourselves, beloved, but give place to wrath,
>   for it is written,
>   'Vengeance is mine; I will repay, says the Lord.'
> But 'If thy enemy is hungry, give him food;
>   if he is thirsty, give him drink;

> For by so doing thou wilt heap coals of fire
>   upon his head.'
> Be not overcome by evil,
>   but overcome evil with good.[23]

Such a description of the love of the members of Christ can be understood only by grasping the unity of those members with Christ and with one another. It is true no less in the pagan world of today than it was in the pagan world known to St. Paul. It is this living, vital view of the Church and her inner life that the doctrine of the Mystical Body aims at giving. It is for this ideal that St. Paul lived out his entire life; it was for this that he suffered and died, "being poured out in sacrifice,"[24] yet being able to exclaim: "I rejoice now in the sufferings I bear for your sake; and what is lacking of the sufferings of Christ I fill up in my flesh for his body, which is the Church."[25] To understand such saints as Paul, we must first of all understand the Church which brought them forth; apart from it, they are an unfathomable mystery.

CHAPTER XI

CHRIST IS THE HEAD
OF THE CHURCH

WE COME next to speak of the relationship of the Catholic Church to Christ. We refer to it always as the "Church of Christ" or the "Mystical Body of Christ." What we ask now is, what justification do we have for speaking in this manner?

In answer, Pope Pius XII gives four different reasons why we may refer to the Church as the Mystical Body *of Christ*. The first reason is that Christ is the *Founder* of the Church. "Thou art Peter, and upon this rock I will build *my* Church."[1] In Chapter VII we treated of the different stages in the founding of the Church of Christ. With this in mind, it is easily seen why it is called His Church. Nothing more need be added.

A second reason for referring to this group as the Body "of Christ" is that He is the *Saviour* of the Church. This explanation is also self-explanatory. The words are found in the Epistle of St. Paul to the Ephesians: "Christ is the head of the Church, being himself saviour of the body."[2] As Pope Pius XII explains in the encyclical on the Mystical Body: "The Samaritans were right in proclaiming Him 'Saviour of the world'; for indeed He most certainly is to be called the 'Saviour of all men,' even though we must add with Paul: 'especially of the faithful,' since, before all others, He has purchased with His blood His members who constitute the Church."[3]

A third reason for speaking of *Christ's* Church is that He is the

Support, the *Sustainer,* of the Mystical Body. He accomplishes this above all through the sending of the Holy Spirit: the Spirit of Christ. Chapter XIV will analyze this reason when treating of the Soul of this divinely sustained Church.

CHRIST, THE HEAD OF THE CHURCH

The fourth reason mentioned in the encyclical for calling the Church the Body "of Christ" is the one which fits most easily into the terminology of St. Paul: namely that Christ is the *Head* of the Church. The Pope devotes eighteen paragraphs to this point.[4]

We are speaking again in rather poetic terms; we are making a comparison between Christ and His relationship to the Church on the one hand, and the head of the human body and its relationship to the various parts on the other. There is only a similarity here; the relationship is somewhat "alike" in both cases. The reason for using the comparison, however, is not merely to become poetic. It is done for the very real purpose of emphasizing the true *union,* the intimate bond linking Christ with those people who make up His Church.

Following the writings of the Scholastic theologians of the Middle Ages, the encyclical bases its comparison on the scientific theories accepted by them at that time. Chief among these is the theory of the ancient doctor, Galen, who lived from about A.D. 130–200. The present-day, complex findings of medicine might differ on many points, but it is well to remember that we are making only a comparison, and it will not do to push the comparison too far. The general outline of Galen's explanation is simple enough to be forceful, and it follows the average person's knowledge of the human body.

The chief source of all the nerves, he wrote, is the brain and the spinal cord; and the source of life for the spinal cord itself is the brain. In this way, the head, being the seat of the brain, is the most important part of the human body. The different nerves are necessary for the body, so that the power of feeling things and sensing things, and of moving about and doing things, might pass from the chief source (the brain) through the spinal cord to the different parts of the body, according to whatever their special purpose in the body might be. Thus the brain will send out the power to the eyes to see or the ears to hear or the hands to work, or the feet to walk; and they in turn would relate to the brain what they see or hear or do — all by means of the spinal cord of the nerves.

Richardus a Mediavilla sums up this general notion very clearly when he writes: "Christ is called the Head of the Church, which is His Mystical Body, by way of comparison with the human head and its relationship to the body. The head holds first place over the body because of its position. Also it is in the head that we are to find the more noble sensitive powers, such as the imagination and the memory; and all the senses are in the head. From it as well do the other members of the body receive their power of sensation and motion; it directs the other members in their actions, and it is one in nature with them; and the body is joined to it. So also is there a certain similarity as regards Christ and the Church."[5]

This similarity might well be summed up in six points, as the encyclical, *Mystici Corporis,* actually does. The idea of: (1) the *dignity* of the head as compared to the other parts of the human body (pre-eminence); (2) the *ruling* and *directing power* of the head; (3) the *continuity* between the head and the body of man, the *mutual need* of one for the other; (4) the conformity, the *sameness* of nature between the head and the other members of the body; (5) the *perfection* of the head as compared to the rest of the body; and (6) the *influence* of the head over the functions and actions of the lesser members.

If we take each of these six reasons separately we can see more clearly how well chosen the comparison is, and what it intends to emphasize for us: reasons why Christ is called the Head of the Church.

1. By reason of His pre-eminence:

The head of our body is in the highest place according to where God put it — highest in position, and highest in many functions. It is the noblest part of our body. Now we are justified in using this comparison because in another order — the supernatural — there is surely no one who holds a higher place than Christ.

This reason is very easily understood. As the Holy Father asks:

"Who is in a higher place than Christ, God, who as the Word of the Eternal Father must be acknowledged to be the 'firstborn of every creature'? Who has reached more lofty heights than Christ, Man, who, though born of the Immaculate Virgin, is the true and natural Son of God, and in virtue of His miraculous and glorious resurrection, a resurrection triumphant over death, has become the 'firstborn of the dead'? Who finally has been so exalted as He, who as 'the one mediator of God and men' has in a most wonderful manner linked earth to heaven; who, raised on the Cross as on a throne of mercy, has drawn all things to Himself; who, as the Son of Man chosen from among thousands, is beloved of God beyond all men, all angels and all created things?"[6]

All this St. Paul also has in mind when he writes: "He [Christ] is the head of his body, the Church; he, who is the beginning, the firstborn from the dead, that in all things he may have the *first place*."[7]

2. By reason of government:

It is the head which governs the rest of the body, deciding what is to be done and directing that action. This comparison is not difficult either, for we often speak of the head of this or that government with the same idea in mind. So now we speak of Christ as the Head of the Church because it is He who rules over it at all times. It was in his advice to wives and husbands that St. Paul referred to this: "But just as the Church is subject to Christ, so also let wives be to their husbands in all things."[8]

AN INVISIBLE MANNER

Christ rules over the Church first of all in an *invisible* and extraordinary manner. Actually He is the only Head of the Church; "He alone by every right rules and governs the Church."[9] The Pope is merely Christ's *Vicar:* one who takes His place in the visible administration of the Church. There are not two heads to this Body, but only one, for the Holy Father is so intimately united to Christ in his *office* and his *official capacity,* that they form but one unit and they act as though one person. St. Catherine of Siena always referred to the Holy Father for this reason as "dear Christ upon earth."

While still on earth, Christ governed and directed the Church through His teaching and warning; by giving counsel and precepts. And He established the ruling power of the Church, by conferring on His Apostles and their successors the power to teach, to govern, to lead men to holiness, making this power the fundamental law of the whole Church.

Peter, after having been appointed by Christ, took over the visible rule of the Church when Christ departed from this earth. But after His Ascension into heaven, Christ did not cease to rule. The Supreme Pontiffs attend to the visible part of that work of preaching to all nations unto the end of the world, representing Christ among men, but our Lord Himself continues to govern and guide this group directly and personally as well. He does that first of all in that He reigns within the minds and hearts of the individuals in the Church. He directs their minds along the right paths, strengthens their wills, and inflames their hearts with love. It is Christ the Head of the Mystical Body who speaks in His own ways to those who are His members.

This interior guidance is not limited to individual souls, but extends to the universal Church as well. At times it will be by enlightening and giving courage to the Church's rulers so that they might perform their duties well, so that they might make the correct decisions. These rulers are not merely individuals, but officials; and in addition to the graces they receive for their own individual lives, they receive what we might call "official" helps for those duties. Chief among them, of course, would be the special gift of infallibility given to keep the Church from error when speaking officially on matters of faith or morals.

At other times Christ will show His authority over His entire Body by raising up saints to point out with special emphasis the way that leads to heaven. At all times and in all places, Christ is watching over His Church without ceasing. Powers of the earth can rise up against it, but they will be powerless. They cannot overcome the Church because they cannot overcome Christ. Should the danger be urgent, Christ will go so far as to speak to the leaders or to some chosen soul Himself, or He will send a messenger from heaven in the person of an angel or even the Queen of Heaven herself.

THE ROMAN PONTIFF

In the *visible* and ordinary manner, it is through the Roman Pontiff that Christ rules over His Church. Christ came to found a visible society, and He would not leave it without a visible head.

Even before His death, Christ had selected Peter as the one to whom He would give the office of Supreme Pontiff. The promise to make Peter the visible head of the Church was made quite some time before the death of Christ. Our Lord and His Apostles were traveling in the north of Palestine, near the city named Caesarea Philippi. Christ happened to ask the disciples what other people thought of Him: "Who do men say the Son of Man is?" And the Apostles answered, saying that many thought that Christ was one of the great men in Jewish history come back to life: "But they said, 'Some say, John the Baptist; and others, Elias; and others, Jeremias, or one of the prophets.'"[10]

Christ then turned to His chosen Twelve and asked: "'But who do you say that I am?' Simon Peter answered and said, 'Thou art the Christ, the Son of the living God.'"[11] Under the inspiration of God, Peter had answered for the group, and confessed to Christ his belief in his Master's divinity. Christ turned to him, then, and spoke those beautiful and important words:

> Blessed art thou, Simon Bar-Jona,
>   for flesh and blood has not revealed this to thee,
>   but my Father in heaven.
> And I say to thee,
>   thou art Peter,
> And upon this rock I will build my Church,
>   and the gates of hell shall not prevail against it.
> And I will give thee the keys of the kingdom of heaven;
>   and whatever thou shalt bind on earth
>   shall be bound in heaven,
>   and whatever thou shalt loose on earth
>   shall be loosed in heaven.[12]

This was a magnificent statement, and one filled with meaning for the Church. In accordance with the Oriental idiom, it makes use of metaphors, but it is not so poetic a manner of speech as might first appear. Christ promised to make Peter the head of the Church He intended to establish. The rock *is* Peter. Christ changed the name of this Apostle from Simon to Peter, that is, the rock, to show the supreme importance of the office which He was going to bestow upon Him. He is to be the basis of the Church in this world, the foundation, solid as rock.

In the original language in which the Gospel of St. Matthew was written, we find the word *Kepha,* which means "rock," but which is also a proper name; it is from this that we have the name "Cephas" which is used for Peter in some of the Epistles. St. Paul uses it in telling the Galatians about his dispute with Peter at Antioch: "But when Cephas came to Antioch, I withstood him to his face."[13] As this text of Matthew was translated, however, first into Greek and then into Latin and English, the close relationship between these two words became less apparent. At first glance the two words "rock" and "Peter" seem to have nothing in common. If we substitute the single word which was originally used, however, it becomes clear at once. Thus we have: "And I say to thee, thou art Kepha, and upon this Kepha I will build my Church," meaning Peter.

The Pope is to rule for Christ, and with a power including not merely temporal but spiritual matters as well. "I will give thee the keys of the kingdom of heaven." This metaphor of the keys had always been associated with power and authority, and thus this imagery was the most emphatic way that Christ had of impressing on the Jewish mind the real meaning and importance of what He was doing. We must always remember in reading the Bible that these truths were adapted to the mentality of those who received them. Today in America we would surely speak more directly on so important a matter, but the Oriental mind always expresses important truths in indirect but emphatic ways; it is not accustomed to expressing things directly. This clearly indicated the promise of real authority to Peter. It was Christ Himself who said, "All power in heaven and on earth has been given to me."[14] He now promises to share that power with the one who was to take His place in the visible administration of His Church. Not that Christ had to do so, but because He wished to associate men even with the greatest powers He possessed. The power of the Roman Pontiff is a power always subordinate to that of Christ, and in no way independent from it; yet it is a real power, loosing and binding on earth and in heaven as well. Nor is there a limit made on the use of that power; it is truly supreme: "whatever thou shalt loose or bind." And also, since the Church is, by the command of Christ, to continue to preach the Gospel over all the world, unto the end of time, there is no time limit on the power of Peter. Thus, since there must necessarily be other Popes after Peter to continue that work for all time, these successors also possess the supreme power given to Peter.

THE PROMISE FULFILLED

It was after His resurrection that Christ actually appointed Peter His vicar. The Apostles were in Galilee, and Christ had appeared to them and had had breakfast with them. Afterward our Lord called Peter aside and spoke to him.

> When, therefore, they had breakfasted,
>   Jesus said to Simon Peter,
> 'Simon, son of John, dost thou love me more than these do?'
>   He said to him, 'Yes, Lord, thou knowest that I love thee.'
> He said to him, 'Feed my lambs.'
>
> He said to him a second time,
>   'Simon, son of John, dost thou love me?'
> He said to him, 'Yes, Lord, thou knowest that I love thee.'
>   He said to him, 'Feed my lambs.'
>
> A third time he said to him,
>   'Simon, son of John, dost thou love me?'
> Peter was grieved because he said to him for the third time,
>   'Dost thou love me?'
> And he said to him, 'Lord, thou knowest all things,
>   thou knowest that I love thee.'
> He said to him, 'Feed my sheep.'[15]

Christ asked Peter these questions as the two of them walked along the seashore. Perhaps the divine irony wished Peter to atone for his three denials of Christ, for this was the Apostle who shortly before Christ died had boasted that, "Even though I should have to die with thee, I will not deny thee."[16] And as Peter humbly replied that he did love Christ, our Lord actually gave to him the lofty honor which He had previously promised.

Again, Christ spoke in a very poetic fashion, but that is the manner of emphasis for the Oriental mind. The Jewish people had often spoken of their heavenly Father as a Shepherd, as when they prayed the beautiful twenty-second psalm:

> The Lord is my shepherd:
>   I want for nothing;
> He makes me rest in green pastures.
>   He leads me to waters where I may rest;
>   He revives my spirit
> He guides me along the right paths
>   for his name's sake.
> Even though I walk in a dark valley,
>   I will fear no evil, for thou art with me.
> Thy rod and thy staff:
>   these comfort me.[17]

The prophet Isaias had made use of this same imagery when describing Christ the Messias, centuries before His birth in Bethlehem: "He shall feed his flock like a shepherd. He shall gather together the lambs with his arm and shall take them up in his bosom, and he himself shall carry them that are with young."[18]

Christ Himself had even spoken in this manner before, likening his followers to a flock of sheep, of which He was the Good Shepherd:

> I am the good shepherd.
>   The good shepherd lays down his life for his sheep.
> But the hireling, who is not a shepherd,
>   whose own the sheep are not,
>   sees the wolf coming and leaves the sheep and flees. . . .
> I am the good shepherd, and I know mine
>   and mine know me,
> Even as the Father knows me
>   and I know the Father;
> And I lay down my life for my sheep.[19]

In this same fashion, Christ gives Peter charge over His flock, the Church. Christ applies the imagery of a shepherd and his flock to the relationship between Himself and His followers; He was making a comparison. Obviously here, as in these other instances, Christ and Peter were not speaking directly about the work of herding sheep. Simon was a fisherman, not a shepherd. He had been trained by Christ for the work of preaching the Gospel, and it was of that that Christ now spoke. The inspired text as it is found in this particular place, with its protestations of highest personal love, would be completely meaningless if understood to refer to the herding of animals.

In giving Peter power over all the members of the Church, Christ included the lowly members (lambs) and the higher (sheep): all the members, the people, the priests, and the bishops are to be subject to Peter. He is to be the vicar of Christ, to rule in His place after He has left the earth. "After His glorious Ascension into heaven," therefore writes Pius XII, "this Church rested not on Christ alone, but on Peter too, its visible foundation stone."[20] The two of them formed only one Head, of course, but the union was so great that we may never separate Christ from His vicar on earth. Christ remains the only one chief Head of this Mystical Body, but He at the same time continues to rule it, not only in an invisible manner, but visibly as well, through His representative on earth. This vicar will attend to the flock, and feed and nourish it, and guide it along the right paths, and watch over it as a true shepherd. Hence the error, singled out by Pius XII, of those "who believe that they can accept Christ as the Head of the Church, while not adhering loyally to His Vicar on earth."[21] The two are one. Christ willed to have a visible Church, for it is that which men need. To take away the visible head, however, would mean to break the visible bonds of unity and leave the Mystical Body of the Redeemer "so obscured and so maimed, that those who are seeking the haven of eternal salvation can neither see it nor find it."[22]

THE BISHOPS

The Holy Father is the Supreme Ruler over the entire Church, but for many he is a name only, and a very distant name. They may often see his picture and may pray for him daily, but many can never hope to see him in person. Christ does, however, appear through the person of other representatives: the bishops. What is said of the Holy Father in regard to the Universal Church must be understood also of the bishop in regard to the particular section of the Church assigned to his rule. The bishops are not simply representatives of the Pope, his helpers, as it were, in the particular diocese given to their care. The bishops immediately represent Christ, and they are rightfully considered the more illustrious members of the Church, for they are united by a very special bond to the divine Head of the whole Body. Each bishop is the vicar of Christ in his own particular diocese, just as the Pope is over the entire Church.

The bishop, of course, is subordinate to the lawful authority of the Roman Pontiff; he receives directly from the Pope the ordinary power of jurisdiction which he possesses. Yet these dioceses are "ruled by Jesus Christ through the voice of their respective Bishops."[23] As the bishop travels about his territory, preaching, confirming, ordaining, he is for all his subjects, "dear Christ on earth in our own city," to use the words of St. Catherine. "As far as his own diocese is concerned, each [bishop] as a true Shepherd feeds the flock entrusted to him and rules it in the name of Christ."[24] The honor and reverence shown to him is shown to Christ, for this is His local vicar. When he speaks it is the voice of Christ; when he commands it is the voice of Christ. When he teaches it is the word of Christ. When we kneel to give reverence to him, it is Christ in him whom we honor. It was because of this that Ignatius of Antioch wrote, "Be subject to your bishop as to Jesus Christ."[25]

3. By reason of mutual need

The third reason for calling Christ the Head of the Church lies in the mutual need of the Body for the Head and even of the divine Head for the Body. The basis for this comparison is fairly obvious as regards the human body, but many people miss it entirely when considering the Church. If a man's head is chopped off, both the head and the torso become rather useless. A body without a head has nothing to direct it; a head without a body has nothing to direct. The mutual need is evident.

The same thing is true as regards Christ and His Church — not, however, because it had to be that way, but because Christ *wanted* it that way. It is easy to understand that the members of the Body need Christ; "Without me you can do nothing," Christ told us.[26] We all realize that, knowing our own weakness. We are so utterly dependent upon Christ; every advance of the Mystical Body, either in individuals or the entire group, derives from Christ the Head. From Him comes its perfection. Galen explained the actions of the human body as beginning always in the head, from which the other members derive their power. In this manner did St. Paul write; the translation of Monsignor Knox brings it out well. "We are to follow the truth, in a spirit of charity, and so grow up, in everything, into a due proportion with Christ, who is our head. On him all the body depends; it is organized and unified by each contact with the source which supplies it; and thus, each limb, receiving the active power it needs, achieves its natural growth, building itself up through charity."[27]

Even more marvelous, however, is the fact that *Christ depends upon the Body*. The Holy Father tells us that "What Paul said of the human organism is to be applied likewise to the Mystical Body: 'The head cannot say to the feet: I have no need of you.'"[28] Remarkable as it may seem, it is true: Christ has need of His members! "This is not because He is indigent and weak, but rather because He has so willed it for the greater glory of His spotless Spouse."[29] Christ could have accomplished all of this work by Himself, but He deigned to associate us with His work. The whole redemption as brought about on the hill of Calvary, of course, was entirely the work of Christ. "Dying on the Cross, He left to His Church the immense treasury of the Redemption, towards which she contributed nothing";[30] the members of the Body had no part to play there, for salvation is from Christ alone.

When it came to distributing these graces, Christ *could* have imparted them directly of Himself. Actually "He willed to do so only through a visible Church made up of men, so that through her all might co-operate with Him in dispensing the graces of Redemption.... He wills to be helped by the members of His Body in carrying out the work of Redemption."[31] Even more than this, the Church was not to be merely a lifeless "channel" of grace. Christ was not content simply to share the work of sanctification with His Church, but more than that, "He wills that in some way it be *due to her action.*"[32] It is a remarkable fact. Christ wills that the Body itself should have a real, an active, a personal role to play in winning the souls of men. In the words of the Holy Father himself: "This is a deep mystery, and in inexhaustible subject of meditation, that *the salvation of many depends* on the *prayers* and *voluntary penances* which the members of the Mystical Body of Jesus Christ offer for this intention, and on the *co-operation* of pastors of souls and of the faithful, especially of fathers and mothers of families, a co-operation which they must offer to our Divine Saviour as though they were *His associates.*"[33]

God wills that this be true of *every* member of His Mystical Body, and not the priests and bishops alone. It is the work of the children and the adults; of the religious and the laity; of the married and the unmarried, as well as of the hierarchy. It is the work of everyone. The world is to be saved through the prayers and labors of all the members of Christ; it cannot be left to the priests alone. The teacher, the student, the lawyer, the factory worker, the army officer, the newspaper writer, the politician, the homemaker — all of these must bring Christ and His teaching to those who labor with them in their respective fields. They are apostles in their own way, and Christ is looking to them for help in saving mankind. The very purpose of the Church is to go out and preach to all, and it is a command given to the complete Church — the laity as well as the priests and bishops. The Church is not made up merely of the hierarchy, and the obligation of the Church to bring Christ to the world cannot rest upon them alone. It is a private obligation of every member of Christ, which each must accept as an individual. Yet this obligation is so basically rooted in the Sacraments of Baptism and Confirmation, that, should the hierarchy assign them to a particular task, the laity may share even in the *official* apostolate of the bishops. This sacramental direction toward the apostolate is what makes Catholic Action organizations possible, but it is the work of all. If anyone becomes cold and indifferent to his duty, the entire Body will suffer for it.

CATHOLIC ACTION

Catholic Action is not primarily a movement; it is the outgrowth of belief — a firm belief in the doctrine of the Mystical Body, of the intimate and active union of all the faithful with Christ and with the work of Christ. Just as the liturgical movement is not simply a movement but rather a collective attempt to grasp the social-mindedness of the prayer-life of Christ's Mystical Body, so also is Catholic Action an attempt to grasp that concept in terms of daily life. The true liturgist is not following a current fad, but rather he hopes to do something to impress the full meaning of the liturgy upon others, and to do what he can to enable them to express that meaning properly in their life of prayer. Rubrics, symbolism, missals, the chant — all of these are means to an end — not ends in themselves. So also, the techniques, the forms of activity of Catholic Action are not ends in themselves, but only means to help men live the doctrine of the Mystical Body in their daily life, and to aid them in fulfilling their individual obligations of drawing others into the life of the Mystic Christ. The techniques may be changed at other times and places, but the aim of such activity remains the same. This union with our Lord in the Church is not solely a personal affair; it does not end with making ourselves better, though it will begin there. It is a union with Christ as He is: Christ, the *Source of all Grace,* but also the *Fisher of Men,* and thus it places upon all certain obligations actually to do something for the building up of the Body of Christ. This is the basis for the entire apostolate, both of priests and laity. If the world is going to be saved and brought to the feet of Christ, it is the concern of every member of Christ's Mystical Body; the divine Head has need of every one of them. Whether they be working in offices or factories, teaching or studying in schools, caring for the sick or managing a home, they are called upon to help Christ in that particular place where they are.

Every member of Christ should put to himself a few simple questions. "If Christ is to reach the workers in factories," for example, "can He ever do so except through those who labor beside them in those factories?" How else? This is especially true in our present day when there is an ever widening breach between the secular and the religious. The priests in so many thousands of instances cannot get to the factory worker; they cannot reach him, often they cannot even contact him. How, then, will Christ come to those workers unless the members of Christ who are not priests, but who are fellow workers in that same factory, accept their responsibility and bring Him to them? And that is the apostolate. The same is true in every other sphere of life. If Christ is to come to the modern doctors, it is His members in the medical profession who must bring Him; it is the teacher, the stenographer, the lawyer, the housewife, the student who must bring Christ to those about them, who must not simply speak of Christ's teaching to them, but who must, above all, mirror Christ in their lives. They must "put on Christ";[34] they must BE Christ in all they are, in all they say and do. They must come to the aid of the hierarchy, and become conscious of their own obligations, and do all they can to extend the kingdom of Christ's love among men.

Both our prayers and our activities are demanded if this is to be accomplished. The prayers must be never ending, and the activities, under the guidance of the hierarchy, ever zealous. Christ wants it that way; He has made Himself and His work dependent upon the co-operation of His members. It is a serious thought, a shocking thought! But a truth which should become a moving force in our lives.

CHAPTER XII

THREE MORE REASONS

THE encyclical on the Mystical Body gives three more reasons why we may liken the relationship of Christ and His Church to that between the human head and its body. The first three were: (1) because of the pre-eminence of the head; (2) because of the governing powers of the head; and (3) because of the mutual need of the head and body for each other. We now go on to consider the last three closely related reasons for calling Christ the Head of the Mystical Body.

4. By reason of the conformity of nature between Christ and the members of the Church.

A *nature* is the answer to the question: "What is it?" A man is recognized by a human body and a human head; a dog by a dog's body and head. There is no mix-up in nature; we do not see the body of a man with the head of a dog, or vice versa. If we are going to compare the relationship of Christ and His Church to that of a human body, we would rightly suspect a comparison on this point also: that the Head and the Body should be of one nature. And so it is. There is a similarity of nature between Christ and us in two ways. The first is obvious: Christ became man to be one of us. More than that, however, and far more remarkable, Christ brought us sanctifying grace so that *we might become one with Him.* He wished not merely to share our human nature, but rather He deigned to let us share His divine nature as well. Thus on two counts there is a sameness between Christ and ourselves: He shares our human nature, and we, through grace, share His divine nature. "Grant that we may become partakers of His divinity who vouchsafed to become partaker of our humanity," the Church prays each day.[1] It is the very essence of Catholicism.

As it was mentioned before,[2] when Christ became man He did so with a very special intention: the intention of representing *all* of mankind. Adam had affected every person in the world through his sin; Christ now willed to act on the part of every single person in atoning for that sin. He thus became the "New Adam." When we speak of Christ in this way we refer to Him as the *Moral Head* of mankind. It was in this role that Christ honored our human nature by the very act of assuming it, and made it possible for us to be of the same nature as He. Even though our human nature is below that of the angels considered in itself, yet it has "through God's goodness, risen above it."[3] Christ became a man and not an angel; He assumed human nature and not the angelic. Christ the God-Man, of course, is the Head of the angels; even in His humanity He is superior to them. And he illumines their intellects and influences their wills. But there is not this oneness in nature which we find between the Son of God and mankind, and so the comparison with which we are dealing now could not apply to the angels. Everything that was said in Chapter VI about the coming of Christ may be recalled here to show us how *truly* Christ shared our human nature.

THE LIFE OF GRACE

This similarity between Christ and His members begins with the possession of the same human nature; it terminates in the possession of the divine nature by both Head and Members. It is this which gives us some notion of the loftiness of the union of mankind with Christ. It is a supernatural bond, changing men, elevating them to new and undeserved heights: making them the true sons of God. "Behold what manner of love the Father has bestowed upon us," writes St. John, "that we should be called children of God; *and such we are.*"[4] Or in the words of St. Paul:

God sent his Son, born of a woman, born under the Law,
   that he might redeem those who were under the Law,
      that we might receive the adoption of sons.
And because you are sons,
   God has sent the Spirit of his Son into our hearts, crying,
      'Abba, Father.'
So that he is no longer a slave,
   but a son;
And if a son,
   an heir also through God.[5]

Sanctifying grace is rightly defined as a sharing in the divine nature itself. We share in this according to our own way; we do not become identical with God. And still we do actually share in the intimate life of God through grace. Grace is not something poured into our soul like water into a glass. It is rather something that God does to our soul; a very real change made in the very depths of our being. Thus grace gives at one and the same time a new dignity and worth to man, a new power, and a new life.

It gives a *new life* by raising man to the supernatural order. The result of this, of course, is a *new power* — a power to know and love God as a friend; to know and love God as He is in Himself, and not simply as we know Him through created things. God is the only one who can fully know and comprehend Himself. If, then, we are to be enabled to know God even partially as He knows Himself, as He is in Himself, it is first of all necessary that something of the divine nature be given to us. We must become like God if we are to know God as a friend. To be a friend with someone demands a certain equality between the two. In some way they must be equal, and the only way that God could bridge the infinite gap between man and Himself is by raising man to this newer and higher way of life: to make man, in some way, divine. As Father Mersch writes: "The Christian teaching concerning this divinisation is explicit and very ancient. The Christians possess in themselves an elevation of the very substance of their soul, which renders them truly Godlike, *partakers of the divine nature;* which makes them intrinsically pleasing to God, objects of His love and worthy of His heaven. But in the eyes of God, God alone has worth. In order that men might be strictly of value before Him, and 'might find favor before His eyes,' it is first of all necessary that God make them like to Himself."[6]

The pattern of this raising up of man's soul is the hypostatic union. In Christ, the divine person took over the humanity completely; it was a substantial union of the human and divine. The man in sanctifying grace, however, possesses an accidental, although an habitual, union with the divine; but it is something very real nevertheless. This new life is possessed in this world through sanctifying grace in an imperfect manner. In heaven, however, we will be united to God in a perfect manner in the beatific vision, where we shall know and love God for all eternity. We shall see him "face to face,"[7] as He is in Himself; and we shall never be in danger again of losing that love. Sanctifying grace results from an accidental modification of the soul; it is a new quality which completely sanctifies the soul. The fullness of that new life, however, will appear only in heaven, and it is for that reason that we say sanctifying grace is the seed of glory.

SONS OF GOD

This new life of the soul also gives a man a *new worth* before God in heaven: it makes him a true son of God. The sanctified soul has a new power of loving God intimately, of knowing Him as He is in Himself. To be able to do that, though, a man must be Godlike; he must share the same nature possessed by God. Grace, therefore, brings that about, and since a man then participates in the very nature of God, he is a true son of God. In this way, those who share in the grace of Christ share also in the divine life of Christ. "I came that they may have life, and have it more abundantly,"[8] said our Lord; "Amen, amen, I say to you, he who hears my word, and believes him who sent me, has life everlasting, and does not come to judgment, but has passed from death to life."[9]

But that life has been given for a purpose; those who share in the divine life of Christ, share also in the *knowledge* and *love* of Christ for the Father, and in the very Sonship of Christ itself. "Just Father, the world has not known thee, but I have *known thee,* and these have known that thou hast sent me. And I have made known to them

thy name, and will make it known, in order that the *love* with which
thou hast loved me may be in them, and I in them."[10] They have been
given this new life that they might also be able to know and love
God as He is in Himself. Raised to the level of a new and supernatural life, they have become one with Christ; they have shared not
only in the *life,* but in the knowledge and love of the Son as well.
They are in truth the sons of the living God.

This is one of the most profound, yet one of the most inspiring
mysteries presented to the mind of man. It means that man might
be able to lift up his head, and cry out in full right, not merely "Our
God," or "Our Creator," but more intimately, *"Our Father";* that
man might possess, within his own soul, the power to know and
love God the Father as Jesus Christ knows Him and loves Him; it
means that through a sharing in the grace of the Son of God, man
might become, in reality, a son of God Himself. The change takes
place entirely in the soul of man, and not at all in God. Grace reaches
down to the very roots of human nature and exalts it to the level
of supernature. Our soul becomes then a truly sanctified soul.

It is only toward setting up this higher similarity of nature that the
entire plan of God has been directed. God wants to draw all of mankind into the intimate nature of the Trinity through grace. The Redemption and all that it entails is not simply a payment for sin; it
was the final and highest establishment of the supernatural order to
which mankind was raised. Christ became Man for our sake, that
we might become gods. We may sum it all up in the words of Pope
Pius XII in saying: " 'If the Word emptied himself taking the form
of a slave,' it was that He might make His brothers according to
the flesh partakers of the divine nature, through sanctifying grace in
this earthly exile, in heaven through the joys of eternal bliss. For the
reason why the only-begotten Son of the Eternal Father willed to be
a son of man was that we might be made conformed to the image
of the Son of God, and be renewed according to the image of Him
who created us."[11]

This *positive* notion of grace is something we ought to remember
also in regard to original sin and baptism. We are in the state of
original sin when we are born, because we do *not* possess sanctifying

grace, although we are *supposed to*. This constitutes us as sinners. When we are baptized, we really receive something rather than simply "lose" original sin. Often we tend to look at it the other way around. We feel that original sin is taken away by baptism, and that ends it. Actually, when we are baptized we receive that which we are supposed to have — sanctifying grace. It is something like an empty glass. When it is filled with water, it is no longer empty. So also, when our soul is filled with grace, we no longer lack it. Thus we are no longer in the state of original sin.

5. By reason of the plenitude of His grace: in Christ Himself

The last two reasons for calling Christ the Head of the Mystical Body are closely related. The first treats of the grace in Christ the Head; the second treats of that grace as received by the members of His Body.

According to the theory of Galen which was mentioned above, the source of all life and action in the body is the head. If we apply this to the Mystical Body in this particular instance, we see that the same is true. There is nothing done by the Body of Christ which does not begin with Christ the divine Head; He is the very Source of life. When Christ became Man, His soul was filled with the plenitude of grace, for, according to the words of St. Paul, "It has pleased God the Father that in him *all* his fullness should dwell."[12] But this grace was given with a very particular purpose in mind. Not only was it to adorn the soul of Christ and make it beautiful, but it was to be the source of grace for all mankind, in which all men would share. Christ was given grace *for us*. We call this complexus of all the gifts and graces in the humanity of Christ the "Grace of Headship"; it is a term used to indicate that He was given grace so as to give it to us, just as He became man to help us. It is always the grace of Christ in which mankind shares.

We owe all things in this way to Christ. No one receives grace except through Christ, and "to each one of us grace was given according to the measure of Christ's bestowal."[13] He determines how many and what graces we shall receive, but He Himself possesses the supernatural gifts without any limit whatsoever, in their fullness and perfection. The Holy Spirit dwells in Him with a fullness of grace than which no greater can be imagined. He has in the highest degree all of the graces and gifts that it is possible for men to have; and, what is important for our present comparison, He possesses these graces "for us": that He might pass them on to us, as the head passes on to the various parts of the body their power of sensing and moving.

When the Holy Spirit came upon Christ, He brought to His soul all those graces which He would need as Head of the Church, and also all of those graces which Christ, as Man, would need so that His humanity might share in the granting of every grace to every man. Today when the Holy Spirit comes upon any individual, He comes "through Christ" the God-Man; there is no other way of obtaining grace. "There is no other name under heaven given to men by which we must be saved."[14] Apart from Christ we are nothing; we become like the branch, torn from the vine, left to wither and to be cast into the fire. He is the Vine and we are the branches, and as He has told us Himself, "Without me you can do nothing."[15]

In the eternal plan of God, all grace comes to man from Christ not only as Moral Head, but also as Mystic Head, that is, as head of the visible Church. No matter what graces men receive today, they still receive them from Christ and through Christ, and even through His Church. The greatest graces, nevertheless, are reserved for those people in whom this comparison is most fully completed, that is, in those who are members of the visible Church. They are able to receive not only certain of the graces which flow from the divine Head, but rather they can receive of that fullness of grace, involving all of those "many heavenly gifts and helps which can only be enjoyed in the Catholic Church."[16] They above all others are able to say with St. John, "And the Word was made flesh, and dwelt among us; and we saw his glory — glory as of the only-begotten of the Father — full of grace and of truth. . . . And of his fullness we have all received, grace for grace."[17]

6. By reason of the communication of His grace and power to us

When we speak of man as sharing in the fullness of Christ, we come to the last reason for calling Christ the Head of the Mystical

Body. In the human body the head is considered the source of all activity for the body, but it is not an inert thing: it *actually* passes on that power to the body. So also is this true in our comparison: Christ, the divine Head, *actually does* pass on the life of grace to His members, and for that reason may be called our Head. As the Holy Father explains: "As the nerves extend from the head to all the parts of the human body and give them power to feel and move, in like manner our Saviour communicates strength and power to His Church so that the things of God are understood more clearly and are more eagerly desired by the faithful. From Him streams into the body of the Church all the light with which those who believe are divinely illumined, and all the grace by which they are made holy as He is holy."[18]

We shall go on now, to look at the influence of Christ in His members. There are two ways in particular in which Christ vivifies them; we may treat of each separately: first, through enlightening our minds, and, second, through sanctifying our lives.

CHRIST ENLIGHTENS OUR MINDS

The union of the Mystical Body is something entirely supernatural; it is a thing of God, and for that reason God must tell us about it before we can do anything at all. We cannot live or act in a Christian manner until we first *know*. That is the beginning of such life, and it is the work of our divine Head to make possible that beginning. It is not enough, of course, just to know; religion does not end there. It is ultimately our will that must be moved and through that our actions. But, as the Holy Father mentions in his encyclical *On the Sacred Liturgy*, "every act of the will presupposes an act of the intelligence, and before one can express the desire and the intention of offering oneself in sacrifice to the eternal Godhead, a knowledge of the facts and truths which make religion a duty is altogether necessary."[19]

Christ taught us what we must believe first of all through His own preaching; He spoke the "words of everlasting life"[20] to us, revealing the mysteries of God and His Church, explaining to us the nature of the Christian life. He continued this work even after

His Ascension into heaven by inspiring the writers of the New Testament to put down in writing the truths He desired to make known. Inspiration is defined as a supernatural influence of the Holy Spirit on the sacred writers, moving and impelling them to write in such a manner that they first rightly understood, then willed faithfully to write down, and finally expressed in apt words and with infallible truth all the things, and those only, which God ordered. When St. Paul wrote, for example, he did not write as an individual, thinking up things to say on his own. In a mysterious manner, while making use of Paul's own mentality and style of expression, God moved him to write down just those truths which He ordered, even though Paul himself might not have been conscious of such inspiration at the time. In all instances, God is the true Author of the Bible. Thus also the evangelists were helped by Christ so much that we can truly say that "as members of Christ they wrote what they had learnt, as it were, at the dictation of the Head."[21]

Again, the gift of faith which every one of us should possess is a *gift* from God. Apart from this special grace, no one can, of his own volition, believe with real faith, no matter how much study he may have put into the religion, or even how much intellectual acceptance of it he might have. Faith is not mere knowledge. In this way, Christ is our Head, since He is both the Author and Finisher of our faith, that precious gift of God through which our mind accepts these divine truths. This faith is the very beginning, the foundation, the root of all justification.

Besides imparting the light of faith to believers, Christ our Head also imparts special gifts to the leaders of the Church: "the supernatural gifts of knowledge, understanding and wisdom, so that they may logically preserve the treasury of faith, defend it vigorously, and explain and confirm it with reverence and devotion."[22] This will include above all the gift of infallibility by which the Holy Father or the assembly of the bishops either gathered together in a Council or in their common teaching throughout the world are preserved from error when speaking on matters of faith or morals. We shall speak of this in greater detail in the following chapter. Yet

Christ grants His special light to all pastors and teachers, helping them to carry out their tasks perfectly; and He does the same for all His members, whatever their station in life, mothers and fathers of families especially.

CHRIST SANCTIFIES OUR SOULS

Christ communicates His grace and power to His members, second, by sanctifying our lives. "Holiness begins from Christ; and Christ is its cause. For no act conducive to salvation can be performed unless it proceeds from Him as from its supernatural source."[23] The full and complete understanding of this is something we could never hope to impart in a book, much less a part of one. It is something we must come gradually to realize more and more. It means grasping the full import of the words of Christ: "Without me you can do nothing"[24] — realizing the absolute, all-inclusive nature of that word "nothing."

A few examples may help. A man may make an act of contrition thinking that if he tells God that he is sorry for his mortal sin, God will in turn forgive him. Actually it is quite the other way around: *it is God who must always take the first step.* Unless God did so, we would never make an act of contrition nor approach the confessional, should we have fallen into mortal sin. Unless God would first grant us the special actual grace to be supernaturally sorry for what we had done, we would never be able to regain the gift of sanctifying grace which we had carelessly cast aside. Everything begins with God, even our sorrow, our returns to Him. If He did not lead us, we would never come back.

The leaders of the Church, the various preachers and teachers, may come to greater and more profound understanding of the truths of God and the meaning of those truths for our lives, so that the whole Body may grow ever more and more in holiness and in integrity of life. But it is not the leaders leading the people; it is God leading the leaders, so that through them He may lead the people. The greatest minds of the Church are not the glory of the individuals who possess them, but rather the glory of the God-Man

Christ, who, through the outpouring of His gifts of wisdom and understanding, of counsel, fortitude, fear, and piety, has brought them about.

A priest will administer the Sacrament of Baptism, or recite the words of absolution over a repentant sinner. The sins are replaced by the freshness of sanctifying grace, but it is not the priest, the human being, who causes this to happen; it is Christ, working through the priest, who is but the instrument of Christ.

Everything that is done in the supernatural order is done by Christ the divine Head. A man may be struggling under tremendous difficulties or terrifying temptation, and he may pray and pray, and wonder if God ever hears him; but he forgets that the simple fact of our continuing to pray shows that God *is* helping us, for without a new actual grace we would not continue to pray. And should that man grow discouraged, forgetting for a moment that his spiritual life began from God, he need only recall the undying spirit of hope which urged St. Paul to write: "I am convinced of this, that he who has begun a good work in you will bring it to perfection until the day of Christ Jesus."[25]

Our divine Saviour longs to be with us to sanctify us, and He does this especially when He nourishes our souls with His own flesh and blood, and thus calms the turbulent passions of our souls. It is in the Eucharist that the members are very especially united with their Head; that they become more and more like to Christ. Those who eat of natural bread incorporate that bread into their own bodies, making it a part of themselves; but those who eat of this Bread from heaven do just the opposite: they are changed into Christ, incorporated as members into His Body, sanctified by contact with the very Source of grace Himself.

St. John Chrysostom has spoken of the meaning of this union with Christ in the Eucharist. "Christ wishes that we become His body, not through charity alone but that we be actually 'mingled' with His own flesh. This union is accomplished by means of the food which he has given us as proof of His love for us. Therefore He has 'mingled' Himself with us, He has implanted His body in us, that we may be one, as a body united with its head. What ardent love this manifests! . . . All this has Christ done, to bring us into closer friendship with Himself and to show His love for us. To those who yearned for Him He has not only appeared, but He has given Himself in the flesh . . . to be 'mingled' with us, and thus to satisfy every desire."[26]

If the sick woman could be restored to health by mere contact with the hem of Christ's garment; and if the ruler's daughter could come back from death to life when Christ but touched her hand, what still more wonderful graces and helps we might expect when we are united to Christ entirely in the Eucharist. Christ wants us to seek those graces. As Pius XII explains: "Christ, as the Eucharistic Victim on earth and the glorified Victim in heaven, through His wounds and His prayers, *pleads our cause* before the Eternal Father"; but even more, "He selects, He determines, He distributes every single grace to every single person 'according to the measure of the giving of Christ.' "[27] The grace of the divine Head thus flows out into all the members, so that they might live and act according to His desires, and that the entire Body might "grow up in all things in Him who is the Head, Christ."[28]

CHAPTER XIII

THE INFALLIBLE CHURCH

THE question of Christ the Head of the Church enlightening our minds from on high, brings before us one particular function of the divine Head that is not always understood in its proper light. It is the question of preserving the Mystical Body from error; the problem of an infallible Church here on this earth. Actually, we can have a proper understanding of what this means only if we see the Church for what it really is: the living Body of Christ, the extension of Jesus Christ in time in space. Unless we perceive the power of Christ behind His Church, its statements on matters of belief can hardly avoid appearing somewhat "arrogant."

There are two questions involved in this problem. *First,* could God preserve a group of human beings from error on matters of revealed truth; and *second, does* such a divinely sustained group actually exist. There are some men who deny the very possibility of a divinely sustained Church; for them, infallibility is out of the question. If, on the other hand, a man admits all that we have noted about the inner nature of the Church thus far, he knows that such divine guidance could be possible; the only other question that remains is: Did God actually give such a privilege to His Church?

SUPERNATURAL TRUTH

The gift of infallibility is one that we might readily suspect God would give to His Church, even had He not told us of it. Since He wished to give a set of *revealed* truths, of *supernatural* truths, to men, there had to be some assurance that the exact meaning of those truths would not be lost. If a man admits Revelation, he must admit some kind of infallibility as well. Left to themselves, human beings and their human language are variable creatures. Men can gather different meanings from the very same words; everyone has had the experience of someone "misunderstanding" his statement, and accepting as an insult what had been meant as praise. Thus if Christianity is to remain, there must be some Force outside of man that will not only reveal these truths, but which will also preserve them. Unless this were so, the entire purpose of Revelation might be frustrated. These truths necessarily *surpass* the understanding of man; that is what the very word "supernatural" means. Should an error creep into our understanding of them, it could be passed on to others, and man would have no power within himself by which he might check the accuracy of his knowledge about the supernatural. Left to himself, he could not tell the truth from the error.

In theory, of course, we might say that once God revealed the basic facts of the supernatural order, He could have watched over those truths in a general way; He might have preserved the entire human race from error in these truths, so that every individual could know the truth. But we are not living in a theoretical world; we are living in a real world, determined by the actual historical state of mankind. We could not accept the fact of such a universal preservation of revealed truth unless we could discover perfect agreement among all believers. God certainly is not preserving these truths in this manner, and still leaving them so vague that we can only remain in doubt as to what they are; and unfortunately, far from showing perfect harmony, there is great and obvious disagreement among men concerning what God intended to say, and the confusion grows yearly.

Since God does not reveal these truths to individuals, nor preserve them intact by a world-wide miracle touching upon each single man upon earth, there must be something else. It would only seem logical that there should be some objective standard of belief. If God has left to the individual to decide the meaning of Revelation, there would be an endless series of such "revelations," differing from man to man. There could be no condemnation for not accepting the truth of Christ, nor any real obligation to do so, because the words of Christ would necessarily be what each individual thought. Yet Christ Himself levied upon every single man, at all times and all places, the obligation of accepting His words. He warned that "he who rejects me, and does not accept my words, has one to condemn him. The word that I have spoken will condemn him on the last day."[1] And the inspired words of St. Paul, speaking of the second coming of Christ, issue a warning "that all may be judged who have not believed the truth, but have preferred wickedness."[2]

WHAT IS TRUTH?

If there be such a terrifying obligation to accept the truth of Christ, there must be some way of knowing with certainty just what that truth is. Indeed, the very word *truth* implies something definite and unchanging; it must be the same for all men. There can be no diversity. The universality and oneness of Christ's teachings must be just as absolute as the universality and oneness of His salvation.

The modern world has a special difficulty in understanding an infallible Church, however, because it has lost, not only the notion of a divinely sustained organization, but it has lost, in so many cases, the very meaning of *truth*. Men have come to measure things by their value rather than their inherent truth, and we may find men claiming that "today we do not care to ascertain whether an opinion is true or false, but only whether it is life-furthering, life-preserving."[3] In other words, our only concern is whether it works well.

Yet in an age which doubts even its ability to know something as true today which will still be true tomorrow, the Church declares her acceptance of truths as eternal and changeless as God. The Church even finds it necessary to affirm her belief in something that common sense would certainly take for granted, that is, "the mind's ability to attain certain and unchangeable truth."[4]

It is for this reason that there must be an infallible Church. Were it a question of purely natural knowledge, we could hope that there could be some final agreement among men, since the truths lie within reach of the human mind. If it were a matter of scientific investigation, we could check and recheck our findings until we attained the fact we had misplaced. Since faith deals with revealed truths, however, the knowledge must come from God alone. Unaided human reason cannot determine what these truths are or what we are to understand by the words in which they find expression. There would be no way of keeping these truths intact, if there were no Power outside of man preserving those truths. Man, changeable as he is, is only too prone to error. Indeed, the very reason why so many oppose the Catholic claim to infallibility is the frank recognition of error and change in human knowledge. Not seeing the divine power which sustains that claim, they see only the weakness of man. They cannot understand, then, how any group of human beings can claim the possession of complete and changeless truth, especially in matters which they claim surpass human understanding.

CHRIST IN HIS CHURCH

The real answer to this quest for supernatural truth lies in seeing Christ in His Church. Infallibility is not a separate problem; it is intimately wrapped up with our acceptance or rejection of the Church as the Body of Christ, as the instrument through which God applies to mankind the salvation of the cross. If we see the Church in that light, far from seeming arrogant, the claim will appear as an expression of humility; it proclaims our complete dependence upon Christ, even in the continued possession of revealed truth.

We find here once again the close resemblance between the life of Christ and the life of His Church. When Christ dwelt upon this earth, He appeared to many to be no more than another human being, for His divinity was hid, as it were, by His humanity. When He claimed divine powers, those who failed to see beyond the appearances to the profound depths of His divine personality cried out, "He has blasphemed!"[5] "How can this Man forgive sin and promise eternal life? By what right does He rule over us, and demand obedience to His commands? How dare He impose upon our minds the yoke of His teachings? He has usurped the power of God, and stands between us and our God; He desires His sanctifying rites to replace the sanctity of our Temple, His Law to supplant the Law of our Fathers, and His truth to replace the truth of God!"

The same thing is true of the Church which extends the words of Christ in time and space. Those who see no more than the human beings who make up that Body, and who fail to see beyond to the divine power that sustains this group, are shocked at its statements. When the Church assumes, through Christ, the duty of sanctifying, ruling, and teaching mankind, the voices are raised again, crying out: "These men blaspheme! How can these men forgive sins and promise eternal life? By what right do they rule over us, and demand obedience to their commands? How dare they impose upon our minds the yoke of their teachings? They have usurped the power of God, and they stand between us and our God; they desire their sanctifying rites to replace the sanctity of the cross, their laws to supplant the Law of the Redeemer, and their truth to replace the Truth of Christ!"

It might be expected that when men failed to look beyond the humanity of the God-Man to see the divine Person that He was, they might also fail to see beyond the frail and faulty human beings whom Christ uses to complete the work of Redemption: that they might fail to see the divine power which sustains that Church, and which speaks and acts through its feebleness. "If the world hates you, know that it has hated me before you. . . . If they have persecuted me, they will persecute you also."[6] A Church which knew no persecution, no rejection would have reason to fear that it had wandered from the path of Christ's truth. Nevertheless it is still Christ who is rejected in His Mystical Body. Until men manage to see Christ the Priest, the King, and the Teacher in His Church, they will miss the sole explanation for the efficacy of her Sacraments, the power of her law, and the truth of her teaching.

INSTRUMENT OF CHRIST

In the Church of Christ we may distinguish the threefold power: the power to rule, to sanctify, and to teach. We call the power to rule the *power of jurisdiction;* the power to sanctify, the *power of orders;* and the power to teach, the *power of teaching.* Basically, it is always Christ who acts through His visible Body in all that is done. We must make a distinction between these three powers, however, since the Church possesses the power to make laws in her own name in certain instances, while in declaring divine law, and in teaching and in sanctifying she acts only as the instrument of Christ.

"Thus it follows," as Father DeGuibert remarks, "that we may not speak of the power of orders, of teaching and of jurisdiction in exactly the same fashion. In the strict and complete sense, only the power of jurisdiction, i.e., the power of ruling over her subjects is a power, and it alone is a *proper* and *principal* power. The power of orders and teaching is a *ministerial* and *instrumental* power, for the Church does not sanctify by her own power nor does she define faith on her own authority; these she does only as the instrument of God. On the other hand, she passes laws on her own authority — an authority received from God, of course, but proper to her nonetheless — and she makes these laws as the principal cause and not as a mere instrument."[7]

MEANING OF INFALLIBILITY

Infallibility is a special gift pertaining to the teaching office of the Church. It means "unerring." Strictly speaking it means that the Holy Father or the assembly of the bishops either gathered together in a Council, or in their common teaching throughout the world, are preserved from error when speaking on matters of faith or morals. It does not mean that the Holy Father is incapable of sin; nor does it have anything to do with freedom from error in purely natural science. It is limited to those matters bearing upon faith and morals, and it is effective only when those who are the official teachers clearly intend to speak in their official capacity. Infallibility does not mean that the bishops or the Pope could not make an error when expressing their *private* opinion, even when speaking on matters of faith or morals.

The Bishop of Rome is a human being, prone to evil no less than other human beings. He could naturally make a mistake in telling time or spelling a word. The story is told how Cardinal Gibbons was once asked by a lady if it were true that the Pope was infallible in everything and could make no mistakes, and he replied: "Well, Madam, I can only assure you that His Holiness always referred to me as Cardinal Jibbons." So also the sinful life of one or another Pontiff that historians note is no proof against the attribute of infallibility. There are also examples of how a pope expressed erroneous views about religion when speaking as a *private* individual. One famous case is that of Pope John XXII, whose private opinion on the nature of the beatific vision was later disapproved by the official teaching of the Church.

What is meant by the infallibility of the Roman Pontiff is that, when the Pope speaks to the whole Church in an official capacity, and clearly desires to exercise the prerogative of infallibility which resides with him in a very special manner, Divine Providence will preserve him from teaching something that is untrue. The Pope is then said to be speaking *ex cathedra,* that is, "from the throne." The Vatican Council expressed this doctrine in these words: "We teach and define it to be a divinely revealed dogma, that the Roman Pontiff when he speaks *ex cathedra* — that is, when in the discharge of his office as pastor and teacher of all Christians, he defines, in virtue of his supreme apostolic authority, a doctrine concerning faith or morals, to be held by the Universal Church — is, through the divine assistance promised to him in Blessed Peter, possessed of that infallibility with which the Divine Redeemer willed His Church to be endowed in defining doctrines concerning faith or morals; and that therefore such definitions of the Roman Pontiff are of themselves, and not through the consent of the Church, irreformable."[8]

Infallibility is a negative thing in a way, in the sense that it keeps the Church from error; it has been compared to a dam holding back the waters, so that when the official teachers of the Church do speak *ex cathedra,* God's providence will hold them back, as it were, from saying what is not true. Yet that does not explain all that is contained in this notion of the teaching authority of the Church. Infallibility also implies something of a more positive nature. It is not, of course, a divine revelation; nor does it mean that the Pope suddenly thinks up a new teaching to give to the world. As Pope Pius XII tells us, the teaching authority of the Church is to "preserve the revealed truths pure and entire throughout every age, in such a way that it presents them undefiled, adding nothing to them, and taking nothing away from them."[9]

DEVELOPMENT OF DOGMA

We must not think of this work of the teaching authority as a purely negative thing, for there actually is within the Body of Christ a legitimate development of dogma. Without adding to the truths of revelation or taking away from them, the Church — under the guidance of the Holy Spirit — comes to an ever clearer understanding of the *content* of revelation. Throughout the long history of the Church's life, there have been many things which have contributed to this process. The progress of mankind, or the development of science, has had an influence. There have been heresies also which have meant that the Church had to explain more clearly *just what* its teaching meant in the most precise terms possible. This demanded discussion and debate *within* the Church. And throughout that process of debate, the Supreme Pontiff would, from time to time, point out some general line of thought to indicate the approved direction; or he would definitely exclude one or another path. Speaking as the supreme teacher in the Church, the Holy Pontiff would demand special respect for his words, although he was not as yet *defining* the truth once and for all.

The Holy Father does this today in different ways, especially in his encyclical letters. Pius XII condemned those theologians, in fact, who passed over these letters as unimportant because the Pope was not speaking infallibly at the time. He spoke of this in his encyclical letter on the errors of modern thought, *Humani Generis,* issued August 12, 1950:

"It must not be thought that what is expounded in Encyclical Letters does not of itself demand consent, since in writing such Letters the Popes do not exercise the supreme power of their Teaching Authority [infallibility]. For these matters are taught with the ordinary teaching authority, of which it is true to say: 'He who heareth you, heareth me'; and generally what is expounded and inculcated in Encyclical Letters already for other reasons appertains to Catholic doctrine. But if the Supreme Pontiffs in their official documents purposely pass judgment on a matter up to that time under dispute, it is obvious that that matter, according to the mind and will of the same Pontiffs, cannot be any longer considered a question open to discussion among theologians."[10]

What this all means is that we cannot divorce the ordinary teaching authority of the popes from the prerogative of infallibility; it is, as the Holy Father says, the "exercise [of] the *supreme power* of their Teaching Authority." We would surely have a faulty notion of infallibility if we thought that the Pope suddenly "stumbled," as it were, on a truth to be defined. The process leading up to the formal definition of a dogma in the Church is a gradual one, and it is only at the end of that process that the Church exercises her supreme power in teaching and speaks infallibly. At that moment, her final statement is irrevocable and unchanging; it is the moment when infallibility in the proper sense is present. But the Holy Spirit does not lead the Church by a series of *errors* to discover the *truth!* The doctrines contained in the various decrees of the Holy Father, in his addresses, or his encyclicals, even though not taught infallibly in themselves, are closely connected with this supreme power; we are being led to an ever clearer understanding and expression of revealed truth. We must therefore listen attentively to those words.

MISUNDERSTANDINGS

There are many men outside the Church who fail to see it as the living Body of Christ. As a result, they fail also to appreciate its role in this matter of teaching divine truth. There are some men, for example, who complain that there is no life, no vitality in the Church; it does nothing, they would say, but hand down a set of doctrines that were fixed once and for all, in their completed form, in the early ages of Christianity. They have the mistaken notion that the Church on earth is supposed to do nothing more than repeat, rote-fashion, what has been handed down from the past.

This much *is* true of the dogmas of our faith, of course: they *are* unchanging from century to century. But there is progress and development and vitality in coming to a clearer understanding of what has been revealed, and in explaining the full application of those truths. As Pius XII points out: "Each source of divinely revealed doctrine contains so many rich treasures of truth, that they can really never be exhausted; hence it is that theology through the study of its sacred sources remains ever fresh."[11] But it does this only by remaining faithful to the teachings of the past and the official teachings of the present. A theology that would cast aside both the past and the official guidance of the present, and set out by itself to solve the questions of faith, would cut itself off from the two sources of Revelation: Scripture and Tradition. The one must explain the other, and the Bible especially, as experience has shown, can lead only to confusion without a legitimate interpreter. And Tradition is the teaching of the living Church.

There are other men who feel that the Church can teach only what was taught explicitly in the first centuries of our era — as though the Holy Ghost abandoned the Church after that time. They cannot bring themselves to believe a truth defined by the Church unless they can find some historical trace of it recorded centuries ago. To them Christian truth is not a living and vital thing; it is dead, archaic. They fail to see the life of the Church, and failing that, they do not see, as Pius XII notes, that "even positive theology cannot be on a par with merely historical science, for, together with the sources of positive theology God has given to His Church a living Teaching Authority to elucidate and explain what is contained in the deposit of faith only obscurely and implicitly."[12]

IMPLICIT AND EXPLICIT

This last word of Pius XII raises another question concerning the manner in which things are revealed. We can understand this process of development of dogma within and through the Church if we can see the difference.

We speak of what theologians call a *formal* revelation, either explicit or implicit. A formal revelation would concern a truth that is stated in proper and express terms; it could be *explicitly* revealed — such, for example, as the doctrine of the divinity of Christ, the Trinity, the Virgin Birth. But such a formal revelation (a revelation formally telling us some supernatural truth) could also be *implicitly* revealed. Sometimes this is comparatively easy, as when a certain truth can be immediately drawn out of some other truth that *is* explicitly stated in the sources of Revelation. It would be contained in it, as they say, as a "part in the whole," or the "particular in the universal." If, for example, we say that Christ is a man, that very phrase also tells us (implicitly) that He has a soul and a body, an intellect and a free will.

On the other hand, there could be cases which would not be so evident. Something that is explicitly stated can be explained more fully as time goes on; and, more often, truths which are implicitly revealed in other dogmas can be seen more clearly with the passing of time and the continued life of the Church. It is on these points, then, that there is growth and development of dogma within the Church; but it is guided always by the Holy Spirit, the Soul of that Body and the Force behind the living Teaching Authority.

This development involves more than simply explaining terms and phrases; it means more than looking at the records of history or the rules of logic. It is something intimately associated with the *inner nature* of the living Church, and it is only when we understand that Church that we can understand her role in teaching mankind.

There is still some discussion among theologians about just what is involved in an implicit revelation. We have, for example, what we call a theological conclusion. By this we mean some truth which we arrive at by certain rules of logic. We know some definite article of faith, and we apply our human reason to this truth. As a result, we conclude that it also involves something more than we would have noticed at first. The discussion, therefore, would center around the question of whether this second truth was "implicitly" revealed or not. It is a question, in other words, of whether this new conclusion was really contained in the first truth all the while, even though we hadn't seen it; or if it is something entirely distinct. This is an especially difficult question for another reason. When we are actually dealing with a truth which was revealed implicitly, we will not realize, as a rule, that it *was* implicitly revealed until the *end* of a long process of growth and development in doctrine. The life of the Church contributes much to this process of unfolding the full content of revelation, and it is only the final decision of the Church which will settle the matter definitively.

If, however, this process of reasoning were to add something completely separate from the truth which was revealed explicitly, the Church would not define it as something to be held on divine faith. There would then be something involved in it which had not been revealed by God. However, the Church could still teach this other truth infallibly (without saying that it is a dogma and that it was formally revealed). This could be so, since the Church could show that all the elements connected with the truth are known to be positively true: the elements which came from revelation and those which came from human experience. Thus we see that the infallibility of the Church extends also to other things not formally revealed, but which are concerned with faith or morals.

GLORY OF THE CHURCH

We can see from all of this the importance of respecting the teaching authority of the Church in all of its day-to-day teaching. It is through that authority that we receive the security we need in the way of faith; it is the voice of Christ speaking to us. As Father Mersch explains: "We may say that the teaching of the Church is not less infallible than the teaching of Jesus, and that nevertheless Jesus alone is infallible, for it is He who is infallible in the Church. . . .

"At all times, the Christian is one who refuses to see anything but Jesus Christ. As regards the bishops as well as the Pope, his docility will be the same: it will be the docility he has toward Christ. For him, the definitions of a Council and the declarations of the Incarnate Word are of absolutely the same worth. Even more: in the unity of the Mystical Body, they are identified. The definitions of a Council but continue the words of Christ, just as the voice which reaches the ear continues the voice which speaks. . . . Indeed, when Jesus Christ promised to remain with His Church all days, He did not speak of such remoteness. It is not only from the heavenly heights that He abides in us and we in Him, but rather, within us and in our Church. The Church is His Body, and when it teaches, it lends Him its lips, its voice, its efforts; but it is Christ alone who speaks."[1]

PROMISE TO PETER

While yet on this earth, our Lord made a special promise to Peter concerning the stability of his faith. "Simon, Simon, behold Satan has desired to have you, that he may sift you as wheat. But I have prayed for thee, that *thy faith may not fail;* and do thou, when once thou hast turned again, *strengthen thy brethren.*"[14] Though Simon might deny the Lord through weakness, yet in his official capacity as supreme teacher of the Church, his faith will never fail. It is upon the rock of Peter that the faith of the Church will be supported until the end of time; and since, when these words were spoken, Peter had already been promised the primacy that was to endure to the end of the world, this promise extends also to those other Peters who are to follow after him, becoming, each in turn, the "rock" upon which the visible edifice will rest.

While the gift of infallibility comes to us through the Pope and the bishops united to him, it benefits the entire Body. It is not so much an infallible Pope as an infallible Church that we know on this earth. Once we see the division of gifts and offices intended by Christ, we will have no difficulty in admitting that those who are the rulers, the official teachers, the shepherds of the flock will be the ones who actively possess the prerogative of infallibility. Yet, as we are all one in Christ, so do we all share in this great gift.

In the words of Father Mersch: "The grandeur is common to all, and all are equally illumined; and this resembles a democracy. But the grandeur comes only through certain ones [the bishops], through one above all [the Pope]; and it is only these certain ones, one above all, who hold aloft the torch: and this is the monarchic principle. But the Pope and the bishops and all are enlightened only because they are within the house (Matt. 5:15); and that is the synthesis of these two aspects. In reality, there are not, on one side, those who teach, and on the other, quite separate, those who are taught; there is but one life, but one Mystical Body, but one Whole Christ, Head, and members. When the Head communicates the light to the members, there is but one Mystic Man who grows in knowledge. And there will be one Christ teaching Himself: *et erit unus Christus docens seipsum.*"[15]

HOW EXERCISED

This prerogative of infallibility in the highest sense is exercised in different ways. Since the bishops share with the Roman Pontiff in this office of official teacher, they also share, in their own way, in this power of infallibility.

When the Pope officially and explicitly defines one or another truth *ex cathedra,* as we say, his decrees are infallible; we have an example of this in the definition of Pope Pius XII of the Assumption of the Blessed Mother, or that of Pius IX of her Immaculate Conception.

However, we also have what we call the General Councils of the Church. These are gatherings of the bishops of the world, in union with the Pope, for the purpose of discussing matters of faith and morals. These General Councils may also define doctrines infallibly; we have an example of that in the decree of the Vatican Council in 1870 concerning the teaching on the infallibility of the Roman Pontiff; or the many definitions of the Council of Trent in the sixteenth century concerning grace or the Sacraments. These Councils cannot define truths infallibly if they are called together *apart* from the Pope, and without his consent; he is the chief teacher in the Church, and no one, not even a gathering of bishops, can ignore him. But a Council that is convened under the authority of the Pope can act infallibly in defining truths of faith.

Yet, as Pius IX explained when speaking of the assent required in matters of divine faith: "It must not be limited to those things which have been defined in express decrees of Ecumenical Councils or of the Roman Pontiffs, but must extend to those things also which are handed down as divinely revealed by the ordinary magisterium of the entire Church throughout the world, and are therefore held by Catholic theologians to pertain to [the content of] faith because of the universal and constant agreement."[16]

Thus, in the classic statement of the Vatican Council: "All those truths must be believed by divine and Catholic faith, which are contained in the written word of God or in tradition, and which the Church proposes for acceptance as divinely revealed, either by solemn definition [of the Pope or a General Council] or through her ordinary and universal teaching."[17] Either this ordinary or the extraordinary teaching of the Church will be infallible if the living Magisterium teaches a certain truth as revealed.

REQUIREMENTS

We might sum up, then, under three headings, the ways in which this divine attribute of infallibility is exercised in the Church; we are speaking here of the exercise of the *supreme power* of the teaching authority in the Church.

First, the Church speaks infallibly through the Pope alone when he speaks *ex cathedra* on matters of faith or morals; this we call papal infallibility. To speak infallibly in this manner certain conditions must be verified:

1. The Holy Father must *intend* to use his official power and to speak infallibly. Thus a private opinion would be excluded, as well as a statement issued as Pope but without the intention of exercising this supreme teaching power.

2. The Holy Father must intend to *define* a particular doctrine; that is, there must be a manifest intention of giving a dogmatic, final, and unchangeable judgment as to the truth to be held on divine faith.

3. The Holy Father must intend to *impose* this belief upon the *universal* Church, and he must clearly signify this intention, so that there may be no doubt as to the obligation imposed.

4. The Holy Father must be speaking on matters of *faith or morals,* including, however, those matters that are so closely connected with revealed truths that they are necessary so as to preserve and explain and defend those truths.

Second, the Church speaks infallibly through the decrees of a General Council which have been sanctioned and approved by the Pope. As with the express definition of the Pope, the Council must also intend to define a doctrine of faith or morals, and must clearly impose this belief upon the Universal Church. Not every word spoken in a Council would be infallible, of course, but only those statements which, with the approval of the successor of Peter, are issued as official decrees.

Third, the Church is infallible in her day-by-day teaching of the bishops throughout the world, who are in union with the Holy Father.

Provided that there is universal agreement that a certain teaching is a truth revealed by God, and it is proposed in that way, the Church's ordinary teaching is infallible even without any solemn definitions of the Pope or the Councils. This highlights, again, the danger of losing touch with the current of revealed truth. One who wishes to "think with the Church" will listen attentively to the day-by-day teachings of that Body. A man, on the other hand, who would discount these teachings, and claim to have regard only for explicitly defined truths, would find that he has entered upon the way of novelty.

RESULTS OF DENYING INFALLIBILITY

Protestant Christianity today gives us the finest example of the dire results of denying an infallible Teaching Authority in the Church. At the start, the Reformation attempted to transfer infallibility to a book, to the Scriptures. This soon proved to be a futile attempt; the wide disagreement about the meaning of the varied texts led only to further confusion and endless division within Protestantism itself.

To try to stop this process of division, some groups became *fundamentalists,* as they say; they imposed certain beliefs upon their members. Since they had denied infallibility, however, it amounted to imposing belief on human authority alone. The Scriptures had failed to solve the entire difficulty as was hoped, and therefore the leaders of particular sects interpreted those Scriptures for their members, and bound them to those beliefs.

Many modern Protestants, however, have realized the incongruity of such a practice, and they have become *liberal* Protestants. For them, there is no special belief to be imposed upon anyone because religious truth is relative rather than absolute. It changes, in other words, from century to century. There is no "true" and no "false," no "right" and no "wrong" — or if there is, they feel we cannot tell the difference.

Thus we have in modern Protestantism but two choices: a fundamental church which denies infallibility but which acts as though it possesses it; or a liberal church which destroys all Christian truth in order to retain the principle of independence. It is difficult to see which is more unfortunate: the situation of those who prefer to admit the illogical position of a creed in a church that claims no infallibility;

or the situation of those who choose the even more astounding view of denying the possibility of unchanging religious truth itself — of those who say it makes no difference whether you believe Christ was God, or only a good man; or whether you believe that baptism saves you from sin or if you look upon it merely as a remnant of early Christian symbolism.

PROTESTANT CONFUSION

This confusion of non-Catholic thought is unavoidable; in the last analysis, Protestantism could not arrive at any other goal. This will always be true, as Father Weigel says, "because the principle of protest cannot admit that the Mystical Body of Christ, the Church, exists with an indestructible structure and an infallible teaching power whose pronouncements are enlightenment for the mind and not objects of criticism. This Protestant situation derives from the Protestant theology's inability to answer Pilate's question: 'What is truth?' "[18]

If it were not that the Catholic populace sees the image of Christ in the Church, there would be no power in Rome nor any binding force to a papal decree. The Catholics of the world are not intellectual myopics duped by their leaders, nor moral cowards enslaved by tyrants. The power of the Roman Church lies not in political force or medieval fear, but in a faith in Christ which far surpasses in depth and content the faith of any protesting body; a faith in Christ as present among us in His Mystical Body.

In accepting the teaching authority of that Body, the Catholics of the world do not do violence to their minds or will. They simply accept the words of Christ, and they do so because they fully realize that this living Church upon earth, with its infallible teaching authority, is the very means by which God would bring security into their way of faith, and eliminate the possibility of doctrinal vagary and confusion which is gnawing at the heart of Protestant Christianity.

Nor do they look upon their leaders as exalted above them, but rather as brothers in Christ, united in one living Body the Church. The penetrating words of the late Emile Mersch remind us of the need of all the members to see Christ in His Church, but also of the dependence of every single member upon the life-giving Head:

"The magisterium of the Church is not the exaltation of a few men above the masses who are kept in tutelage; it is the means by which God raises up the entire populace. Like the others, the Pope and the Bishops need to be taught by Christ. But in their case only, Jesus Christ teaches them by means of the office which they themselves fulfill. Thus, as private persons, they are subject to the power which, as public persons, they exercise in the name of God. This reveals much about the exact nature of the magisterium. It shows us that the Church's power of teaching is purely an action which *Christ performs through men, and not an action of men.* They can teach, or rather they must teach; but the truth which they express comes from Christ and that truth surpasses them. They have been but a channel; what they have spoken is not the result of their own thoughts; they are the thoughts of Him, who, in the flesh hypostatically united to the Word, has given us the doctrine of truth. . . .

"The office of Popes and Bishops will pass away, and it is not because they have taught that, in heaven, they will see the light. It will be only because, like any of the faithful, they have believed."[19]

CHAPTER XIV

THE SOUL OF THE MYSTICAL BODY

WE HAVE seen the reason for referring to the Church as the Body of Christ, and the reason for naming Christ the Head of this Mystical Body. It still remains for us to see why we are justified in making a comparison between the Holy Spirit and His relationship to the Church, and the human soul and its relationship to the physical body. We must see why we refer to the Holy Spirit as the "Soul of the Mystical Body."

It is evident by now that when we speak of the "soul" of the Church, it is not to be understood in a strict sense, as though the Church had a soul just as the human body has. We are only making a comparison, saying that on certain points there is a marked similarity between what the soul does for the human body and what the Holy Spirit does for the Church. The reason for using such language is that it brings out in bold relief some particular truth we wish to emphasize: in this case, the complete dependence of the Church upon God. It is a divinely sustained Church; that is the sole explanation for its vitality, for its endurance through 2000 years. Were this divine assistance to be taken away from it, the Church would be nothing more than any other merely human organization, and it would wither and die away no less quickly than does the human body when the soul departs from it.

THE TRINITY

Actually the work of preserving the Church, like all the works of God, is proper to the entire Trinity. The sole exception to this is the Redemption wrought by Christ; the Second Person of the Trinity alone assumed the human nature through which He died upon the cross. But even there, it was the entire Trinity which brought about that union of the two natures. When speaking of the works of the Trinity, however, we do speak of one or another work as being more proper to one of the Three Persons; we call this "appropriation." It means that we speak *as if* one of the Persons did perform this or that particular work. Thus we appropriate the work of creation to the Father, the work of redemption to the Son, and the work of sanctification to the Holy Spirit. And we speak of power and majesty and omnipotence as being of the Father, while we appropriate wisdom and design to the Son, and goodness, mercy, and love to the Holy Spirit. In line with this, we have the division by which we attribute to the Father the decree or decision to redeem mankind, to the Son the carrying out of that decree, and to the Holy Spirit the perfecting of this work of redemption.

Since the work of sustaining the Church and preserving her from evil and sanctifying her members is a work of Love, we appropriate it in a special way to the Holy Spirit. This work of sanctification was made possible through the sufferings of Christ upon the cross, and when He returned in triumph to the Father, with the work that was given to Him completed, *He promised to send* the Paraclete: "another Advocate to dwell with you forever, the Spirit of truth . . . whom I will send you from the Father."[1] It is for this reason that we call this divine principle of life and power in the Mystical Body the "Spirit of Christ," by which the Church lives the supernatural life of Christ, and through which the divine Saviour "permeates His whole Body and nourishes and sustains each of the members according to the place which they occupy in the Body, in the same way as the vine nourishes and makes fruitful the branches which are joined to it."[2] It is really the Trinity which accomplishes these things, but we appropriate it to the Holy Spirit; He acts as the Spirit of Christ, through which the Head sustains His members. When we say that the Holy Spirit descended upon the Church on Pentecost, we mean that the entire Trinity gave to those people a special outpouring of graces. Since we appropriate such sanctifying works of the Trinity to the Third Person, we say that the Holy Spirit came upon them. This has a basis in what happened, for when granting these graces, the Holy Spirit made known His presence in a distinct manner through the sound of roaring wind and the parted tongues of fire.

WHY CALLED THE SPIRIT OF CHRIST

If we look a little closer, we will find a number of reasons for referring to the Third Person of the Trinity as the Spirit of Christ in this instance. The encyclical on the Mystical Body gives us seven of these, each based upon some special relationship between Christ and the Holy Spirit.

1. It was by the Holy Ghost that Christ's soul *was made beautiful* from the first moment of His human existence. The Holy Spirit, the Sanctifier, showered upon the human soul of Christ more graces than were ever granted to any other person, and for that reason may He be called especially the Spirit of Christ. The soul of Christ was adorned with the fullness of grace — that fullness of which we have all received. If grace makes the soul beautiful and pleasing to God, then Christ possessed the fullness of that beauty also. His soul was the very masterpiece of the handiwork of the Holy Spirit, and this from the very first moment of His existence in the womb of His Mother. St. John Chrysostom has spoken of the extent of the graces possessed by Christ. "Christ," he tells us, "does not possess grace by way of participation, but He is the very source, the very root of all good things; He is Life itself, Light itself, Truth itself. He does not keep these abundant gifts to Himself, but extends them to all others; yet after He has done so, He is still filled with them. He is still no poorer as a result of His generosity; despite the fact that He is constantly giving away and communicating His goods to all, He possesses the same plenitude. . . . If we take a drop of water from the sea, the sea is diminished, tiny though the loss may be. But with this source the case is quite different; no matter how much we draw from it, it is as abundant as before."[3]

2. The Holy Ghost loved to dwell in the human soul of Christ as His most *cherished shrine*. The Holy Spirit dwells in the souls of all the just; a person in the state of sanctifying grace is then a

temple of the Holy Spirit. "If anyone love me," said our Lord, "he will keep my word, and my Father will love him, and we will come to him and make our abode with him."[4] Or as St. Paul asked: "Do you not know that your members are the temple of the Holy Spirit, who is in you, whom you have from God, and that you are not your own?"[5] The degree of sanctifying grace which a person possesses and the intimacy of this union are commensurate, so that we can easily see how profound, how very intimate would be this union of the Holy Spirit with the human soul of Christ, which possessed the very fullness of grace. There above all the Spirit would take up His abode; there above all would He love to dwell as in His most beautiful of temples; the Spirit of Christ.

3. Christ *merited* the Holy Spirit *for us* by His Death upon the cross, thus adding another reason for referring to the Holy Spirit as the Spirit "of Christ." It was through Christ's death that it became possible for us to receive the Holy Spirit and His gifts into our souls, and thus escape the burden of original sin. Christ paid the price of our redemption, and through His death He merited the reward of eternal life for all: "In Him we have the redemption through His blood, the remission of sins, according to the riches of his grace."[6] Thus it is that the Holy Father writes: "If our Saviour, by His death, became, in the full and complete sense of the word, the Head of the Church, it was likewise through His blood that the Church was enriched with the fullest communication of the Holy Spirit, through which, from the time when the Son of man was lifted up and glorified on the Cross by His sufferings, she is divinely illumined."[7] The Holy Ghost is the Spirit of Christ, that is, the Spirit which Christ merited for His Church.

4. Christ *gave* the Holy Spirit to the Church *for the remission of sins,* and so again we may speak of "His" Spirit in a special way. "Receive the Holy Spirit; whose sins you shall forgive, they are forgiven them; and whose sins you shall retain, they are retained."[8] One of the greatest works of the Church of Christ was to be the forgiving of sins and the reconciling of the sinner with God. It might be expected, since that was the very work of Christ Himself: "I have not come to call the just, but sinners to repentance."[9] The

Mystical Body continues the work of Christ in time and space, even the forgiving of sins. Christ wished to do this through the Holy Ghost, so that the Holy Spirit is truly the Spirit of Christ; it is through Him that the work of Christ is accomplished.

5. Christ alone received this Spirit into His soul *without limit;* all others are limited in the graces they receive, and limited according to the measure of Christ's giving. This flows from what was said above, about the beauty of Christ's soul, adorned with the fullness of grace. Since He possesses the Holy Spirit and His gifts without any limit, we may give another reason for calling this Spirit the Spirit of Christ more than of anyone else. Indeed all others only share in this plenitude of grace in Christ: "Of his fullness we have all received."[10] All others, then, share in the Spirit of Christ, but He alone possesses the Spirit of Himself and is able to make others share with Him: He alone really possesses this Spirit, His Spirit; others only participate in it.

6. Again, it is the Spirit of Christ that has made us the *adopted sons of God.* Christ, the eternal Son of the Father, in sharing His Spirit with us, has shared also His *sonship;* we become in truth the brothers of Christ, sons of God. St. Paul tells us this in his Letter to the Galatians: "And because you are sons, God has sent the Spirit of his Son into our hearts, crying, 'Abba, Father.' "[11]

7. Lastly, we may refer to the Holy Spirit as the Spirit of Christ because of the *effect* of His coming into our souls. He is given to us in order to make us more *like Christ.* The Holy Spirit dwells in us as individuals, as well as in the universal Church, but His purpose is to make every man more Christlike in his individual life, and, as we shall see more clearly in the final chapter, to make the picture of the entire Church grow more and more into a true representation of the God-Man.

THE HOLY SPIRIT: THE SOUL OF THE CHURCH

This Spirit of Christ is closely linked to the life of the Mystical Christ, just as it was in the life of the historical Christ. Indeed, since Christ wished to continue His work through a divinely sustained

Church, it is only to be expected that this same Spirit should also become the divine Principle of life and power in that Church. In completing our comparison, then, "Let it suffice to say," as Leo XIII wrote, "that as Christ is the Head of the Church, so is the Holy Spirit her soul."[12] He is the very *Source* of every gift and created grace in the Church. It is to this that we refer when we think of the Soul of the Church *in itself*. If, however, we were to speak of the Soul of the Church in its *created effects;* were we to ask exactly what is the immediate result of the presence of this Soul in the Church, we would have in mind all of the gifts mentioned above,[13] through which Christ and His Spirit enlighten and sanctify the Church.

The human soul has certain relationships to the human body which are similar to those between the Church and the Holy Ghost. Once more, following the encyclical on the Mystical Body, we may outline five of these to help us understand a bit more the reason for making this comparison — remembering it is just a comparison.

1. First of all, the human soul infuses the entire body; it is there in the body as a whole, but it is also in every single part of the body — not just a bit of it, but all of it in each part. This is possible because the human soul is something nonmaterial, something spiritual. The presence of the soul in the body differs, however, from the presence of water poured into a bottle; when that is done, the *whole* of that water is in the whole bottle, but not in each part of it. The soul, on the other hand, is entirely present anywhere that it actually is present.

Something very similar is found in the Church, for the Holy Spirit is present to the Church as a whole, but He is also present completely to each and every one of the members. The Church possesses the Holy Spirit; the individual members possess the Holy Spirit; He is entire in the Head, entire in the Body, and entire in each of the members. The result of this, as in the human body, is that all the parts of the Body are joined *one with the other,* and with their exalted Head, Christ. In the human body it is the soul which, being present in the entire body, becomes the source of unity. When water is poured into a bottle, the right side of the bottle is not thereby joined or united to the left side as a living thing. In the

Church, however, the Holy Spirit is more like the human soul, for He becomes the source of unity in the Church, joining the members to one another and to Christ. Were He to leave the Church, deprive it of His gifts, that bond of union would be broken, as was said, and the Church would begin to wither away as does the human body after the soul leaves it in death.

2. While it is true that the human soul is entire in each part of the body, it is obvious that not all of the soul's powers are exercised in each part of that body. The legs cannot be used for seeing, or the eyes for hearing. The soul acts in each member according to the purpose which it is to serve in the body, enabling the eye to see, the ear to hear, and the feet to walk.

So also in the Church, the Holy Spirit is present and assists the different members according to the various duties and offices which they hold, and according to the greater or less degree of spiritual health which they enjoy. The Holy Father and the bishops, for example, have need of special gifts from the Holy Spirit to perform the tasks assigned to them. The laity, on the other hand, will have needs proper to their own state of life. The Holy Spirit will not be present to mothers and fathers of families in such a way that they might be able to forgive sins, for that is the work of priests. The eye and the ear have different jobs to perform in the human body, and this is true of the different members in the Church. Yet the Holy Spirit *is* there also to help mothers and fathers perform their important tasks, for it is to them that "our Saviour has entrusted the youngest members of His Mystical Body."[14] They need the special gifts of the Holy Spirit to give them the courage to found a family; and to enlighten them on the manifold decisions which fall to parents in instructing, reproving, and guiding their children. So also with the other members of the Body of Christ. The special graces of God will enable them all to perform the particular tasks which fall to their lot.

3. In the human body, once more, it is the soul which is ultimately the source of every single action performed by any part of the body. Without the soul, the body is lifeless, powerless to act. The head may determine what to do, and send its impulse to the

other members, provided always that it is alive; the head of a corpse is not the source of any action.

Now, in the Mystical Body, Christ the divine Head has determined that He would act always through the Holy Spirit, the Soul of His Mystic Body. This Soul is to be the very principle of *life* just as the human soul is to man's body. There is not a single action performed in the proper order of the Church (that is, the supernatural order) which does not spring from this Breath of Life which is her divine Soul. Whether it be the prayers of a humble scrub woman or an infallible definition of the Roman Pontiff, there is not a single supernatural act performed in any part of the Body which does not begin with the Holy Spirit. Every act, high and low, large and small, depends entirely upon the impulse of the Soul, through whom Christ acts.

This relationship between Christ the Head and the Holy Spirit is explained by Pius XII: "Christ is in us through His Spirit, whom He gives to us and through whom He acts within us in such a way that all divine activity of the Holy Spirit within our souls must also be attributed to Christ. 'If anyone does not have the Spirit of Christ, he does not belong to Christ,' says the Apostle, 'but if Christ is in you . . . the spirit is life by reason of justification.' This communication of the Spirit of Christ is the channel through which all the gifts, powers, and extraordinary graces found superabundantly in the Head as in their source flow into all the members of the Church, and are perfected daily in them according to the place they hold in the Mystical Body of Jesus Christ."[15]

4. While the human soul is present entirely in each part of the body, yet it does not always act directly in those parts, but rather indirectly through the higher members. The soul is the ultimate source of all life and activity, yet it is through the mind (deciding what to do) and the will (saying, "Go ahead and do it") that the feet will walk or the lips speak or the hands open a door. These higher, loftier members of the human being have something very real to contribute to the actions of the lower members. The soul does not act independently of them when giving life to the hands and feet and lips.

A comparison is in order between this fact and the action of the Holy Spirit upon the Church, for there also the Soul of the Church deigns to give His gifts to men through the ministry of the higher members of the Body. This Soul is present in all the members, but He acts through the bishops and priests especially when giving help to the lesser members of the Church. The hierarchy have something very real to contribute to the spiritual life of the Mystical Body; the divine Soul does not act entirely independently of them, but "while He is personally present and divinely active in all the members, nevertheless in the inferior members, He acts also through the ministry of the higher members."[16] This hierarchy, or holy ordering of different offices, is something which belongs to the very nature of the Church; Christ decreed in instituting it that it should always be so. For this reason, Pius XII has written in his encyclical *On the Sacred Liturgy:* "Let all, then, who would live in Christ, flock to their priests. By them they will be supplied with the comforts and food of the spiritual life. From them they will procure the medicine of salvation assuring their cure and happy recovery from the fatal sickness of their sins. The priest, finally, will bless their homes, consecrate their families and help them, as they breathe their last, across the threshold of eternal happiness."[17]

5. Lastly, the comparison between the human soul and the Holy Spirit is verified in the easily understood fact that the human soul does not dwell outside the body. It infuses the body entirely, but goes no further than that. And the same is true of the Soul of the Church. The Holy Spirit may indeed dwell in the souls of those who, through no fault of their own, are not members of this Body, provided they are in the state of sanctifying grace, but He does *not dwell* in them precisely *as* the Soul of the Church. He does not thereby bind them together in that special union with Christ and the other members of His Body; nor does He give them those gifts and graces flowing from the Mass and the Sacraments, which can only be had in the Church. He may dwell in them as a Spirit, but not as the Soul of the Church — that unifying principle of the Mystical Body.

Even more, "He yet refuses to dwell through sanctifying grace in those members that are wholly severed from the Body,"[18] that is, in those who knowingly and willingly reject such membership. In rejecting the Body, they also reject the Soul which dwells within it. Because of this, the Sanctifier can dwell in them neither as Spirit nor as Soul of the Mystical Body.

The Holy Spirit does constantly give grace to *draw* all men to the Church; "by His grace He provides for the continual growth of the Church,"[19] the visible Body. The highest ideal of the Church is that one day all men might be united in organic oneness in the Body of Christ; that all might be animated by the Soul of that Body. It is toward that goal that the Holy Spirit will work through His gifts of grace, toward the fulfillment of that divine prayer of our Saviour to the heavenly Father: "That all may be one, even as thou, Father, in me and I in thee; that they also may be one in us, that the world may believe that thou hast sent me."[20]

It is from the Holy Spirit that this apostolic zeal must proceed on all levels. The Church Militant is fighting a battle upon this earth, striving to extend the Kingdom of God — the Church; but it is a battle of love. All of the zeal of the Catholic world is based upon this truth. She longs to bring men to Christ, to help them freely submit through faith and love to the rule of the Mystic Head. She longs to see the Body of Christ grow both quantitatively (in the number of members) and qualitatively (in the increased sanctity of the members' lives). It is the Holy Spirit who promotes this growth; it is His work of love. As St. Paul reminds us: "Christ himself gave some men as apostles, and some as prophets, others again as evangelists, and others as pastors and teachers, in order to perfect the saints for a work of ministry, for *building up the body of Christ,* until we *all* attain to the unity of the faith and of the deep knowledge of the Son of God, to perfect manhood, to the mature measure of the fullness of Christ."[21]

CHAPTER XV

THE MOTHER OF CHRIST

WHEN we speak of Christ, in any way, we cannot help but speak of His Blessed Mother as well, for there was no one more closely associated with Him in the work of salvation than the Virgin Mary. So also, since the Church — the Mystical Christ — is to continue the work of the God-Man for all time, it might only be expected that Mary would also have her role to play in the life of that Church. So complete is our oneness with Christ in His Church that we can call her in all truth Mother of the Mystical Christ, born on the hill of Calvary, just as she is the Mother of the Child of Bethlehem. Because Christ *in His fullness* includes so many others, to be the Mother of Christ means to be the Mother of those other men as well, and it is a motherhood as real as is our identification with Christ.

"Thus," our Holy Father tells us, "she who, according to the flesh, was the mother of our Head, through the added title of pain and glory became, according to the Spirit, the mother of all His members . . . and she continues to have for the Mystical Body of Christ, born of the pierced Heart of the Saviour, the same motherly care and ardent love with which she cherished and fed the Infant Jesus in the crib."[1]

MARY'S ROLE, A ROLE OF LOVE

Mary, of course, held no priestly office in the Church, yet her work was tremendously important. It was entirely a work of love, and it continues down to this very hour. That is why some writers have spoken of Mary as the "Heart" of the Mystical Body, for the duty of any mother is to foster love in her family, and the same is true in the family of Christ. Mary has always lavished upon those who are members of the Mystical Christ that same attention and devotion which she gave to the Christ Child Himself. And those children, "weeping and crying in this vale of tears," have run with confidence to that same Mother who rocked the Infant in her arms and who received His bruised body from the cross.

The silent figure of Mary appeared throughout the life of Christ, a figure glowing with the warmth and tenderness of a mother. When the Magi came from the East asking, "Where is the newly born king of the Jews?" they were sent to Bethlehem, and when they had entered the house, "they found the child *with Mary his mother*."[2] And thus it always was, down until that hour when "there were standing by the cross of Jesus, *his mother* and his mother's sister, Mary of Cleophas, and Mary Magdalene."[3]

Since the Church, however, is to be nothing more than the extension of Christ in time and space, should it be a cause for amazement that when we search for it, we should find it, like the Christ Child, with its mother, Mary? She who had so intimate a role to play in the life of the historic Christ cannot be pushed aside from the life of that Christ in His fullness; she who shared so closely in the labor of redeeming mankind objectively will only continue, as we might expect, to share closely in the labor of the Mystical Christ in applying that redemption to the souls of individual men. Since the shining figure of Mary appears throughout the life of the Church, a study of the Church would not be complete should we ignore that figure. Indeed, from the first moment on the hill of Calvary down to the present day, she has played a large role in the life of the Mystical Body. All the devotion of the Church to Mary throughout the centuries; all of the Marian dogmas of the Catholic creed; all of the magnificent cathedrals of the world named in her honor indicate the truth of this statement. We cannot ignore Mary, for the love which Catholics of all times have directed to her is only too much in evidence.

REASONS FOR HONORING MARY

If we try to find the ultimate explanation for this devotion to Mary, we will find that it does not lead us away from Christ and the Church as some may think. Rather, it is only the intense realization of what the Church is that enables the Catholic to pray to Mary as he does; it is only the realization of that deep, organic *oneness with Christ* that he has in the Church, which urges him to cry out to Mary in all simplicity that meaningful word "Mother."

The devotion of the Church to Mary is a stumbling block for many of those outside the Church, for they fear that in honoring her we are forgetting her Son, and giving less honor to God. Yet the very opposite is true. Mary does not stand between us and Christ, nor does she take His place. We find her with Christ; and we find Him with His Mother, Mary. A Catholic who understands what the Church is, will be able to call upon Mary as his "Mother" only after he has learned the profound meaning of his Baptism, through which he has become another Christ, and a true Son of God. It is through this that he obtains the right to address Mary as his Mother, for that eternal Son of God is also the Child of Mary. He must first of all learn what it means to "put on Christ." When once we realize our oneness with Christ, then we can properly honor Mary as Christ did. As Origen wrote centuries ago: "According to those who reason rightly, no one is Mary's son except Jesus; and if Jesus said to His Mother, 'Woman, behold thy son,' instead of saying, 'Behold, this one [John] is also thy son,' it is as if He had said: 'Behold Jesus whom thou hast begotten.'" No distinction need be made, for the two are one; and the same is true of every member of Christ. Being one with Christ, we are also — in Him — the son of Mary. "Truly," he goes on to explain, "he that is perfect no longer lives, but Jesus lives in him. And since Jesus does live in him, we may say to Mary of such a person: 'Behold thy son, Christ.'"[4]

It is true, of course, that Mary is the Mother of Christ and our Mother on different counts, but she is no less truly our Mother. In becoming other Christs, we accept for our own that Mother whom Christ chose from all eternity, and whom He gave to us as He hung upon the cross. The Word of God deigned to share His eternal Father with us in making us children of God through grace; and when that divine Son became Man to unite us to Himself more closely as a partaker of our nature, He willed to share with us as well the Mother from whom He received that nature.

When the Church prays to Mary, then, she is praying to her own Mother, and in giving honor to her, she is simply following the example of the eternal Father Himself, for God first honored Mary when He chose her from all eternity to be the Mother of Christ. That is why the liturgy on the feast of the Immaculate Conception applies to Mary the words of Scripture which properly refer to Christ; she dwelt eternally in the Mind of God long before she was even born into this world, for God intended her always to be the Mother of His Son:

> The Lord possessed me in the beginning of his ways,
>   before he made anything from the beginning.
> I was set up from eternity,
>   and of old before the earth was made.
> The depths were not as yet, and I was already conceived;
>   neither had the fountains of waters as yet sprung out.
> The mountains with their huge bulk had not as yet been established:
>   before the hills I was brought forth.
> He had not yet made the earth, nor the rivers,
>   nor the poles of the world.
> When he prepared the heavens, I was present:
>   when with a certain law and compass he enclosed the depths:
> When he established the sky above,
>   and poised the fountains of waters:
> When he compassed the sea with its bounds,
>   and set a law to the waters
>   that they should not pass their limits:
>   when he balanced the foundations of the earth:
> I was with him forming all things:
>   and was delighted every day, playing before him at all times;
>   playing in the world.
> , And my delights were to be
>   with the children of men.[5]

God continued to honor Mary from the first moment of her existence in all of the manifold graces which He bestowed upon her.

The Immaculate Conception, by which her soul was preserved from the stain of original sin; the Virgin Birth by which she miraculously became the Mother of God while remaining ever a virgin; the Assumption by which her body was saved from the corruption of the grave and granted an anticipated resurrection without awaiting the end of the world — all of these were granted so that Christ might have for His Mother the fairest and most perfect of all creatures.

Mary herself realized the tremendous and unmerited favors which God bestowed upon her; she expressed that realization in those words of hers which have now become one of the favorite prayers of the Church, the *Magnificat:*

> My soul magnifies the Lord,
>   and my spirit rejoices in God my Saviour;
> Because he has regarded the lowliness
>   of his handmaid;
> For, behold, henceforth all generations
>   shall call me blessed;
> Because he who is mighty
>   has done great things for me,
> And holy is his name.[6]

Thus, when the Church goes on honoring Mary today, she is really giving honor to God by paying tribute to this masterpiece of His divine craftsmanship, "our tainted nature's solitary boast," as Wordsworth has put it. It is not, however, simply the reverence given to a chosen one of God; it is the love and honor of a child for its mother as well. It would surely be sufficient reason for honoring Mary to say that God has honored her first; but there is all the more reason for doing so when we say that she is in truth our own Mother, for the love she gives to us demands a proper return.

THE MOTHER OF CHRIST

The relationship between Mary and the Church is very similar to that between Mary and Christ. Naturally, we are only making a comparison once again, and what we say must be understood in that light. What is meant is simply that there is a very close resemblance between the physical motherhood of Mary in regard to Christ and her spiritual motherhood in regard to the Church — the Mystical

Christ. Yet it is something very real that is involved, and it helps to explain the attitude of the Church toward Mary. To understand that relationship, we need only understand the role of any mother in any family. There is surely no more appealing example of love than that of a mother for her children, and in Mary we have the noblest example of that mother love. There is no one who does not receive the benefits of her care. She is constantly turning to her Son to plead for others, even though these very people might not have asked. A mother does not always wait until her children cry to her; rather, she looks ahead and sees what they need. As one day at the marriage feast at Cana, Mary turned to Jesus and told Him, "They have no wine,"[7] so now she turns to Him and tells Him that the hungry have no food, that the homeless need shelter, the tempted need strength, and the sinners, forgiveness. Mary is acclaimed as the Coredemptrix because she too shared in the *saving* of mankind; and she bears the title of "Mediatrix of all graces" because she continues at every moment to share in *applying* that salvation to the souls of her children.

On these two scores, Mary is very close to us. A number of reasons are set forth to explain this — reasons of love, of suffering, of prayer. Our Holy Father enumerates different ways in which she has been linked to the entire human race, so as to become Mother of us all, and especially of those who are the members of Christ.

MARY BRINGS CHRIST TO US

There is first of all the very fact of her choice from all eternity as the Mother of Christ, and the graces showered upon her for that reason. In this way, "she whose sinless soul was filled with the divine Spirit of Jesus Christ above all other created souls," was able to act in our name because of her dignity, and to give her consent "for a spiritual marriage between the Son of God and human nature."[8] When Mary consented to become the Mother of Christ, her simple words, "Be it done to me according to thy word,"[9] contained, in a way, the consent of the entire human race, of all her spiritual children, to that marvelous union of the divine and human nature in Christ, and the overflow of that union into our souls through grace.

Second, when Christ assumed His sacred body from the Blessed

Virgin, He did so not merely that He might become man, but also *that as man* He might be the Head of the Church. Actually the Church had its very first beginnings at the moment of the Incarnation when "within the virginal womb of Mary, Christ our Lord already bore the exalted title of Head of the Church,"[10] and possessed all the gifts and graces given to Him for the ruling and the sanctification of the faithful. Thus, in becoming man, the divine Head sought to join the whole human race to Himself so that in Him they might be saved. Therefore, through Mary the sinful world received Christ the Redeemer.

Third, when Mary brought forth the Christ Child, it was "as the source of all supernatural life"; and she presented Him, newly born, as "Prophet, King, and Priest to those who, from among Jews and Gentiles, were the first to come to adore Him"[11] — the very work which the Church continues today: to bring supernatural life to all, and to exercise the triple role of Christ in teaching, ruling, and sanctifying mankind. Mary brought grace to the world in presenting to it the Fountain of Grace Himself.

MARY BRINGS GRACE TO US

In these ways, Mary was bound to mankind by giving her Son to them as the Source of grace. The encyclical also speaks, however, of the value of Mary's intercession on our behalf, since her only Son, "condescending to His mother's prayer in 'Cana of Galilee,' performed the miracle by which 'his disciples believed in him.' "[12] From that beginning, Mary has continued to bring blessings down upon the followers of Christ, as she does today; her intercession is continuous.

Worthy of mention in regard to the Church and Mary's relation to it, is the day of Pentecost. After the Ascension of Christ into heaven, the Apostles had returned to the upper room in Jerusalem, and there, as we read in the Acts of the Apostles, "all these with one mind continued steadfastly in prayer with the women and Mary, the mother of Jesus, and with his brethren."[13] It was then especially that the motherly love of Mary for the Church was shown, for as the Holy Father tells us: "She it was who through her powerful prayers obtained that the Spirit of our Divine Redeemer, already given on the Cross, should be bestowed, accompanied by miraculous gifts, on the newly founded Church at Pentecost."[14]

Not satisfied with simply praying for us, Mary also shared in offering her Son upon the cross, and joined her own anguish and sorrow to the sufferings of Christ. It is for this reason that she is hailed as the Coredemptrix. She shared intimately in the act of redemption itself upon the hill of Calvary, and thus for one more reason became the Mother of the redeemed. As the encyclical explains: "It was she, the second Eve who, free from all sin, original or personal, and always most intimately united with her Son, offered Him on Golgotha to the Eternal Father for all the children of Adam, sin-stained by his unhappy fall, and her mother's rights and mother's love were included in the holocaust."[15]

There is a note of gratitude, for that reason, in the devotion of Catholics to their heavenly Mother, from whom, after God, they expect all assistance, in life and in death. It is the fullness of Catholic belief which impels them to fall upon their knees and call out to their Mother, the Mother of the Mystical Christ. It implies a realization of the role she played in giving Christ to us so that we might receive from Him the life of grace; a realization of the power of her intercession before the throne of God; and a realization of her share in the sacrifice of Calvary where, according to Pope St. Pius X, through the "community of will and suffering between Christ and Mary, she merited to become most worthily the Reparatrix of the lost world, and Dispensatrix of all the gifts our Saviour purchased for us by His death and by His blood."[16] It was there, especially, at the foot of the Cross that Mary gained the title of Mother of us all. As the encyclical on the Mystical Body explains: "Thus she who, according to the flesh, was the mother of our Head, through the added title of pain and glory became, according to the Spirit, the mother of all His members . . . and bearing with courage and confidence the tremendous burden of her sorrows and desolation, she, truly the Queen of Martyrs, more than all the faithful 'filled up those things that are wanting of the sufferings of Christ . . . for His Body, which is the Church'; and she continues to have for the Mystical Body of Christ, born of the pierced Heart of the Saviour, the same motherly

care and ardent love with which she cherished and fed the Infant
Jesus in the crib."[17]

Surely Mary is the "Mother of Christ," but we are one with Christ
in the Church, and so that means she is our Mother as well. She is
the "Mother of divine grace," and we ask her to obtain for us a
generous sharing in that grace possessed in its fullness by her Son.
She is the "Mother most pure, most chaste; Mother inviolate and
undefiled," and we raise up our voices to ask her help to overcome the
world and sin. She is the "Mother most amiable, most admirable":
one whom we can love and whom we can imitate; the "Virgin most
powerful," who will plead our cause before God; the "Mother of
good counsel," to whom we can go in our fears, and who, as the
"Morning Star," will lead us on to that divine Son of hers, and to
the glorious daybreak of eternity in heaven.

CHAPTER XVI

THE LIVING CHRIST

WE HAVE looked at the various parts of the Mystical Body one by one in the hope of understanding just what is meant by the terminology. It remains now to stand apart and view the whole picture; to see it in its entirety. There is danger of becoming involved in words to the extent that we think this is merely a metaphor; a very nice figure of speech, but nothing more. We may know what is meant by the Head of the Mystical Body, and the Soul, and the requirements for membership in that Body; but we might still fail to see it in ourselves, in those about us, in our parish church. The terms are to help us understand the reality; we must not be content with merely understanding the terms, and let our thinking end there. It is the reality of the Living Christ that we must seek, and as was mentioned at the outset, to grasp that reality is a result not merely of study, but of the grace of God through prayer and meditation. Unless we approach this truth in a religious attitude, we will only be "studying" the Mystical Body, and we run the risk of becoming like those thinkers, censured by Etienne Gilson, who "have fallen into the error of philosophizing on philosophies instead of philosophizing on real problems." And he adds a word of warning: "As soon as we turn our backs on reality and begin to think about the formulae that express it, we turn our backs on the sole possible centre of unity, and philosophy dissipates itself into an anarchic verbalism."[1] The same is true of a study of the Mystical Body. If the doctrine is to be anything more than just so many words, we must look for the *reality itself* — a search which will succeed, in this case, only with the help of God's grace.

Actually this teaching means that Christ is not departed from this earth. He lives on as really and actively today as He did 2000 years ago, and He will remain even unto the consummation of the world. There are three ways of considering Christ: first, as true God; second, as Christ the God-Man; third, not as an individual but in His fullness: the Mystical Christ. In the first way, Christ always was and always will be true God, the Second Person of the Trinity. At the moment of the Incarnation, He began to exist in the second way, by assuming to Himself a human nature. Unchanged as God, He began to exist as Man as well, the Son of the Virgin Mary. As God-Man, He is the Head of the Church, as He exists at once in both His natures.

THE MYSTICAL CHRIST

In the third manner of considering Christ, we do not consider Him just as an individual, either with a divine nature, or a divine and human nature, but rather in a social way: in His fullness, taking into account both Christ and His members. Christ, the God-Man, in His body and blood, soul and divinity, is the Head; the Roman Catholic Church is His Body; *together* they make that unique organism, the *Mystical Christ,* the *Whole Christ,* the *Living Christ.*

Everything that has been said thus far contributes to this sublime notion, for it is the Church, living by the life of Christ, united to Him through the Holy Spirit, which is the Body of this Mystical Christ. And we may speak simply of "Christ" when we speak of the Church because of this intimate union between them. St. Paul leads the way in doing this. Speaking to the Galatians, he reminds them that they are no longer either Jew or Greek, slave or freeman, but "you are all one [person] in Christ Jesus."[2] Or to the Ephesians: "For Christ himself is our peace, he it is who has made both [peoples: Jew and Gentile] one, has broken down the intervening wall of the enclosure, the enmity, in his flesh. The Law of the commandments expressed in decrees he has made void, that of the two [peoples] he might create in himself [as Head] *one new man* [the Mystical Christ], and make peace and reconcile both [peoples] in one body [the Mystical Body: the Church] to God by the cross, having slain the enmity in himself."[3]

This was always something very real to Paul from the day that he first came into vital contact with the Mystical Christ. The divine Head appeared to him, striking him blind, and asked him, "Why dost thou persecute *me?*"[4] Paul was not injuring the God-Man who was in heaven; yet he was persecuting *Christ:* the Mystic Christ. When the Body was struck, the Head cried out in protest.

He spoke of this also to the Corinthians, when he passed without warning, as it were, from speaking of the Church to speaking of Christ. When the Church at Corinth was disturbed by small factions which threatened to split the unity of the group, Paul wrote back, "Has *Christ* been divided up?"[5] And when he spoke later of the quarrels over the value of having one office in the Church rather than another, he made the comparison with the human body, and ended up by saying, "So also is it with *Christ.*"[6] According to all that he had written in the first twelve verses he should have said, "So also is it with the Church," but for Paul the Church was Christ, this Mystic Christ which lives on in the world, undying though persecuted, triumphant though suffering.

When St. Paul was in prison in Rome, he thought often of this mystery, and as he suffered much, he offered it all up for the members of Christ upon this earth. "I rejoice now," he wrote, "in the sufferings I bear for your sake; and what is lacking of the sufferings of Christ I fill up in my flesh for his body, which is the Church."[7] Surely there was absolutely nothing lacking to the sufferings of the God-Man considered as an individual; what He had suffered upon Calvary was more than sufficient to redeem all of mankind. But there was a lack on the side of the Church — the Body of the Mystic Christ. Christ did not desire to save men without anything contributed on their part; the free will of men comes between Calvary and salvation, and there is a certain number of good actions to be performed, and a certain amount of penance, and a certain amount of suffering due on the part of each individual. Some of the members, however, did not do

penance, and rebelled against the suffering sent them by God. It was for
them that Paul suffered, making up for what was lacking to the sufferings of the *Mystical Christ,* not as regards its divine Head, but on the
side of its only too human Body. Such a thing as reparation is possible
because of the intimate union between the various members of this
Body. They act as one individual, and what one does or suffers will
have its effect upon the whole Body.

To see Christ in the Church, then, is a very great blessing. The
Body is something real and vital. If a man wishes to *see* the Mystical
Body, he need do no more than stop in his parish church, and there
he will find Christ at prayer — the Mystic Christ living on this
earth. One need not feel sorry that he had no opportunity to rejoice
with Christ and the angels at His birth, or to grieve with Him at
His death. Christ lives on today, in sorrow and in joy. The man
of faith must learn to rejoice at the goodness and success of the
members of Christ; there is no room for envy or jealousy. Nor may
the other members of the Church be indifferent to those who suffer,
for it is *Christ* who is suffering, and like Veronica and Simon they
have been called upon to help Him. They are asked to comfort Him
in His suffering members, no less than the Apostles were asked to
watch with Him in the Garden of Olives. We may apply to the
Church in full vigor the beautiful words of Pascal concerning our
Lord: "Christ is in agony until the end of the world; and we must not
sleep the while."[8]

THE LIVING CHRIST

This unity of the Church with Christ does not limit itself to
merely *being* one with Christ; it extends also to *actions,* for all
that is done in the Church is done in union with Christ. It is really
Christ who acts, and it is for that reason that we can truly say
Christ lives yet upon this earth. There was no discontinuity between
the historical life and the mystical life of Christ. When, at the
moment of death, His mortal life was ended, at that same instant
the Mystical Christ began to live, and that mystical life of Christ
began. "The Holy Books always end with the same indication,"
states Father Mersch. "Their content, their Christ, does not leave

them, but passes into the Church. To separate the Scriptures from the Church would be to take them out of their context, and to rob them of both their meaning and their Author."[9] Christ has willed to unite mankind to Himself most intimately in the Church. The faithful are not merely in Christ, nor are they simply one in Christ: they are Christ Himself, the one Christ, the Mystical Christ. Indeed, because of this will of our Saviour, Christ is not complete without the Church, just as this Body cannot be complete without Him. The Church is the fullness of Christ; and the Whole Christ, the complete Christ, is the Head together with the Body.

There is something of the human and the divine in all that the Church does. We speak of this as the "theandric" nature of the Church. The term comes from two Greek words, *theos* meaning "God," and *aner, andros* meaning "man." The theandric actions of the God-Man were those which were placed by Him who was at the same time both God and Man: the actions in which both natures participated. Something similar is found in the Church, for every supernatural act of the Body of Christ is performed by God and man. God Himself is the Author of all that is done in the Church, but it is done by men — men who are intimately united to God. "Christ is Head of the universal Church as He exists at once in both His natures,"[10] that is, the human and divine. When Christ became Man, He made use of His humanity as an *instrument* in the redeeming of mankind; it was something He used to achieve His purpose, and that humanity had something of its own to contribute to that work. In the distributing of the graces of that redemption, He now makes use of a new human instrument, the Church. As Pius XII expresses it: "Just as at the first moment of the Incarnation the Son of the Eternal Father adorned with the fullness of the Holy Spirit the human nature which was substantially united to Him, that it might be a fitting *instrument* of the Divinity in the sanguinary work of the Redemption, so at the hour of His precious death He willed that His Church should be enriched with the abundant gifts of the Paraclete in order that in dispensing the divine fruits of the Redemption she might be, for the Incarnate Word, a powerful *instrument* that would never fail."[11]

The Church thus extends the theandric actions of Christ throughout time and space; it becomes an extension, as it were, of the humanity of Christ. In the Church, of course, we do not find a hypostatic union of the human and divine nature, but the Church does have its human and divine sides, its visible and invisible elements, and there is a very real union between the two. The Body of Christ is intimately united to its divine Head through the work of the Holy Spirit. This theandric nature of the Church is tremendously important; it is what Father Bluett has called "the core, the central truth of ecclesiology, apart from which nothing else in the Church can be understood for what it really is."[12]

It is this union of the human and divine in the Church which explains why the Body of Christ is so different from any other group of people in the world, for no other group was chosen by Christ as the means, the instrument He was to use to complete His work. Thus the coming of the Holy Spirit upon the Mystical Body had far-reaching effects. Father Gruden sums it all up nicely. "The offices Christ exercised in his physical body he continues to exercise through the instrumentality of his mystical body. Hence when the church teaches, Christ teaches, when the church rules, Christ rules, and when the church sanctifies, it is Christ himself who sanctifies. The actions of the church are the actions of the God-man Jesus Christ extended in space and time. The actions of the church are, therefore, truly theandric actions, but it is the Holy Spirit who makes them so, for it is he who is the bond of union between the human and the divine, between the natural and supernatural, the visible and invisible, between the members and organs and Christ their head. It is the Holy Spirit who elevates the natural and human elements to the level of the supernatural and divine order of being."[13]

INDIVIDUALS

This life of unity with Christ will become apparent first of all in the lives of the individual members, for they must strive little by little to become more like Christ; to reproduce in their own lives as far as possible the life of Christ. "Be imitators of me as I am of Christ," wrote St. Paul.[14] That is the goal of every Christian life: to live again in our own way, in our own circumstances, the life of Christ.

Paul was filled with this ideal, and even went so far as to make up new words to express this idea, compounding verbs by making use of the preposition "with" (the Greek *syn,* the Latin *cum*). To die *with* Christ to this world, to be buried *with* Him, and to arise gloriously *with* Him. Through the cross and penance in our life, we mortify ourselves: "*with* Christ I am nailed to the cross."[15] When that mortification shall have become complete, we shall be perfectly detached from this world and what it has to offer us; we shall truly die to this world, knowing full well, however, that "if we have died *with* him, we shall also live *with* him."[16] But death comes always with a reason; it marks a beginning, and not an end, and so we know again that though "we were buried *with* him," we will arise to a new life of grace, the supernatural life, where "we also may walk in newness of life."[17] From then on, that is the only life we really know; it consumes our earthly existence so completely that we "use this world, as though not using it, for this world as we see it is passing away."[18] We realize fully our own obligations to do this, for "if you have risen *with* Christ," wrote St. Paul, "seek the things that are above."[19] It is there that our true life lies; we belong more to heaven than to earth, for "our citizenship is in heaven."[20]

Much of the symbolism of the Church in her prayers and ceremonies is based upon these notions. We are to reproduce in our lives the life of Christ; we are to live again His life in ours. We also will have our Bethlehems and our Calvarys, our Resurrection and our glorious Ascension. The Church Year itself aims at instilling into our hearts the proper dispositions: "It strives to make all believers take their part in the mysteries of Jesus Christ so that the divine Head of the Mystical Body may live in all the members with the fullness of His holiness."[21] It looks forward to that time when every member of Christ might be so filled with the Spirit of Christ that he may call out with St. Paul: "It is now no longer I that live, but Christ lives in me."[22]

Pius XII presents a striking outline of this plan of the Church Year in his encyclical *On the Sacred Liturgy* which is well worth quoting: "In the period of Advent, for instance, the Church arouses in us the consciousness of the sins we have had the misfortune to commit, and urges us, by restraining our desires and practicing voluntary mortification of the body, to recollect ourselves in meditation, and experience a longing desire to return to God Who alone can free us by His grace from the stain of sin and from its evil consequences. With the coming of the birthday of the Redeemer, she would bring us to the cave of Bethlehem and there teach that we must be born again and undergo a complete reformation; that will only happen when we are intimately and vitally united to the Word of God made man and participate in His divine nature, to which we have been elevated.

"At the solemnity of the Epiphany, in putting before us the call of the Gentiles to the Christian faith, she wishes us daily to give thanks to the Lord for such a blessing; she wishes us to seek with lively faith the living and true God, to penetrate deeply and religiously the things of heaven, to love silence and meditation in order to perceive and grasp more easily heavenly gifts.

"During the days of Septuagesima and Lent, our Holy Mother the Church over and over again strives to make each of us seriously consider our misery, so that we may be urged to a practical emendation of our lives, detest our sins heartily and expiate them by prayer and penance. For constant prayer and penance done for past sins obtain for us divine help, without which every work of ours is useless and unavailing. In Holy Week, when the most bitter sufferings of Jesus Christ are put before us by the liturgy, the Church invites us to come to Calvary and follow in the blood-stained footsteps of the Divine Redeemer, to carry the cross willingly with Him, to reproduce in our own hearts His spirit of expiation and atonement, and to die together with Him.

"At the Paschal season, which commemorates the triumph of Christ, our souls are filled with deep interior joy: we, accordingly, should also consider that we must rise, in union with the Redeemer, from our cold and slothful life to one of greater fervour and holiness by giving ourselves completely and generously to God, and by forgetting this wretched world in order to aspire only to the things of heaven. . . .

"Finally, during the time of Pentecost, the Church by her precept and practice urges us to be more docile to the action of the Holy Spirit who wishes us to be on fire with divine love so that we may daily strive to advance more in virtue and thus become holy as Christ our Lord and His Father are holy."[23]

THE SOCIAL BODY

Besides this individual imitation of Christ, there is also the representation of His life in a social way by the Church. Different groups will be formed, each assuming to themselves the imitation of some particular phase in the life of Christ; they "specialize," as it were, in order to bring out in all its beauty this or that particular virtue of Christ. It is something like the varicolored coat of Joseph in the Old Testament,[24] each group contributing its own special "color." Taken altogether, it becomes a thing of overwhelming beauty.

There is so much to imitate in the life of Christ that no man could hope to do a perfect job of it alone; for Christ was also God. There must be a division of labor, then, and, while all must in their individual lives bear a resemblance to the divine Head, yet the same characteristic will not be equally prominent in all. Her supreme Pontiff makes visible Christ's unending governance of His kingdom on earth. Her priests are to make visible His presence at the altar, to make audible his words of forgiveness. Her religious perpetuate a poverty, an obedience, and an utter purity which began at Bethlehem. And her lay men and women, each according to his state in life, will exemplify above all some particular virtue of the Master.

Christ was the great Healer of the sick, and so there are communities of Sisters and Brothers, and Catholic nurses and doctors, who give over their lives to this Christlike work. They labor not for themselves alone but for the entire Body, performing those works of mercy which others, because of their own duties, cannot perform. They are Christ; and as they keep all-night vigil in the dark corridors of large city hospitals, it is Christ in them who keeps watch, guarding the sick: Christ living on this earth.

A priest sits in a dark confessional, turning from side to side, as the mumbled whisperings of other Magdalenes and thieves pour out the horrors of sin and the happiness of repentant love; and Christ speaks to each of them in turn, "Thy sins are forgiven . . . thy faith has saved thee; go in peace."[25]

During the long centuries of waiting before the coming of Christ, the psalmist had said of Him in prophecy, "Thou lovest justice and hatest iniquity,"[26] and he described what the work of Christ would be:

> May he rule thy people with justice,
>   and thy poor with equity. . . .
> He shall protect the lowly among the people,
>   he shall save the children of the poor
>   and shall crush the oppressor. . . .
> For he shall deliver the needy one, when he cries,
>   and the poor man, who has no helper.
> He shall take pity on the needy and the poor,
>   and save the life of the poor.
> He shall redeem them from harm and oppression,
>   and precious shall be their blood in his sight.[27]

Thus even today does that work go on, carried forth by those good and conscientious legislators and lawyers and judges, who have freed themselves from the legalistic verbiage of the Pharisees, both ancient and modern, and who have learned to love justice and hate iniquity. In them, as well as in good political leaders, Christ will rise up to rule the people with justice and equity; through them Christ will continue to protect the lowly and to crush the oppressors of this world.

Christ was a Teacher of eternal truths, and today He continues to do that in the persons of priests and Brothers and Sisters and zealous laymen who stand before the youth who fill our classrooms and the people who fill our churches, and speak to them of God and of the world in relation to God. Christ speaks to men today with as strong and persuasive a voice as He used 2000 years ago. Christ the Teacher lives on.

And as the whistles blow in a hundred thousand factories throughout the world, Christ the Worker picks up his lunch bucket and takes his place; or seats himself at a desk in an office to give to God that glory of labor once offered up daily by the divine Carpenter of Nazareth.

Christ was also the Good Shepherd, seeking the sinner and the unfortunate; lifting them up so that they might see God. And so today we have groups of men and women, engaged in social work and the work of bringing the fallen back to God. They are the ones who, like Christ their Head, do not wait for these unfortunates to come, but rather, "leaving the ninety-nine,"[28] go out to seek the one or the million that are lost and downtrodden and so covered up by sin or the hardships of this life that they look in vain for God. Christ is there to lift them up.

A soldier, far from home, stands looking into the pitch-black night, but he does not stand alone; Christ keeps watch in him this hour. Christ the lone, the weary; Christ suffering and afraid; Christ the Strength of the helpless and the Defender of the weak, keeps a vigil for freedom. Christ, having taken up the "armor of God" and the "shield of faith," and "having put on the breastplate of justice,"[29] stands alert to push back the powers of evil darkness which threaten the children of God.

In a sickroom somewhere a child or a man or a woman lies helpless but not hopeless on a bed of pain. Christ suffers on, and the unbelievers, unable to see the value of suffering, stand about that cross and mock and laugh and jeer. "If there is a God, why does He not take this man down from his cross and put an end to his suffering!" But like Paul and the Virgin Mary, he rejoices in the sufferings he now bears for others, and what is lacking of the sufferings of Christ, he fills up in his flesh for His body, which is the Church; and he answers to those who stand about: "O foolish ones and slow of heart . . . ! Did not the Christ have to suffer these things before entering into his glory?"[30] The sufferings of thousands of sick men and women are of value to the entire Mystical Body. If only we admit that Christ accomplished His greatest work through suffering, we can see its place in the life of His Church.

Out in some quiet valley, or high upon some lonely mountain, a silver bell breaks the silence of the night, and Christ arises and prays. Not all men can devote their lives to intense devotion; some must live a life of action. But the Mystical Christ, even as its divine Head, must go up to the mountaintop, alone, and spend the long nights in prayer. The priests of the world and the communities of monks and nuns attend to that work as they recite the Divine Office. Every prayer of every individual, of course, benefits the entire Body, but these are the "official" representatives, reciting the official prayer of the Church. Far from living wasted, useless lives, these courageous men and women who devote their entire lives to prayer, are among the most important members of the Mystical Christ. Unless one wishes to admit that the long nights of prayer in the life of our Redeemer were useless, he must admit the urgent need of them in the life of the Mystical Christ as well.

CHRIST LIVES ON

There is no side of the life of Christ which is not represented in some way in the Mystic Christ. The life of the God-Man continues in all things and without change in the life of the Church. His exiled life, His life as a laborer, His hidden life, His life of prayer, His public life, His life of suffering, His triumphs, His humiliations, His ascent to Calvary, His bloody immolation — all are repeated in the daily existence of the Living Christ. In Him and with Him and through Him — in union with its divine Head — the Whole Christ continues to save the world.

This work itself will go on from age to age, from soul to soul, always under the guidance of the Holy Spirit, Himself the Soul of the Mystical Body. There will be times of joy and times of sadness. The Church will have her Palm Sundays and her Easter mornings, but her Good Fridays as well. Since she is to parallel everything in the life of the God-Man, "What wonder," asks our Holy Father, "if while on this earth, she, like Christ, suffer persecutions, insults and sorrows."[31] It is a slow and tedious work, but a glorious work that belongs to the Church: to extend the life and activities of Christ in time and space. It will go on until the day of its blessed completion, when Christ shall be all things and in all; when all things shall be truly re-established in Christ, and the triumph and victory of the Whole Christ — the God-Man and His members — shall be complete, and the Living Christ will raise its collective voice for all eternity in songs of praise and adoration in that city of pure gold, like pure glass, which "has no need of the sun or the moon to shine upon it, for the glory of God lights it up, and the Lamb is the lamp thereof"; that city in which the servants of Christ "shall see his face and his name shall be on their foreheads . . . for the Lord God will shed light upon them; and they shall reign forever and ever."[32]

FOOTNOTES

Introduction

1. Bossuet, in John C. Gruden, *The Mystical Christ* (St. Louis: Herder, 1938), p. 2.

2. Pope Pius XII, *Mystici Corporis: On the Mystical Body of Christ*, June 29, 1943; translation published by the National Catholic Welfare Conference, Washington 5, D. C. In further references this work will be cited simply by paragraph number, for example, "paragh. 57."

Chapter I: It's the Church We're Talking About

1. Paragh. 13.

2. Emmanuel Cardinal Suhard, *Growth or Decline?*, translated by James A. Corbett (South Bend: Fides Publishers, 1948), p. 28.

3. Pius XII, Allocution to the Newly-created Cardinals, "La elevatezza," February 20, 1946 (*AAS*, Vol. 38, p. 149).

4. Cardinal Suhard, *Growth or Decline?*, pp. 21–22.

5. Denzinger, 1794.

6. Thomas Babington Macaulay, *Essay on Von Ranke's History of the Popes*, October, 1840 (*Miscellaneous Works of Lord Macaulay*: Putnam, Vol. 4, p. 398).

Chapter II: What's This "Mystical" About?

1. Acts 9:1–9.

2. Matt. 25:40.

3. Gal. 3:27.

4. Luke 15:11–24.

5. John 15:4–6.

6. Rom. 11:16.

7. Matt. 9:14–15.

8. Eph. 5:21–29.

9. Eph. 2:21.

10. I Pet. 2:5.

11. I Cor. 3:16.

12. I Cor. 10:17.

13. Paragh. 86.

14. E. Myers, *The Mystical Body of Christ* (Macmillan, 1931), p. 29.

15. Paragh. 63.

16. Paragh. 91.

Chapter III: I Never Heard of It

1. *Encyclopaedia Britannica*, 11 ed. (Cambridge, England, 1911), "Reformation," Vol. 23, p. 11.

2. *Augsburg Confession, No. 7* (in Philip Schaff, *The Creeds of Christendom*, New York, 1878, I, 534).

3. *Westminster Confession, Chapter XXV* (in Schaff, *The Creeds of Christendom*, I, 765).

4. E. Myers, *The Mystical Body of Christ*, p. 3.

5. Pius XI, *On Atheistic Communism*, March 19, 1937 (America Press ed.), paragh. 8.

6. Alban Goodier, S.J., "The Mystical Body," *The Month*, 159:289 (1932), p. 289.

7. John J. Galvin, "Survey of Modern Conceptions of Doctrinal Development," *Proceedings of the Catholic Theological Society of America* (Washington, D. C., 1950), p. 46.

8. Carl Feckes, *Die Kirche Als Herrenleib* (Köln: Bachem, 1949), p. 14.

9. *Ibid.*, p. 15.

10. Paragh. 10.

Chapter IV: How Confused Should We Be?

1. Cf. Feckes, *op. cit.*, pp. 15–28.

2. Joseph Bluett, S.J., "Introduction" to the encyclical, *The Mystical Body of Christ* (American Press ed.: New York, 1943), p. 1.

3. Sebastian Tromp, S.J., *Corpus Christi Quod Est Ecclesia* (Rome: Gregorian University, 1946).

4. John 1:14.

5. 2 Cor. 4:4.

6. Heb. 1:3.

7. Col. 1:16.

8. John 1:3.

9. Heb. 10:5, 10.

10. Acts 4:12.

11. 1 Tim. 2:5.

12. Paragh. 12.

13. Rom. 11:34.

14. Emile Mersch, S.J., *La théologie du corps mystique* (Paris: Desclée, De Brouwer, 1946), II, p. 195. Since this book was written an English translation has appeared: *The Theology of the Mystical Body,* translated by Cyril Vollert, S.J. (St. Louis: Herder, 1951).

15. Friedrich Jurgensmeier, *The Mystical Body of Christ,* translated by H. G. Curtis (Milwaukee: Bruce, 1947), p. 49. The book has, however, been reissued, completely corrected, by Sheed and Ward (1955).

16. Mersch, *La théologie du corps mystique,* II, p. 196.

17. Tromp, *Corpus Christi Quod Est Ecclesia,* p. 170.

18. Paragh. 1.

19. Paragh. 91.

Chapter V: And Adam Ate of the Fruit

1. Gen. 1:26.

2. St. Augustine, *Confessions,* I, i.

3. 2 Pet. 1:4.

4. Pohle-Preuss, *God: The Author of Nature and the Supernatural* (St. Louis: Herder, 1944), p. 306.

5. *Ibid.*

6. Heb. 1:1.

7. Col. 3:1.

8. Rom. 7:19.

9. Denzinger, 792.

10. The *Exsultet* of Holy Saturday.

11. Rom. 5:12–21.

12. Rom. 8:22.

Chapter VI: Salvation This Way

1. 2 Tim. 2:8.

2. 1 Tim. 2:5.

3. Gen. 3:15.
4. Isa. 61:1.
5. Luke 4:16.
6. John 4:25.
7. Matt. 2:5.
8. Luke 18:31–33; cf. Ps. 21; Isa. 50:6; 63:1; Ps. 68; Dan. 9:26; Zach. 11:12; 12:10; 13:6; Ps. 15:9–10.
9. Heb. 4:15.
10. Matt. 13:55.
11. Phil. 2:5.
12. John 15:13.
13. Luke 2:34.
14. John 14:31.
15. Phil. 2:8.
16. 1 Cor. 6:20; 1 Pet. 1:18.
17. Rom. 5:12, 18.
18. Cf. Chap. IV, pp. 47, 48.
19. Paragh. 12.
20. Paragh. 12.
21. Paragh. 46, 96.
22. Mal. 1:11.
23. Pius XII, *On the Sacred Liturgy*, November 20, 1947 (N.C.W.C. ed.), paragh. 77, 79; Secret Prayer, 9th Sun. after Pentecost; Mal. 1:11.
24. Cf. paragh. 18–20.
25. Eph. 4:13.

Chapter VII: The Church Is Born

1. Vesper hymn, Feast of the Sacred Heart: "Ex corde scisso Ecclesia, Christo jugata, nascitur": "O wounded Heart, whence sprang the Church, the Saviour's bride."
2. Cf. above, p. 26.
3. Leo XIII, *On the Holy Spirit*, May 9, 1897 (America Press ed.), paragh. 22.
4. Paragh. 26.
5. Paragh. 2, 3.
6. John 15:20.
7. Paragh. 31.
8. Pius II, *In minoribus agentes*, 26 April, 1463, in Tromp, *op. cit.*, p. 39.
9. Acts 1:4, 14, 5.
10. Matt. 3:11.
11. Matt. 3:14.
12. Matt. 3:17.
13. Paragh. 33.
14. Exod. 19:16.
15. Acts 2:2.
16. Voltaire, in Hervé, *Manuale Theologiae Dogmaticae*, 12 ed. (Paris, 1935), I, 186.

Chapter VIII: The Church Is a Visible Body

1. Paragh. 22.
2. Paragh. 23.
3. Paragh. 22.
4. Canons 1070, 1099.
5. Paragh. 103.
6. Pius XII, *Humani Generis*, August 12, 1950 (N.C.W.C. ed.), paragh. 20.

7. *Ibid.*, paragh. 27–28.

8. Paragh. 14.

9. Jurgensmeier, *The Mystical Body of Christ*, p. 49.

10. Joseph Clifford Fenton, "The Encyclical *Mystici Corporis Christi*," *The American Ecclesiastical Review*, 110:48 (1944), p. 48.

Chapter IX: The Church and Salvation

1. Bossuet, in Gruden, *op. cit.*, p. 2.

2. Cf. above, p. 81 sq.

3. Paragh. 44.

4. *Ibid.*

5. Cf. Denzinger, 423, 430, 468–469, 714, 1646, 1647, 1677; also Fenton, "The Holy Office Letter on the Necessity of the Catholic Church," *The American Ecclesiastical Review*, 127:459 sq. (1952).

6. *Letter of the Holy Office*, to the Most Reverend Richard James Cushing, Archbishop of Boston, August 8, 1949: in *The American Ecclesiastical Review*, 126:307–315 (1952), pp. 312–313.

7. Pius XII, *Humani Generis* (N.C.W.C. ed.), paragh. 27.

8. *Letter, loc cit.*, p. 312.

9. *Ibid.*, p. 313.

10. *Ibid.*

11. Paragh. 103: Qui *pertinent* ad ecclesiam, (or) Qui *membra* sunt. . . Qui inscio quodam desiderio ac voto ad mysticum Redemptoris Corpus *ordinentur* (*AAS* Vol. 35, 1943), pp. 242–243).

12. *Letter, loc. cit.*, p. 308: Incorporetur . . . adhaereat.

13. Luke 10:16.

14. Pius IX, *Allocution*, December 9, 1854; Denzinger, 1647.

15. *Letter, loc. cit.*, p. 313.

16. *Ibid.*, p. 314.

17. Denzinger 1789.

18. Rom. 10:17.

19. Paragh. 61.

20. Eph. 1:11–12.

21. Eph. 4:13.

22. E. Myers, *The Mystical Body of Christ*, p. 48.

23. Paragh. 103.

24. Henri de Lubac, S.J., *Catholicism*, translated by L. C. Sheppard (London: Burns, Oates & Washbourne, 1950), pp. 117–118.

25. Dom Anscar Vonier, O.S.B., *Key to the Doctrine of the Eucharist* (Westminster, Md.: Newman, 1946), p. 228.

26. Eph. 4:13.

Chapter X: The Church Is a Living Body

1. Paragh. 61.

2. Paragh. 86.

3. Emmanuel Cardinal Suhard, *Growth or Decline?*, p. 21; Matt. 13:31.

4. *Ibid.*, pp. 24, 28, 29, 32.

5. Paragh. 15.

6. Rom. 12:4–6.

7. Eph. 2:15.

8. Eph. 2:19.

9. Eph. 5:23, 25.
10. 1 Cor. 6:15.
11. 1 Cor. 6:20.
12. 1 Cor. 12:3.
13. 1 Cor. 12:4–11.
14. 1 Cor. 12:12.
15. 1 Cor. 12:13.
16. 1 Cor. 12:14–16.
17. 1 Cor. 12:17–21.
18. Paragh. 17.
19. 1 Cor. 12:21–25.
20. 1 Cor. 12:26.
21. 1 Cor. 12:27–31.
22. Rom. 12:3–8.
23. Rom. 12:9–21.
24. 2 Tim. 4:6.
25. Col. 1:24.

Chapter XI: Christ Is the Head of the Church

1. Matt. 16:16.
2. Eph. 5:23.
3. Paragh. 59
4. Paragh. 34–51.
5. Richardus a Mediavilla, *Sent. III,* in *Textus et Documenta,* Series Theologica, No. 26: "Mystici Corporis Christi" (Rome: Gregorian University, 1943), p. 91.
6. Paragh. 36.
7. Col. 1:18.
8. Eph. 5:24.
9. Paragh. 37.
10. Matt. 16:13–14.
11. Matt. 16:15–16.
12. Matt. 16:17–19.
13. Gal. 2:11.
14. Matt. 28:18.
15. John 21:15–17.
16. Matt. 26:35.
17. Ps. 22:1–4.
18. Isa. 40:11.
19. John 10:11–15.
20. Paragh. 40.
21. Paragh. 41.
22. Paragh. 41.
23. Paragh. 42.
24. Paragh. 42.
25. Ignatius of Antioch, *Tral. II, i;* in *Textus et Documenta,* p. 97.
26. John 15:6.
27. Eph. 4:16, from the translation by Ronald Knox, copyright Sheed and Ward, New York.
28. Paragh. 44.
29. Paragh. 44.
30. Paragh. 44.
31. Paragh. 12, 44.

32. Paragh. 44.
33. Paragh. 44.
34. Gal. 3:27.

Chapter XII: Three More Reasons

1. Offertory Prayer.
2. Chap. IV, p. 47.
3. Paragh. 46.
4. 1 John 3:1.
5. Gal. 4:4–7.
6. Mersch, *La théologie du corps mystique,* II, 360.
7. 1 Cor. 13:12.
8. John 10:10.
9. John 5:24.
10. John 17:25–26.
11. Paragh. 46.
12. Col. 1:19.
13. Eph. 4:7.
14. Acts 4:12.
15. John 15:5.
16. Paragh. 103.
17. John 1:14, 16.
18. Paragh. 49.
19. Pius XII, *On the Sacred Liturgy* (N.C.W.C. ed.), paragh. 32.
20. John 6:69.
21. Paragh. 50.
22. Paragh. 50.
23. Paragh. 51.
24. John 15:5.
25. Phil. 1:6.
26. St. John Chrysostom, *In Joh. Hom.,* 46, in Mersch, *The Whole Christ,* translated by John R. Kelly, S.J. (Milwaukee: Bruce, 1938), p. 326.
27. Paragh. 51.
28. Eph. 4:15.

Chapter XIII: The Infallible Church

1. John 12:48.
2. 2 Thess. 2:12.
3. Cf. Fulton J. Sheen, *God and Intelligence* (London: Longmans, Green and Co., 1925), p. 19.
4. Pius XII, *Humani Generis* (N.C.W.C. ed.), paragh. 29.
5. Matt. 26:65.
6. John 15:18, 20.
7. Joseph DeGuibert, S.J., *De Christi Ecclesia* (Rome: Gregorian University, 1928), No. 217.
8. Vatican Council, Session IV, Chap. 4; Denzinger, 1839.
9. Pius XII, *Munificentissimus Deus,* November 1, 1950; *The Catholic Mind,* Vol. 49 (January, 1951), p. 67.
10. Pius XII, *Humani Generis,* paragh. 20.
11. *Ibid.,* paragh. 21.
12. *Ibid.*

13. Mersch, *La théologie du corps mystique*, II, 247, 249, 246.
14. Luke 22:31–32.
15. Mersch, *op. cit.*, II, 257.
16. Pius IX, *Tuas libenter*, December 21, 1863; Denzinger, 1683.
17. Denzinger, 1792.
18. Gustave Weigel, S.J., "Protestant Theological Positions Today," *Theological Studies*, Vol. 11 (1950), p. 565; Murphy, "Protestantism Today," *Sign*, Dec., 1954, p. 11.
19. Mersch, *op. cit.*, II, 257, 258, 257.

Chapter XIV: The Soul of the Mystical Body

1. John 14:16; 15:26.
2. Paragh. 55.
3. St. John Chrysostom, *In Joh. Hom.*, 14, in Mersch, *The Whole Christ*, p. 335.
4. John 14:23.
5. 1 Cor. 6:19.
6. Eph. 1:7.
7. Paragh. 31.
8. John 20:22.
9. Luke 5:32.
10. John 1:16.
11. Gal. 4:6.
12. Paragh. 57; Leo XIII, *On the Holy Spirit* (America Press ed.), paragh. 26.
13. Cf. above, Chap. XII, p. 160 ff.
14. Paragh. 99.
15. Paragh. 76–77.
16. Paragh. 57.
17. Pius XII, *On the Sacred Liturgy* (N.C.W.C. ed.), paragh. 43.
18. Paragh. 57.
19. Paragh. 57.
20. John 17:21.
21. Eph. 4:11–13.

Chapter XV: The Mother of Christ

1. Paragh. 110.
2. Matt. 2:11.
3. John 19:25.
4. Origen, *Comment. in Joh.*, in Mersch, *The Whole Christ*, p. 257.
5. Prov. 8:22–31.
6. Luke 1:47–49.
7. John 2:4.
8. Paragh. 110.
9. Luke 1:38.
10. Paragh. 110.
11. *Ibid.*
12. *Ibid.*
13. Acts 1:14.
14. Paragh. 110.
15. *Ibid.*
16. Denzinger, 1978a.
17. Paragh. 110.

Chapter XVI: The Living Christ

1. Etienne Gilson, *The Spirit of Mediaeval Philosophy,* translated by A. H. C. Downes (New York: Scribner, 1940), p. 480.

2. Gal. 3:28.

3. Eph. 2:14–17.

4. Acts 9:4.

5. 1 Cor. 1:13.

6. 1 Cor. 12:12.

7. Col. 1:24.

8. Blaise Pascal, *Pensées,* VII, in *The Wisdom of Catholicism* (New York: Random House, 1949), p. 639.

9. Mersch, *The Whole Christ,* p. 205.

10. Paragh. 90.

11. Paragh. 31.

12. Joseph Bluett, S.J., *Proceedings of the Catholic Theological Society of America* (New York, 1946), p. 54.

13. Gruden, *The Mystical Christ,* p. 195.

14. 1 Cor. 11:1.

15. Gal. 2:20.

16. 2 Tim. 2:11.

17. Rom. 6:4.

18. 1 Cor. 7:31.

19. Col. 3:1.

20. Phil. 3:20.

21. Pius XII, *On the Sacred Liturgy* (N.C.W.C. ed.), paragh. 152.

22. Gal. 2:20.

23. Pius XII, *On the Sacred Liturgy,* paragh. 154–160.

24. Gen. 37:3.

25. Luke 7:49–50.

26. Ps. 44:8.

27. Ps. 71:2, 4, 12–14.

28. Matt. 18:12.

29. Eph. 6:15.

30. Luke 24:25; cf. Col. 1:24.

31. Paragh. 47.

32. Apoc. 21:23; 22:4–5.

INDEX

Abstract terms, 7
Accidental union, 77, 157
Adam, Christ the new, 81; condition given to, 65; representative of all men, 66; sin of, 66
"Adhere" to the Church, 110
Analogies, meaning of, 44
Angels, illumined by Christ, 155
Apologetics, meaning of, 31
Apostate, meaning of term, 98; not member of Church, 98
Apostolic work of Church, 193
Applied concepts of Mystical Body, 42–43; 45–55
Appropriation, meaning of, 185
Ascension, and rule of Peter, 91, 148
Assumption, definition of, 179; meaning of, 198
Augsburg Confession, 31

Baptism, effects intrinsic change, 19–20; and membership in Church, 96–97; and original sin, 159
Baptism of blood and desire, not sacraments, 97
Beatific vision, and grace, 114, 157
Bible, the Church's book, 37; God Author of, 162; inspiration of, 162; and Protestantism, 181; source of revelation, 175
Bishops, and exercise of infallibility, 179; Ignatius of Antioch and, 149; and infallibility, 178; jurisdiction directly from Pope, 149; local vicars of Christ, 149; representatives of Christ, 148
Bluett, J., on importance of encyclical on Mystical Body, 44; on theandric nature of Church, 208
Bonds of union, theological and juridical, 4
Bossuet, definition of Church, vii
"Brothers according to the flesh," 82–83, 158

Catholic Action, and Church, 134; notion of, 152; and sacramental seal, 151
Cephas, from *Kepha,* 145
Charismatic gifts, nature of, 131
Charity, necessity for salvation, 114
Chastity, and Mystical Body, 130
Christ, acts through priest, 164; baptism of, 92; and bestowal of grace, 159; birth of, and Mary, 200; brought to us through Mary, 199; communicates grace to us, 160; continues redemptive work through Church, 105; continuity between historical and mystical, 195, 206; death climax of life, 81; divinity hid by humanity, 169; enlightens minds, 161, 163; every action an act of God, 79–80; first visible Head of Church, 91; Founder of Church, 139; fullness of grace, 159; fullness of grace in, 186; 188; governs Church, 142–143; grace of, 186; had grace for us, 160; had true human nature, 74; Head of Church, 207, 140 ff; Holy Spirit the Spirit of, 186; human body of, 24; human nature of, 154; identified with Church, 111, 132, 196, 204; imitation of, 208 ff; infallibility an act of 183; infallibility an action of, 183; invisible rule of, 142–143; King, Priest, Teacher, 170; Mediator between God and men, 71; the Messias, 72–73; moral Head, 47–49, 82–83; moral headship of, 155; Mother of, 194; mystic head, 48–49, 82–83; need of Church for, 150; not a human *person,* 76; and objective redemption, 150; our brother through grace, 188; pre-eminence of, 141; reasons why Head of Church, 141; relationship to soul of Church, 191; representative of every man, 81; sanctifies souls, 163; Saviour of Church, 139; shows love by Cross, 80; similarity of nature with, 154; soul of, 186; speaks in infallibility, 177, 182; Sustainer of Church, 140; in synagogue at Nazareth, 72; theandric actions of, 207; three ways of considering, 204; in what sense sufferings lacking, 205; the Worker, 212

Church, adaptability of, 10; apostolic work of, 83, 123, 193; attitude toward non-Catholics, 101; beginning of public life on Pentecost, 93; and bestowal of grace, 121; born on Good Friday, 86, 90; Bossuet's definition of, vii; and Catholic Action, 134, 152; Christ first visible Head of, 91; Christ Founder of, 139; Christ Head of, 140 ff; Christ Saviour of, 139; Christ Sustainer of, 140; City of God, 116; continues work of Christ, 87; defends power of intellect, 168; definition in regular catechism inadequate, 33; different from physical organ-

225